The Politics of Compromise:
State and Religion in Israel

The Politics of Compromise:

State and Religion in Israel

Ervin Birnbaum

Rutherford • *Madison* • *Teaneck*
Fairleigh Dickinson University Press

Associated University Presses, Inc.
Cranbury, New Jersey 08512

SBN: 8386 7567 0
Printed in the United States of America

to

HELEN

Contents

Preface

As this book goes to press, the storm raised by a national election in Israel has simmered down somewhat. The vote has been tallied and the composition of the Seventh Kneset has been announced to the expectant population. As is usually the case in a political contest, shouts of jubilation mingled with sighs of disappointment.

The election list with the greatest expectation was the combined one of the four major socialist parties. Upon formulating their merger-alignment, they commanded 63 votes in the outgoing Kneset. They had high hopes of being the first list in Israel's history ever to gain a clear parliamentary majority that would enable it to form a government unencumbered by protracted coalition bargaining and compromise. The high hopes of the allied parties, particularly the Mapai, were shattered on the Israeli voters' unwillingness to yield the reins of government to any one party or list.

Five votes short of a majority does not seem like much. But former Mapai Prime Minister Ben Gurion's efforts to alter Israel's electoral system were frustrated by a mere one vote in November 1959. And so Mapai, or the Israel Labor Party of which it is a part, is back at the old "coalition chess game" on which this book focuses.*

Once again the religious parties find themselves in the enviable position of being ideal partners to the socialist group. They

---

* After the merger with other socialist parties, Mapai's identity continued to be recognizable, and it remained the mainstay of coalition government. Hence, though referred to by the name of Labor Party or Alignment once the merger materialized, it is nonetheless the old Mapai in a new garb.

offer their support—if they get something in return. This seems like a perfectly normal and reasonable business transaction, except that the give and take appear to be in two different realms. They give in the realm of politics, and they take in the realm of religion. To those to whom religion is a matter of private conscience this seems like an unfair deal. The support offered to Mapai in the maintenance of socialist policies and its power stance in public affairs seems to be repaid to the National Religious Party by interference in private affairs. A most recent example is the Sabbath TV affair.

In May 1969, the Cabinet, with the endorsement of the Kneset, agreed to extend television broadcasting from the current three days to seven days a week. This was found necessary in order to counteract the blast of propaganda from neighboring Arab lands that penetrates virtually every home, to bring TV broadcasting in line with the ongoing seven-day-a-week radio programming, and to satisfy public demand. The religious parties were opposed to the breach of Sabbath. Confident in their ultimate victory at the polls, the Labor majority in the Cabinet determined to initiate the Sabbath broadcast the week after the Kneset elections. When the election results and the Labor Party's inevitable dependence on a coalition became known, the National Religious Party informed Prime Minister Meir that the price of their support would be the revocation of the Cabinet decision regarding Sabbath television broadcasting. Mrs. Meir thereupon ordered the Broadcasting Authority to rescind the Cabinet order. To the great consternation of the interested political parties and to the great delight of the secular public, a private citizen obtained a court order according to which the original decision of the Cabinet was to be enforced. Sabbath TV programs were on. It could possibly be only a matter of time, however, before the nonreligious socialist parties find a way out of this embarrassing dilemma and solve the Sabbath TV affair to the satisfaction of the religionists.

A less spectacular example of squeeze tactics in coalition bargaining, but one of greater import was the NRP (National Religious Party) demand for concessions in religious education. Finding its hands temporarily tied by the court order regarding Sabbath TV, the NRP began insisting on the Deputy-Ministership of Education with special far-reaching powers attached to it. Yigal Allon, the leader of ex-Ahdut ha-'Avodah who was slated to become the new Minister of Education, thereupon refused to accept the new portfolio. He claimed that a religious Deputy Minister with special powers would split his Ministry, making it for all practical purposes two Ministries. The issue was resolved by granting the Deputy Ministership to the NRP, but without special powers.

Despite the national emergency, it took the Prime Minister designate, Golda Meir, six weeks to establish a viable Cabinet. Contrary to general expectations, the right wing Gahal proved very cooperative. The greatest obstacles to forming a new Cabinet came from Mapam, which feared a "Gahal-Dayan" takeover, and from Yigal Allon, who was apprehensive of his rival's, Moshe Dayan's, rising influence with the strengthening of the Gahal and NRP in the government.

On December 15, 1969, Prime Minister designate Golda Meir received the Kneset's confidence in her newly constituted government. As its predecessor, the Sixteenth Government of Israel was a Government of National Unity. It differed from its predecessor in reflecting more realistically the parliamentary strength of the parties supporting the coalition, with the ratio of one Minister for roughly every four representatives in the Kneset. Overriding Mapam objections, right wing representation in the Cabinet increased.

The composition of the new Cabinet developed as follows: Israel Labor Party, 12 Ministers (ex-Mapai, 8; ex-Rafi, 2; ex-Ahdut ha-'Avodah, 2) ; Gahal, 6; NRP, 3; Mapam, 2; Independent Liberals, 1. Mapam joined the government with the stipulation that the rule of collective cabinet responsibility will not apply to it on social and economic issues where it feared undue Gahal influence. Thus, under strong pressure from the minority coalition partners, Mrs. Meir had no choice but to create the largest Cabinet in Israel's history, consisting of 24 Ministers.

And so the game this book deals with—a game played in many countries on several continents—is on in Israel in the 1970s as it has been since the country's pre-independence days. Only the variations differ.

Acknowledgments

I wish to thank the following publishers for having given me permission to quote from published works:

Cambridge University Press, for permission to quote from Sir Ivor Jennings, *The British Constitution*, 1961, and Sir Ivor Jennings, *Cabinet Government*, 1951.

Thomas Crowell, for permission to quote from Norman Kogan, *The Government of Italy*, 1965.

Duke University Press, for permission to quote from Helen Miller Davis, ed., *Constitutions, Electoral Laws, Treaties and States in the Near and Middle East*, 1953.

Harvard University Press, for permission to quote from Stanley Hoffman, ed., *In Search of France; Paradoxes of the French Political Community*, 1963.

Holt, Rinehart and Winston, Inc., for permission to quote from Pendleton Herring, *The Politics of Democracy*, 1940. Reprinted by special permission of the publisher, Holt, Rinehart and Winston, Inc.

The *Jewish Frontier*, for permission to quote from Mendel Kohansky, "A Problem of Religion," February, 1958.

The Jewish Publication Society of America, for permission to quote from *American Jewish Year Book 5684*, 1923.

Oxford University Press, for permission to quote from Beckham Sweet-Escott, *Greece* (London: Royal Institute of International Affairs), 1954. Reprinted by permission of Oxford University Press.

Frederick A. Praeger, for permission to quote from Dorothy Pickles, *The Fifth French Republic*, 1962, and Alex Rubner, *The Economy of Israel; A Critical Account of the First Ten Years*, 1960.

Midstream, for permission to quote from Maurice Friedberg, "The Split in Israel's Communist Party," February, 1966. (Quoted by permission of Professor Friedberg also, whom I also thank.)

The *New York Times,* for permission to quote from "Court Overrules Israel Rabbinate," August 12, 1964. © 1964 by The New York Times Company. Reprinted by permission.

Princeton University Press, for permission to quote from J. La Palombara and Myron Weiner, eds., *Political Parties and Political Development,* 1966, published for Social Science Research Council. Also for permission to quote from *The Politics of Israel,* by Marver H. Bernstein (Copyright © 1957 by Princeton University Press).

Twayne Publishers, for permission to quote from Joseph Badi, *Religion in Israel Today,* 1959 (New York: Bookman Associates). Reprinted by permission of Twayne Publishers, Inc.

John Wiley and Sons, for permission to quote from Maurice Duverger, *Political Parties,* Science Edition, 1963. Reprinted by permission of John Wiley and Sons, New York.

The World Mizrahi and ha-Po'el ha-Mizrahi Organization for permission to quote from Bezalel Cohen, *Iyunim b'Ba'ayot Dat u-M'dinah,* 1964.

Yale University Press, for permission to quote from Robert A. Dahl, ed., *Political Opposition in Western Democracies,* 1966.

The Zionist Organization, Youth and Hechalutz Department, Jerusalem, for permission to quote from Eliezer Goldman, *Religious Issues in Israel's Political Life,* 1964.

I wish to thank the marvelous director and staff of the Zionist Archives, Sylvia Landress, Ro Schechtman, Esther Togman, and Rebecca Zapinsky, who immeasurably facilitated my research by making materials at their disposal readily accessible to me. Of the Israeli parties, the former Herut and Mapam were particularly cooperative with their prompt reply to my queries. I owe a special debt of gratitude to Professor J. C. Hurewitz for his guidance and constructive criticism, and to Professor

Dankwart A. Rustow for his critical reading of the manuscript and encouragement to see it through publication. I am indebted to Michael Birnbaum and Jules (Buddy) Granat for their invaluable help in constructing the tables and reviewing several chapters. To Mrs. Mathilde E. Finch, Associate Editor, Associated University Presses, Inc., I wish to convey my warmest feelings of gratitude for guiding me through the maze of editing, updating, and proofreading the manuscript. I would like to express my deep appreciation to my wife, without whose constant prodding, selflessness, and help this book might never have seen the light of day, and to Aiton, Lee, and Daniel, who were virtually bereft of their father while he was involved in this labor of love.

The Politics of Compromise:
State and Religion in Israel

Introduction

The Six Day Arab-Israel War in June 1967 demonstrated Israel's capability to maintain its democratic institutions despite external threats and complex domestic problems. Although Israel's military victory was spectacular, equally significant, even if at first sight less dramatic, was the victory of democracy in the country.

Many of the democratic institutions, like the party system, the electoral process, popular representative government and a loyal opposition are inventions of the Western world. Their success among the nations of Asia and Africa is crucial to American foreign policy and to the development of the free bloc. Those who anxiously follow the ups and downs of the cold (and sometimes not so cold) war, want to know how successful the new nations have been in transplanting Western democratic institutions into a non-Western setting. The difficulties encountered by them in the grafting of democratic processes on their body politic is a cause of serious concern. Israel offers a valuable case study of the problems encountered and the techniques employed in promoting the evolution of a democratic system of government. This study deals with one aspect of the problem: the position of the minority parties in the government, their influence on the process of decision-making, and their effect upon political stability and democracy.

Newly created states have shared conditions of crisis not entirely dissimilar to those of Israel. The saga of most of these states would relate dangers lurking beyond the border and threats lurking within. Few would care to question, however, that in Israel these threats and dangers became acutely accentuated owing to its geopolitical isolation. Israel is surrounded by a ring of hostile neighbors who deny its existence and who appear ready to wipe it off the map. To the threat of bloody conflict an array of factors can be added that have fostered intermittently a condition of crisis. Among these have been widespread economic instability, unemployment, and demands of austerity. No less significant in producing a climate of unrest are deeply entrenched and radically divergent national loyalties (Arab versus Jew), religious differences (Orthodox versus liberal Jew, and Jew versus Muslim), linguistic differences (Hebrew versus Arabic), and clashing ideologies. Yet Israel managed to maintain a democratic government without ever being threatened by a takeover from its efficient military machine or by the imposition of a dictatorship. The experience of Israel demonstrated that a democratic government can be maintained in the face of unfavorable geopolitical and economic circumstances and deep national divisions.

Israel's achievement is all the more noteworthy since it coincided with a decline of democracy on a global scale. Impatient with the slow and halting process of decision-making that seems to be so often inherent in a democratic system, a number of states have submitted to dictatorships and to military government. Of 79 member states in the United Nations in 1955 as many as 47 experienced military rule. It is obvious that any type of government that assures stability and order seems to be preferable to internal conflict and lawlessness.

It would, of course, be premature to assume that democracy is safe and secure in Israel. Israel's democratic processes suffer from many shortcomings. The governmental system has been adapted to the multiplicity of parties, yet dependence on the minority parties for the establishment of government has on several occasions pushed the country to the brink of paralysis. Similarly, the lack of a vital opposition that could pose as a legitimate alternative government to the parties in power offers a major challenge to the preservation of a democratic system. The demands of the religious parties that Jewish religious law become the law of the state has threatened to replace democracy with theocracy.

These shortcomings, and many more, in Israel's democratic structure make a study of Israel all the more instructive and valuable. They prove that circumstances need not always be ideal for a nation to aspire to, and achieve, a democratic representative government.

An examination of the bargaining power of minority parties in the government of Israel and the resultant compromise politics call for an inquiry into the formation and functioning of the coalition cabinet. It also requires a study of the ideologies, behavior, and activities of the numerous parties, all of whom have governmental aspirations.

Among the minority parties, the religious parties are the most significant political group. With only 15 per cent of the popular vote they participated in all governments. They achieved substantial concessions from the socialist and secularist Mapai, the party that has dominated all governmental coalitions in the twenty years following Israel's declaration of independence.

Owing to the constant participation of religious parties in the coalition cabinets, they offer the best case study of minority pressure on the dominant Mapai. Focusing on the religious parties in this work attains a double objective: it offers insight into the functioning of democratic government and simultaneously clarifies the relationship of state and religion in Israel.

The first five chapters of the study examine the basis of coalition government in Israel, relating the particular type of government to institutional factors, historical antecedents, ideology, ethnic composition, the interaction of events on the domestic front and to regional and international developments. They also discuss the role of the parties and the constitutional and political bases of the Cabinet and of religion. Eight chapters offer case studies of government crises and of attempts at forming new coalitions. Though the stress is on the bargaining for power between Mapai and the religious parties and on the technique of the religious parties in extracting concessions from the majority, the complete process of government formation and the participation of the other parties are subjected to analytical scrutiny. The remaining three chapters summarize the problems of stable democratic government in a crisis setup and discuss the prospects for a solution of the religious impasse.

The State of Israel is the product of unusual historical circumstances, not the least of which is the return of the Jewish people to its homeland after an absence of 1800 years. Similarly, the government of Israel is a product of problems and circumstances unique in their conglomerate aspect. Yet many of the problems and characteristics are, feature by feature, shared by other governments. It is therefore hoped that this work will prove useful for comparative governmental studies and that it will contribute to the further exploration of the safeguarding of representative government in an era of perpetual crisis to the system of democracy.

Part I

The Basis of
Coalition Government

Since the establishment of the State of Israel in May 1948, no fewer than fourteen and as many as twenty-four parties have been striving to attain power and control of government in six parliamentary elections held to date. Of these parties, the Mapai (short for Mifleget Po'alei Erez Israel, Party of Israel's Workers) consistently emerged the strongest. Though it never gained more than 38.2 per cent of the popular vote, with the exception of the election to the Seventh Kneset in October 1969 when it ran on a joint list with three other labor parties, it dominated all the governments of Israel.

Government in Israel is by coalition, hence by mutual concession and compromise among the participating parties. Political parties play a vital role in Israel politics. They determine the composition and functioning of the government. Ministers serving in the Cabinet are neither elected by the nation nor chosen by the Prime Minister; they are appointed by their respective parties. Therefore, their loyalty is apt to be to the party first and to the government second, a situation not conducive to government stability.

To assure reasonable Cabinet stability despite party differences on ideological, economic, political, social, and religious matters, Mapai has tried to secure control of the coalition by keeping a majority of the ministerial posts for itself. To accomplish this, Mapai has had to pay a price in the form of concessions to the minor parties, particularly the NRP (National Religious Party).

Hoping to exert strong religious influence in spite of an overwhelmingly secular majority, the NRP offered Mapai qualified support. This arrangement gave Mapai uncontested supremacy in the Cabinet equivalent to a majority party and enabled the religious parties to strengthen the religious establishment in the state. It went contrary, however, to the outlook of the majority of the population, which has been outspokenly secular, and introduced elements of tension into the political system that brought about frequent Cabinet crises and government changes.

Institutional factors, historic antecedents, ideology, ethnic composition, and the interaction of events on the domestic front play a vital role in shaping the government. Equally significant, however, in their effect on governmental organization and stability are regional and international developments. The sensitivity of a government to circumstances prevailing, and to changes occurring, outside the borders of the state is in inverse ratio to its economic and military self-sufficiency.

Israel is a small state. It shares a long border with an aggressively inclined foe. It possesses a significant Arab minority whose inclination is to be more loyal to the enemy than to its own government. It is, further, economically and militarily dependent on outside support. Its government reacts, therefore, with seismographic sensitivity to global developments and to changes taking place outside its borders.

In this respect Israel is not unlike Czechoslovakia in the period between the two world wars. Czechoslovakia, too, was a small state, sharing a long border with expansionist Germany and harboring in its midst a powerful German minority that clamored for "reunification" (*Anschluss*) with the German Reich against the interests of its own state. In the face of this direct threat of secession Czechoslovakia lacked economic and military self-sufficiency. These circumstances had a substantial effect on the stability of the Czechoslovak government which, just as Israel is, happened to be a coalition.

Thus, regional or geopolitical considerations and matters of international concern have contributed to maintaining the balance of coalition government in Israel. Of these external factors, the Arab threats, the cold war, and the sensitivity of the nations of the world to the status of religion and the holy places in Israel are paramount.

Geopolitically, Israel is isolated from the world by a ring of

Arab states. Prior to the Six Day War of June 1967, Israel, with a territory one-third the size of Lake Michigan, had a 590-mile-long land frontier with hostile neighbors who had denied Israel's right to exist as an independent Jewish state. The Arab states maintained an attitude of active belligerency toward Israel from the moment of its inception. Their persistent threats to Israel's survival have made security the major problem of the state. This circumstance has had a restraining effect on the parties and dampened internal disputes. It is ironic that just as the existence of Israel has furthered the aspirations of Arab unity and solidarity, so the Arab threat to Israel's existence has contributed to the cooperation of the left and right wing, and the secular and religious elements in the country.[1]

The Arab threat has imposed on Israel a severe burden of national defense, compelling it to search for arms, supplies, and allies among the nations. Dependence on the scarce resources available, and the uncertainty of shifting alliances in a conflict which has taken on the unmistakable aspect of a big power struggle, has had a sobering effect on Israel politics. Though debates and clashes in this ideologically oriented society ordinarily would have led to turmoil and possible violence, dependence on outside opinion and help and on the goodwill of present and potential allies has forced the politically conscious elements to subordinate their party loyalties to national interests. This has had a stabilizing influence on Israel's coalition government and prevented any radical departure from the existing situation.

Equally important to the maintenance of coalition government is the stance of the international community and its supersensitivity to religious crises affecting the Holy Land. The predominantly secular leadership of Israel felt compelled from the outset to establish a separate ministerial department, the

---

1. With minor variations, the term "left" in this study designates a socialist, unionist (Histadrut) and pro-collectivist stance. The term "center" denotes support of private initiative and investment side by side with support for collective enterprise. The "right" assumes an anti-socialist attitude, the curbing of labor unions, and reliance on private economic initiative and capital investment. The designation "militant" is occasionally applied to parties who have shown greater than usual zeal and aggressiveness in their attitude, pronouncements, or actions toward the attainment of their partisan objectives.

Ministry of Religious Affairs, in order to palliate the fears of its foreign supporters and of its opponents on matters involving the three major faiths that have a special interest in the Holy Land. The Ministry became the stronghold of the NRP. Though the practical need of the existence of the Ministry of Religious Affairs has often been questioned, and the alternative of shifting its competence to the Ministry of the Interior has repeatedly been proposed by its secular critics, the Ministry has endured as a focus and symbol of the power of the religious establishment and its ability to extract concessions from Mapai.

Thus, the Arab threats, the problem of national defense, and the watchful posture of the international community, in conjunction with the configuration of the political forces in the state, have contributed to the shaping of Israel's brand of coalition government.

1

The Political System and the Religious Establishment

The political system and the religious establishment have co-existed in Israel uneasily under what has been termed the "status quo." If the religious militants could have their way, they would discard the existing parliamentary system of democracy and substitute theocracy for it. If the secular parties could triumph over the religious militants, they would rid the state of what they consider unnecessary encumbrances of a religious past that hamper the full flowering of the "rule of law" and of "freedom of conscience" in the country.

These terms need to be carefully defined within this particular context. The "rule of law" is used by the secularists in reference to laws passed by the duly elected representatives in parliament assembled. This is in contradistinction to the "rule of the Torah," or religious law, held sacred and supreme by the religious elements. According to the secularists, the "rule of law" must be supreme in a democratic state with the clear implication that secular parliament has a right to pass laws that will supersede any law of the Torah which may be in conflict with them.

The term "freedom of conscience," as used in Israel, may have an implication exactly the opposite of that in the United States and in the Western European countries. Since its meaning depends on who is using it, the term is a source of much confusion. To the secular parties, "freedom of conscience" entails freedom from *religious* infringement upon the lives of the secular population. They militate against the imposition of kosher (religiously permissible) food in the armed forces and governmental establishments. They consider this a breach of the "freedom of conscience" of the majority who are then constrained to eat kosher food instead of what they really like. For the same reason and under the slogan of "freedom of conscience," the secular parties object to any constraint on Sabbath travel, pig raising, marriage and divorce practices, and many more. As far as the religious parties are concerned, the exact opposite holds true. To them a Jew can safeguard his "freedom of conscience" only if he lives in obedience to the law of the Torah, which bans Sabbath travel, the consumption of nonkosher food, or certain types of conjugal combinations.

The "rule of law" and the "rule of the Torah" have been, on several occasions, only a hair's breadth from an explosive clash; indeed such clashes did occur in isolated instances. The contradictory approach to "freedom of conscience" has produced equally tense moments that threatened the political order in the country.

Responsible political leaders have done their utmost to prevent open clashes on these lines, and when they did occur, to dull their edge and eliminate their cause. Yet, a *modus vivendi* between the two camps, the religious and the secular, had to be established. For this purpose they have introduced the status quo. Religious life was to be left "as is" in May 1948, when the state declared its independence. However, despite the agreement on the status quo, both camps have claimed that inroads are being made by their opponent into their realm, infringing upon their "freedom of conscience."

Now, though all this may sound somewhat peculiar to the Western mind, the situation becomes even more perplexing when one realizes that the secular parties control 85 percent of the popular vote and of parliamentary representation, and the religious parties muster altogether 15 percent. It becomes obvious that the religious elements, through the medium of the religious parties, exercise a disproportionate influence in Israel politics despite their minority status.

What forces Mapai to make concessions to the religious parties instead of entering into a working agreement with secular parties? How do the religious parties attain their objectives? What are the parties' principal characteristics, goals, and strategies? What political factors work in favor of the religious parties and prevent the assertion of the will of the majority? What possible changes would be necessary to free Mapai of its dependence on the NRP (National Religious Party)? In the circumstances of a possible coercion by a minority, what prevents continual social and political upheaval?

These are some of the questions that we shall attempt to answer in this study. The present study deliberately focuses on the Cabinet, for in this central institution of the Israel political system the techniques of negotiation and compromise enable the religious parties to attain their goals.

Prologue to Conflict and Compromise

The politics of compromise in Israel antedates the creation of the state. It was already well developed in the two organizations that laid the groundwork for the state's independence: the Kneset Israel (Jewish Community) and the Zionist Organization. In the Kneset Israel under the British Mandate in Palestine (1920–1948), several parties joined in a governing coalition. Despite their recurrent hostility toward each other, they exercised their limited power of home rule by mutual concession and accommodation.[1] In the Zionist Organization, which literally fathered the Jewish State by mobilizing the masses of world Jewry into a political front for an independent Israel, politics of compromise was the rule since its inception in 1897.[2]

The situation did not change with Israel's Declaration of Independence in May 1948. The character of government, together with the political party system, the electoral system, and party relationships was inherited by the new state from its predecessors. Thus Israel received a legacy which has radically affected its constitutional and political development.

---

1. Moshe Attias, *Kneset Israel b'Erez Israel: Y'esodah v'Irgunah* (The Jewish Community in Palestine) , (Jerusalem: Va'ad Leumi, 1944) .
2. See the minutes of Zionist Congresses, i.e., *XI. Zionisten–Kongress* (1913) , p. 86; *XII. Zionisten–Kongress* (1921) , pp. 555 ff.

Another legacy left to the state by its forerunners was the religious establishment. The problems it has caused have been infinitely complex. Some of its roots reach back into the distant past. It also carries with it deep-seated psychological and emotional involvements, whose reactions and consequences could not be objectively calculated.

The inherited system of government, as well as the religious establishment, are deeply entrenched in the new state. Attempts have been made to change them, so far with little success. One of the major problems and perhaps one of the greatest obstacles in the path of political change is the interdependence of the government and the religious establishment. This interdependence is characteristic of the Israel system of government. It contributes to the perpetuation of the politics of compromise.

The phrase "politics of compromise," as used in this context, describes a situation where the official position of the government does not reflect the stand of one single party, but is, as far as possible, an amalgam of views of the various parties who together form the government. The extent to which a party can affect the program of the government, if its views are not shared by the other partners of the coalition, depends on its indispensability, size, and influence.

Until now, the religious parties have managed to extract substantial concessions from their main coalition partner, the Mapai. The Mapai has been the sole party that has so far been capable of forming a government in Israel. It has, for reasons yet to be explored, given preference to the religious parties in governmental partnership, despite the concessions it has had to grant them.

The Importance of Compromise

"No matter what men's visions may be, where their goals differ and where a peaceful adjustment is sought, compromise is the product. In a world already bitterly divided in many areas and easily capable of further cleavages, a system that gives us half a loaf is a system to be cherished."[3]

3. Pendleton Herring, *The Politics of Democracy* (New York; Rinehart and Co., 1940) , p. 422.

Unanimity of opinion is neither possible nor desirable in the conduct of state, but it is, nevertheless, necessary when opinions have to be translated into political action. Political action in Israel, as in any other state, on governmental level must be decisive, definitive, and not weakened by internal discord if stability is to be preserved.

Varied opinions become embodied into unity of action through compromise. In that sense, every government is the product of compromise. A writer on Great Britain, with its virtual two-party system, recently stated that "British politics is by nature the politics of compromise."[4] Politics and government in the United States are also subject to compromise, despite its two-party system.

Compromise in a two-party system arises from diverse opinions and points of view in a party that often becomes crystallized into factions. These demand to be recognized and heard and cannot be neglected if the party is to survive. Great Britain's Labour Party has to contend with its powerful trade unions, and the American Democratic Party must take into account the Southern Democrats.

Yet, though a two-party system cannot avoid compromise any more than a multiple-party system, it usually manages to submerge the differences within the party. This holds true even at the time when differences are most likely to break into the open, immediately before national elections. Within the party the rough-and-tumble of bargaining reaches its climax behind the scenes at a national convention from which the party emerges with one document, its election platform. The people who vote for that party know what position the party may be expected to take when assuming the responsibilities of government, though the position evolved from various avenues of thought and from conflicting attitudes.

In Israel, with its multiple-party system where none of the parties has gained a majority in the national elections, the voter may know his favorite party's ideology, but this often gives him only a vague notion of what the party's stand would

---

4. Allan Potter, "Opposition with a Capital 'O': Great Britain," in R. A. Dahl, *Political Opposition in Western Democracies* (New Haven,: Yale University Press, 1966), p. 33.

be if it became a member of the government. The process of hard bargaining, the give-and-take leading to a compromise, can begin only after all the votes are counted and the numerical strength of each party becomes known. At that point a government must be formed that would command the support of the majority in parliament. This is a complicated and often protracted task that taxes to the utmost the ingenuity of the politician no less than the patience of the population. Yet, a government must be established for the purpose of orderly administration and the survival of the state. That government must agree on a working program and set forth its goals.

In a multiple-party system coalition bargaining does not end when the parties agree on a government program. Each party in the coalition continues to press daily for its own advantages, always assuming the attentive posture of a combatant. There is one main difference between parties that are in the coalition and those outside it. Only "national interests" are a restraining factor in the behavior of parties outside the coalition. Within the coalition, however, the parties are, in addition, expected to abide by the rules of the game, namely, by joint cabinet responsibility.

Thus, a multiple-party system, in contrast to a two-party system, has a tendency to produce a blurred image of authority. Government policy is rarely clear-cut; approaches to controversial issues are indirect; and no one ever knows if the same government with the same policies will be in power tomorrow. This is perhaps the principal feature of the politics of compromise in Israel and in other multiple-party systems.

Of course, this distinctive characteristic may be a conspicuous handicap to sound government. It may breed violence in patriotic circles, despairing of slow action. It may grind the machinery of government to an occasional standstill. It may endanger the democratic processes in the country. All these threats are more potential than real in Israel because of historical and socio-economic factors, the international situation and the security position of the state, and the acceptance of compromise as a technique of problem solving in the political process.

Part II
Political Pluralism

In order properly to assess the political system of Israel and the relationship of state and religion within it, we shall examine the basic elements that molded the Israel government's version of politics of compromise. We shall first review some of the determinant sociological and institutional factors. We shall then investigate the role of parties in the political system, since they are important elements of coalition government. Finally, we shall inquire into the constitutional and political basis of the Israel version of coalition government, in which Israel's religious problem is rooted.

Part II

Political Pluralism

2

Demographic, Ideological and Institutional Components

The determinant factors in the politics of compromise in the State of Israel are the heterogeneity of the society, the ideological diversity, the national character, the institution of the electoral system the society allows to operate, and the multiple-party system it produces.

Demographic Considerations

Israel has a heterogeneous society. More than half its population arrived to the country after May 14, 1948, when it was declared independent.[1] The people came from a bewildering variety of backgrounds. Inevitably, they brought with them the cultures, mores, and patterns of behavior (including often political behavior) of their countries of origin.

The heterogeneity resulting from the variety of backgrounds of the immigrants has been complicated by divisions on ethnic, color, or religious lines.[2] Rifts between Oriental and European

---

1. *Statistical Abstract of Israel* No. 17 (Jerusalem: Central Bureau of Statistics, 1966), p. 21. Israel's Jewish population in May 1948 was 649,600. In 1966 its population stood at 2,299,100. Of these, 1,086,700 immigrated since 1948.

2. Moshe Sicron, *Immigration to Israel* 1948–1953, Statistical Supplement (Jerusalem: Central Bureau of Statistics, 1957), p. 22. See also S. N. Eisenstadt, *The Absorption of Immigrants* (London: Routledge, 1954), p. 106.

Jews, between Jews and Arabs, and between the black Jews of
India and the white Jews have contributed to the fragmentation
of the population.

The background of the recent immigrants is only one of
several reasons for diversity in the state. Economic status also
plays a significant role. The society that was once egalitarian
(till the early 1950s), has begun to develop rapidly its ex-
tremes of poverty and the *nouveaux riches*.[3]

Such a varied population has contributed to a pattern of
diversity in the state, making an impact on its socio-political
dynamics. Perhaps its most important result has been the great
heterogeneity of the electorate.

Ideological Considerations

The electorate is further affected and divided by the great
ideological diversity, whose roots go back to the Zionist Organization and to the Jewish Community Rule under the Mandate. Since these organizations were dependent on voluntary
participation, they could not enforce the allegiance of their
members. Therefore, they had to allow freedom of expression
to the fullest possible extent, in order not to alienate any faction operating within their framework. This, in turn, encouraged ideological fragmentation and the establishment of a
machinery of government that responded to the great variety
of interests and loyalties of its membership. Indeed, the organizations succeeded in satisfying most of the parties operating
within their framework, but they also perpetuated political diversity in the institutions of the organizations and, eventually,
in the state.[4]

Ideological splits have crystalized around political, economic,
religious, or ethnic lines. These have by no means been clear-
cut divisions. Two groups may take an identical stand on economic matters, yet be bitter enemies on political or religious
issues. This contributes to the proliferation of parties.[5]

3. Nadav Safran, *The United States and Israel* (Cambridge, Mass.
Harvard University Press, 1963), p. 79.
4. For a concise presentation of the Zionist Organization see Israel
Cohen, *A Short History of Zionism* (London: F. Muller, 1951).
5. Safran, p. 98. He speaks about multi-axial divisions of opinion.

Ideology plays an important role in Israel's political life. Every party, if it wishes to be worthy of the attention of the electorate, must be an ideological unit, advocating, teaching and propagating its own ideological approach and deprecating that of other parties. This does not mean that there is no consensus of opinion among most of the parties regarding certain issues, like the need of securing the borders, defending the sovereignty of the state or promoting Jewish immigration. Such consensus must exist if the nation is to survive. But aside from a few issues embraced by all parties, differences on fundamental questions concerning the character of the society and the state outweigh the agreements so decisively as to pose almost insurmountable obstacles to working together.

To the same extent that each party meets its counterparts with poorly disguised hostility, it shuns variations in ideological interpretation also within its own ranks. Any deviation in ideological approach within a party is considered akin to apostasy and would usually result in the creation of a new splinter party.[6]

Ideological diversity, as well as the heterogeneous structure of the society, have fostered a multiplicity of parties.

National Character

Winston Churchill was quoted as saying that "the Greeks rival the Jews in being the most politically minded race in the world. No matter how forlorn their circumstances, or how grave the peril to their countries, they are always divided into many parties, with many leaders who fight among themselves with desperate vigor."[7]

The history of political divisiveness among Jews is very old. The Pharisees and the Sadducees are but one famous example, the former representing the commoner and the latter the nobility in the Sanhedrin (the judicial and political assembly of Judea) during the two centuries preceding the Christian era.

---

6. A recent example of the formation of a new party as a result of a split is the Rafi Party, the "young" faction of Mapai, which split off in 1965 under the leadership of David Ben-Gurion.

7. Phillip Gillon in *Jerusalem Post,* 30 October, 1959, Supplement.

Already in that age compromise assured that the two presiding officers of the Sanhedrin should each be elected from a different party.

Another example of political divisiveness is that of the Zealots, who would not make peace with their opponents in beleaguered Jerusalem even while the defenses of the city were being eroded by the attacking Romans.

A charactristic trait of Jewish scholarship lies in its polemics. Laws and traditions were argued about by divergent "schools" of thought, the most famous of them being the "schools" of Hillel and Shammai. These schools debated and fought among themselves "with desperate vigor," agreeing on few issues and differing very frequently.

It would be safe to state that the Jewish people has a predilection to debate, argumentation and divisiveness in politics as well as in scholarship. This, too, encourages the creation of multiple parties and the politics of compromise in Israel.

The Electoral System

The machinery of state that best embodies, expresses, and perpetuates the ideological diversity of the society is the electoral system. The electoral system in Israel is one of proportional representation (PR) with a single national constituency.[8] It is the same system that was used in the Zionist Organization and in the Jewish Community Organization under the Mandate. When the independence of the state was declared, the necessity of continuing the same electoral system was not even disputed. The tremendous ideological diversity, the low level of literacy, and the heterogeneity of the population called for proportional representation.

The PR system in Israel is the simplest of all available electoral devices. The voter has to choose only one symbol, which stands for his favorite party, and deposits it in the ballot box. He need not be literate for the task, which requires only the recognition of one letter (occasionally a combination of two or three letters) . Voting is by party lists and not by candidates.

---

8. *Laws of the State of Israel,* "Constituent Assembly Elections Ordinance," vol. 2 (November 19, 1948) : 24.

It is left in the hands of the party machine to decide on the slate of individuals who would be the party's representatives in the Kneset, if the party is successful in the elections.

Since the whole country is a single constituency, the voter is reasonably assured that his vote will not be wasted. Results of Kneset elections are tabulated in proportion to the number of votes cast for each party throughout the whole country. This contrasts sharply with the majority system used in English or American elections, where the votes cast for a losing candidate in one constituency become valueless to the party (even though the loser may have drawn 49 percent of the votes to the winner's 51 percent).[9]

Although this makes every vote precious under the PR system and may seem to be democracy at its best, it also encourages the proliferation of parties that need to acquire only a few thousand votes to be represented in Parliament.[10]

In the United States, under the constituency system, a small party or splinter group, standing little chance to win, would pool its resources with a big party. In Israel, however, until recently it was worthwhile for a splinter group to undergo the expense and the trouble of an election campaign. Under the PR system it stood a good chance to gain, especially since in Israel, contrary to some other countries, the candidate or the party did not even forfeit any deposit, no matter how few votes it may have attracted. The only limitation imposed upon the parties was the requirement of the 1951 Election Law Amendment of at least 1 percent of the popular vote in order to gain a seat in the Kneset.[11] A recent change in the law provides that a candidate forfeits a deposit of 5,000 pounds if he does not gain at least 1 percent of the vote.[12]

While on the one hand the electoral system in Israel is particularly well suited to the tremendous ideological diversity in the state, on the other hand it perpetuates this diversity by

---

9. *Ibid.*, ch. 6, art. 30, details the distribution of votes.

10. In the First Kneset election (1949) the quotient was 3592. In the Seventh Kneset election (1969) it was 11,274.

11. "Second Kneset Elections Law, 5711-1651," vol. 5, art. 38a, (April 12, 1951), p. 991.

12. "Kneset Elections (Amendment No. 3) Law 5721-1961," vol. 15 (May 23, 1961): 129.

strongly encouraging fragmentation among the parties. Historical, sociological, political, and institutional factors work together to preserve a multiple-party system in which none of the party is able to gain a majority in the Kneset. Inevitably, Israel's PR system leads to the formation of coalition government and to the politics of compromise.

Multiplicity of Parties

The heterogeneity of the electorate and its ideological diversity take on meaning at the polls. There, the electoral system of proportional representation helps to translate these, often inchoate, social forces into political forces whose power can be measured by size and influence. What emerges in the political spectrum is a conglomeration as colorful in its diversity as it is bewildering in numbers. In the seven Kneset elections since the attainment of statehood, 21, 17, 18, 24, 14, 17 and 16 parties ran.[13]

In order for a party to survive in such a competitive political climate, it must foster intense partisanship in its followers. Party allegiance is sustained by party newspapers, youth movements, social clubs, convalescent homes; there are even housing projects and various recreational facilities and welfare institutions, all offering avenues for intense political indoctrination.

The electoral law of the state strengthens the party apparatus by providing that the voter is to vote for party lists and not for individual candidates. The candidate is placed on the list by the party machine. The dependence of the representative on his party encourages strong party discipline and party centralization and fosters greater allegiance to the party than to constituents or, perhaps, even to the nation. In a state deeply divided by ideological cleavages, this institutional support of the party results in the strengthening and perpetuation of the multiple-party system.

Undoubtedly, the influence of the multiple-party system on the politics of compromise is great. What makes government by compromise an unavoidable necessity is the presence of a

13. See Appendix for corresponding table.

sufficient number of parties who manage to split the electoral vote to such an extent that a majority party is not able to emerge. In such circumstances, the country can aspire only for a coalition government of several parties. This gives the smaller parties an excellent chance to attain their objectives in the process of hard bargaining. Goals that they could never attain through popular endorsement may be realized through a barter of supporting votes to the Prime Minister and his party. Thus the cycle is completed. The multiplicity of parties fosters a climate for politics of compromise and this, in turn, encourages the small parties to hope for eventual attainment of their objectives within a coalition.

3

The Centrality of Parties

Owing to demographic, ideological, and procedural factors, the largest party, the Mapai, when running on an independent list, managed to gain only slightly more than one-third of the valid votes cast in the elections. Even in conjunction with its three Labor partners in the elections to the Seventh Kneset it fell short of a majority. It was therefore unable to form a Mapai government and remained continually dependent on the support of the other parties. Yet, owing to their fragmentation, the other parties were unable to establish a government without Mapai's participation. Thus, while Mapai was not given the chance to govern by itself, neither was an effective opposition allowed to develop into a possible alternate government.

In the United States it is generally understood that if the Democrats lose an election the Republicans win it. In England the alternative to a Labour government would be a Conservative government. In Israel no similar clear-cut assumption can be made. If anything emerges clearly from a study of the party spectrum, it is the desire of the electorate not to entrust the fate of the nation into the hands of any one party and, simultaneously, to avoid creating a vital opposition to the Government.

It is a distinctive feature of Israel politics that the most effective critique of, and brake on, government action is found within the coalition itself. Maurice Duverger spoke about the confusion in a multiple-party system where "a distinction has to be made between an external opposition provided by the parties of the minority and an internal opposition existing among the majority parties themselves."[1] The parties in the coalition are those on which the government is dependent. Their pressures and desires, therefore, take the place of opposition surveillance and introduce checks and balances into the country's political system. Until an effective opposition is allowed to develop, democracy in Israel may depend on the preservation of coalition government and on the perpetuation of the politics of compromise.

Political Parties: Some General Observations

Parties do not change easily in their program and ideology, especially not in Israel where the assumption seems to be that the country is a "federation of sovereign parties and the Kneset is a kind of United Nations."[2] More often than not, party symbols, slogans, doctrines, and goals become vested with a measure of sanctity. This held true to a large extent in the Zionist movement and in the British Mandate of Palestine, where party and party ideology were taken very seriously. The creation of the State of Israel introduced little change. The state was shackled with a proliferation of parties, doctrinaire ideologies, intense party loyalties, and a political machine to perpetuate the power, centralization, and multiplicity of parties. Nevertheless, changes have taken place both in the total party spectrum of the country and within individual political parties in the first twenty years of Israel's existence.

The most significant change in the party spectrum has been the ever increasing interest in party mergers. While in the Fourth Kneset elections twenty-four parties competed, in the elections to the Seventh Kneset only sixteen lists entered the race. The tendency of parties has been to forge alliances with those factions placed immediately on the right or on the left of the party line-up. Such alliances have been numerous.

In the First (1949) and Second (1951) Kneset elections Mapam and Ahdut ha-'Avodah ran on a joint list; in the Fifth

---

1. M. Duverger, *Political Parties* (Science Edition, 1963) , p. 43.
2. Professor Talmon in *Ha-Arez*, February 17, 1961.

Kneset election (1961) the union of the General Zionist and Progressive parties formed the Liberal Party. In the campaign for the Sixth Kneset (1965), the Liberal Party and the Herut came together in the newly formed Gahal (Herut-Liberal) movement, and the Mapai and the Ahdut ha-'Avodah formed the Ma'arakh (Alignment). In the aftermath of the Arab-Israeli war in June 1967, the Mapai, Ahdut ha-'Avodah, and Rafi parties merged into the new Israel Labor Party and Mapam agreed to run on a joint list with the new party in the forthcoming parliamentary elections. With the exception of the Second Kneset election (1951), the four religious parties amalgamated either into one bloc (1949) or two blocs. Party strategy aimed at strengthening party ranks through the process of fusion.

Few of the alliances, however, proved lasting and often contributed to the creation of splinter factions who either launched their own party on a platform hardly distinguishable from the mother party or remained a source of discontent from within. Nevertheless, the trend seems to indicate a tendency toward party alliances and mergers, leading to an eventual polarization of parties.

The most outstanding ideological changes within individual parties occurred in the leading party in the state, the Mapai. It has, with the outcome of the elections to the Seventh Kneset, run a complete cycle, from left to center and back to left. The most aggressive right-wing party, the Herut, has also made a basic change. Having fought the Histadrut (General Federation of Labor) futilely for over a decade and a half, it decided, prior to the 1965 elections, to join the Histadrut. In the Kneset election of 1965, Herut openly aspired to capture a majority that would have given it control over the Cabinet.

Coalition Groupings

Political parties in Israel can be divided broadly into three groups: the socialist parties, the nonsocialist parties, and the religious parties. The socialist parties include the Israel Labor Party, an amalgam of Mapai, Ahdut ha-'Avodah and Rafi; Mapam, the Communists and the Arab lists. The newly formed

State List could, by its personnel if not program, be assigned to this group. The nonsocialist parties include the Herut and the Liberal Party, who together form the Gahal; the Independent Liberal Party; and the Free Centre. The religious parties are the National Religious Party, Agudat Israel, and Po'alei Agudat Israel.

Although individual parties have encountered changes of fortune from one Kneset election to the next, the coalition groupings have remained very stable. The combined socialist parties' strength in the seven Kneset elections fluctuated between 64 and 69 seats, the nonsocialist parties' strength between 30 and 34 seats, and the religious parties' strength between 15 and 18 seats.[3]

Of the three party groupings, the religious was the only one that would enter into coalition with any of the parties of the other two groupings. Except for the Mapai, none of the socialist parties were in a governmental coalition with the nonsocialist Liberal Party or Herut Party. Except for the Independent Liberal Party, none of the nonsocialist parties was ever in a government coalition with the socialist Ahdut ha-'Avodah, Mapam, or the Communists. This, of course, was not a coincidence. Except for the Mapai and the Independent Liberals, the two groups drew around themselves rigid doctrinaire boundaries that forbade constructive party intercommunication and interaction between the two groupings. The sole exception was the Fourteenth Government, formed on the eve of the Arab-Israeli war in June 1967, when all parties represented in the Kneset aside from the Communists joined in a Government of National Unity to ward off a severe threat to Israel's survival.[4]

This situation forced Mapai to rely either solely on the socialist grouping or exclusively on the nonsocialist grouping

3. The figures include the Sefardi Party in the nonsocialist grouping, while it pursued an independent existence. They do not include the Arab parties in the socialist grouping, limiting the figures to Jewish parties only.

4. When Golda Meir became Prime Minister in March 1969, she established a "government of continuity" in view of the national emergency. For further information on coalition groupings see Appendix, chart on "Fluctuation of Coalition Alignments."

in the formation of government. Neither choice was palatable. It repeatedly, futilely, attempted to bring Mapam and the General Zionists (Liberal Party) together in one coalition. The result was that Mapai had to rely consistently on the religious parties because of their readiness to bargain, their willingness to join with other parties of any vintage, and their usefulness in countermanding any pressure within a one-sided coalition.

The classification of parties according to coalition groupings seems to be the most practical when viewed from the vantage point of the formation and functioning of coalition government. It is therefore utilized in the consideration of the parties in the following pages.

SOCIALIST PARTIES

Toward Formation of a United Labor Front

On January 20, 1969, on the first anniversary of the emergence of the Israel Labor Party, Mapam signed a "covenant of alliance" with it, thus bringing into being the largest single political force in Israel's history and the first faction ever to enjoy a clear majority of 63 seats in the Kneset. The process of fusion, however, was not complete. Members of the Israel Labor Party are often still identified by their former party labels as "ex-Mapai," "ex-Ahdut ha'-Avodah," and "ex-Rafi." Each party maintained its newspaper and kibbutz movement. In line with an unwritten law of Israel party life, the merger of parties produced its splinter group. The discontented element within Rafi that opposed the merger formed the new State List.

Despite these signals of discord the four Labor parties entered the election for the Seventh Kneset on one list, each confidently expecting a sweeping victory that would free it from coalition pressures.

The Mapai Party

The most important party from the point of view of the formation and functioning of the Cabinet is the Mapai. Just as the Cabinet is the axis of political life in Israel, so is the Mapai the axis of the Cabinet. To this day all the Cabinets were formed by Mapai. The country's four Prime Ministers— Ben Gurion, Moshe Sharett, Levi Eshkol, and Golda Meir— were leaders of the Mapai and of the Histadrut, Israel's most powerful labor union, with which the fate of Mapai has been intimately associated. Mapai is also the party with the greatest plurality of electoral votes in the state, having the backing of from one-quarter to one-third of the population.[5]

The founders of the Mapai established cooperative settlements, introducing the unique institutions of Kibbutz and Moshav into the Israel economy and society. They created cooperatives in every facet of economic endeavor; they established units of Jewish self-defense, and by 1920 they had built the powerful organization that made socialism invincible in the country: the Histadrut.

The Mapai was forged into a political instrument in 1929 through the merger of ha-Po'el ha-Za'ir, a non-Marxist labor group, and Po'alei Zion, a faction of the labor movement that adhered to orthodox Marxism with its principles of class struggle and revolutionary socialism. The merger did not eliminate ideological differences between the two factions of the newly formed Mapai Party and in 1944, on the eve of a Histadrut election, the radical (Po'alei Zion) wing of Mapai broke off, forming the new Ahdut ha-'Avodah Party.

Until the creation of the state in 1948, the Mapai could clearly be designated as a left-wing party.[6] The pressures of austerity and the mass absorption of immigrants following the declaration of independence gradually forced the Mapai to accept a milder version of the socialist plank. Investment of private capital and private initiative in all branches of the economy had to be encouraged. Thus, Mapai gradually shifted its position and became a center party, endeavoring simultaneously to encourage the collective as well as the private

5. In the seven Kneset elections Mapai gained respectively 35.7, 37.3, 32.2, 38.2, 34.7, 36.7, and 46.2 percent of the total vote. In the last two elections it was part of an alignment and so the last two figures do not represent Mapai's true strength.

6. J. C. Hurewitz, *Struggle for Palestine* (New York: Norton & Co., 1950), p. 44.

sector of the economy, defending the interests of the worker and the union, as well as of the employer and investor.[7]

The party's success in politics has been noteworthy. In the five Kneset elections between 1948 and 1961 it won 46, 45, 40, 47, and 42 seats out of a total of 120. It has been almost as successful in the municipal elections. Mapai's predominance can be attributed to its large plurality of votes and to its monopoly in establishing a viable Cabinet. Though theoretically the other parties could have pulled together to form a coalition without Mapai, in practice this was not possible. In a certain sense, therefore, the fate of the nation was deposited in its hands. An awareness of this by the average voter contributed greatly to the prestige of the party.

The outbreak of internal feuds, beginning with the "Lavon Affair" in 1960, and culminating in the expulsion of Mapai's founder, David Ben-Gurion, from the party on the eve of national elections in 1965, marked a crucial turning point in Mapai's history.[8]

Mapai and the Histadrut

Mapai's power has mainly derived from its intimate association with the Histadrut. The Histadrut is a veritable "State within the Jewish Community,"[9] controlling certain vital strategic areas of endeavor to the possible exclusion of the state itself. It was the most important single political factor in Israel for three decades preceding independence and has maintained its dominant position ever since. It superimposed the character of the labor movement on practically all institutions of the state. Its ideology has dominated the thinking of much of the population, and it has commanded the loyalty of three-quarters of the productive forces in the country. It was recognized as early as the Mandatory period that "Labor is

---

7. M. H. Bernstein, *The Politics of Israel* (Princeton, N. J.; Princeton University Press, 1957) , p. 60.

8. Elyiahu Hasin, *Ha-Parashah* (The Affair) (Tel Aviv: Am Ha-Sefer, 1961) . See also *Ma'ariv*, March 11, 1965. "The Mapai, since the 'Affair' started, is in a constant state of crisis," p. 5.

9. Alex Rubner, *The Economy of Israel*, A Critical Account of the First Ten Years (New York: Frederick A. Praeger, 1960) , p. 41.

the strongest organized factor in the land,"[10] a status which it has continued to enjoy in the period of sovereignty. It seems to have been an accepted axiom in Israel politics that the party in control of the Histadrut is also in control of the government.

The Histadrut attained monopoly of power and control by providing for all the economic and socio-cultural needs of the members of the labor force, making them completely dependent on the organization. "It became practically compulsory for a worker looking for work to be a member of the Histadrut; and it is even more important that only members of the Histadrut could make use of the services of its medical insurance, the Qupat Holim."[11] But the Histadrut is more than a labor union and a source of medical insurance. It is also in charge of many enterprises that make it the biggest employer in the land, rivaling the government itself. These extend into all areas of endeavor: industry and agriculture; commerce and banking; transportation by land, sea, and air; construction; and housing. The Histadrut has fulfilled socio-cultural needs by providing for education (until the abolition of the trend system), running its own theater, publishing its own periodicals and daily news media, keeping up its own rest homes and cultural centers, and providing comprehensive insurance coverage to its members

As long as Mapai had a majority in the Histadrut, it could control the nation. It was limited only by the alliances it was forced to seek to secure a controlling majority in the political arena, as it already had in the economic arena. Herein could be found the Achilles' heel of the Mapai Party: with a capacity to control the economy of the land through the Histadrut, it still depended on minor parties, among them most prominently the religious parties, to secure its political position. The concessions it has had to grant to the minor parties in return for their political support did not always reflect the socialist and secularist ideals on which the Histadrut and the Israel Labor movement was founded. This had given rise to inner tensions

10. Walter Preuss, *Die Judische Arbeiterbewegung in Palastina* (Vienna: Fiba-Verlag, 1936) , p. 327.
11. Rubner, p. 42.

and feuds within the Labor movement before the establishment of the state; these problems have grown worse in recent years.

Interested in a more clear-cut socialist and secularist policy, all the labor parties demanded reforms.[12] As a result, in the Histadrut elections of September 1965, Mapai, the party that was held responsible for Histadrut policies, suffered a serious setback.[13] For the first time, Mapai became dependent on a coalition in the Histadrut to safeguard its leadership within it.[14] The situation did not improve with the September 1969 elections. Mapai's gradual loss of control of the Histadrut and of its Central Committee may have results whose effect on the political system will be profound. It may mean the loss of the unique position that the Mapai has enjoyed in the country's political life. It may introduce a cleavage between the state and the Histadrut. It may result in the weakening of the government. These somewhat bleak prospects may force the Mapai to lean more heavily than it originally intended to on its partners in the newly created Israel Labor Party.

The Ahdut ha-'Avodah (Unity of Labor)

Mapai's partner in the Israel Labor Party, and its former partner in the Ma'arakh (Alignment), the Ahdut ha-'Avodah, has been sandwiched in ideologically between the Mapai and the Mapam. It is immediately to the left of the former and to the right of the latter. Its close ideological ties with both parties caused it to bounce back and forth between them. Indeed, the Ahdut ha-'Avodah followed the law of the pendulum; it broke away from the Mapai in 1944 because of doctrinal differ-

---

12. *Jerusalem Post*, September 10, 1965.

13. *Ibid.*, September 21, 1965. In the Histadrut elections in 1959, Mapai and Ahdut ha-'Avodah had a combined majority of 74%; in 1965 the Alignment barely swung over the 50% critical line. The Mapai alone had 55% in 1959, while in 1965 it received only 32%. In 1969, Mapai, Ahdut ha-'Avodah and Mapam jointly gained 62%, as compared to 87% a decade earlier.

14. In order to circumvent a coalition cabinet in the Histadrut, Ma'arakh sources suggested that the Histadrut Cabinet be considerably expanded from its present nine members so that Mapai could retain control of the organization. *Jerusalem Post*, November 25, 1965.

ences. It then joined the party on its left, the ha-Shomer ha-Zair, forming the Mapam in 1948. In 1954 it parted company with Mapam as a result of anti-Semitism behind the Iron Curtain. It completed the swing of the pendulum in 1965, when it rejoined Mapai in the Ma'arakh.

"The Ma'arakh was created by Mapai and the Ahdut ha-'Avodah for the purpose of uniting the workers into a major force that will realize the establishment of a working society."[15] This was the goal. In fact, the road to the Ma'arakh was paved by internal strife and a party split within Mapai ranks that produced the Rafi Party. Mapai, when it ran in former elections unaligned, twice emerged stronger, twice weaker, and once equal to its strength of 45 members in the Sixth Kneset, when it was aligned for the first time.[16]

In the Third Kneset election (1955), when Ahdut ha-'Avodah ran for the first time on an independent platform, and in the Fourth and Fifth Kneset elections (1959 and 1961), the party won, respectively, 10, 7, and 8 seats. This was not quite sufficient to put it in a strong parliamentary bargaining position. Yet, from its inception it participated in all the coalitions, sharing responsibility with Mapai for government policy and drawing closer to the leading party.

Though the influence of Ahdut ha-'Avodah in the Kneset was limited by its small representation, in the Histadrut it occupied the position of second largest party, and as such, wielded considerable influence.[17]

It is questionable whether the party has found a permanent place in the Israel Labor Party. In a country where institutions and individuals react with seismographic sensitivity to the slightest variations in political program and outlook, the Ahdut ha-'Avodah continues to stand as far from its present ally, the Mapai, as it has stood from its former partner, the Mapam.

---

15. *Davar*, September 10, 1965. Platform of the Alignment for the Histadrut elections.

16. Mapai representation in the Kneset: 46 (1949); 45 (1951); 40 (1950); 47 (1959); 42 (1961).

17. In the 1959 Histadrut election Ahdut ha-'Avodah gained 17 percent of the vote. Only the Mapai, with 55.4 percent emerged stronger. Mapam placed third, with 14.9 percent. *Jerusalem Post*, September 20, 1965.

Inevitably, it will be consistently outvoted in joint party councils, a most frustrating and demoralizing experience to party diehards, as it was consistently outvoted within Mapam.

The party, which has been called by an observer the "*Naturei Qarta* (the firebrand) of the Histadrut," is militant in its defense of labor interests, yet it has not been doctrinaire and it has not been ideologically entirely unbending. It is strongly opposed to infringement by religious institutions and parties upon the way of life of the nonreligious element in the country.

The Rafi Party

Rafi (Reshimat Po'alei Israel or Israel Labor List) came into being as a result of a revolt within the ranks of the Mapai that culminated in a party split in 1965.[18] One faction, led by Ben-Gurion, protested organizational irregularities and the alleged disregard of party organs by the Prime Minister in the process of decision making. It also deplored Mapai's intention to abandon one of its basic tenets, which was to promise to change the prevailing electoral system. However, neither organizational nor ideological differences in themselves could have produced a split had they not been aggravated by a personal feud between Prime Minister Eshkol and former Prime Minister Ben-Gurion. The latter's followers claimed that the party was being subjected to a systematic process of "de-Ben-Gurionization" by its present leadership.

Rafi spokesmen did their best to give the split a doctrinal and ideological coloring. They denounced Mapai leadership as autocratic, dominating Histadrut in a dictatorial fashion, indifferent to the welfare of the people and taking its power too much for granted. "The party is not to be an end in itself. It is obvious, that she is not an end that sanctifies all means," charged Rafi leader Shimon Peres.[19] "That is the danger that can bring Begin [leader of right-wing Herut] to power. To forestall it, we must make the Party what it was in the past;

---

18. *Jerusalem Post*, July 2, 1965.
19. *Ha-'Arez*, October 1, 1965.

a bearer of a vision, of progress, of freedom, of free speech and criticism, and of good fellowship."[20]

The new party claimed to run on sound and progressive Mapai ideology from which Mapai itself had recently strayed and which it abandoned upon forming the Ma'arakh with Ahdut ha-'Avodah. Rafi members, as a faction of Mapai, opposed the Alignment with Ahdut ha-'Avodah, which openly voiced its dislike of Ben-Gurion, its interest in absolving Pinhas Lavon from guilt, and its opposition to changes in the existing electoral law. A new electoral law is the keynote of the Rafi program.

The Mapai split and the consequent Alignment-Rafi battle occupied the center of the political scene and resulted in the bitterest election campaign in Israel's history. The hopes of Rafi and the dread of Mapai that Rafi would emerge as a major party from the national election, did not materialize. Rafi gained ten seats in the Sixth Kneset, which made it the fourth largest party in the country. The expectations of Rafi that "there is no hope to establish a stable government without Rafi's participation"[21] remained unfounded. In the Sixth Kneset, the choice not being its own, Rafi entered the ranks of the opposition.

On the eve of the Six Day War, however, in June 1967, Premier Eshkol invited all parties with the exception of the Communists to join a Government of National Unity. Moshe Dayan of Rafi became Minister of Defense. It was the first time that Mapai relinquished its hold on that Ministry.

Mifleget ha-'Avodah ha-Israelit (Israel Labor Party)

On January 21, 1968, the biggest party merger was effected in the history of the State of Israel. Three Labor parties, the Mapai, Ahdut ha-'Avodah, and Rafi, after seven months of arduous negotiations, signed the foundation scroll of the most powerful political force yet created in Israel, the new Israel Labor Party.[22] Together with the Mapai-affiliated Arabs, it

---

20. Ben-Gurion, as quoted in *Jerusalem Post,* June 20, 1965.
21. Josef Almogi, as quoted in *Ha-'Arez,* October 5, 1965.
22. *Jerusalem Post,* January 22, 1968.

commanded 58 out of the 120 votes in the Kneset, only three short of a majority. The best results shown by any party to date was Mapai's control of 52 votes in the Fourth Kneset. No wonder that the Mapai Minister of Posts, Israel Yeshayahu, declared triumphantly in the aftermath of the merger: "We are the people!"[23]

The turning point that led to active negotiations for the merger of the three Labor parties was the Six Day War in June 1967. The threat to Israel's survival posited by the neighboring Arab states forced Prime Minister Levi Eshkol and his dominant Mapai Party to call for the establishment of a new broadly based Government of National Unity. The speedy termination of the war did not bring in its wake guarantees for peace. Prudence dictated the safeguarding of the new government to present a solid front in international negotiations. The need for cooperation for reasons of security and defense contributed greatly to the creation of a climate suitable to the consummation of the merger.

The objectives the parties sought to attain in the merger could be succinctly stated. Rafi agreed to the merger in order to increase its framework of influence and eventually to attain control within the united party. Mapai wanted the merger in its aspiration for a numerical controlling majority in the Kneset under its aegis. Ahdut ha-'Avodah went along with the merger in order to maintain its position within the Labor bloc and to keep a watchful eye on Rafi's ambitious young element.

The creation of the new superparty may indicate a radically new departure in the political dynamics of Israel. It could lead to the polarization of parties into three, possibly only two blocs: the socialist, and the nonsocialist and religious blocs. It could bring about the demise of coalition government with its concomitant bargaining and compromise. It could free the government from its dependence on the religious parties and alter the relationship between state and religion. These are substantive changes whose effect on the political development of Israel may be profound. However, though all these prospects, and more, may be realized, the political experience of

---

23. *Ha-Doar,* February 9, 1968, p. 234.

Israel does not offer sufficient cause for unbounded optimism.[24]

The Mapam Party

The Mapam (Mifleget Po'alim Meuhedet or United Labor Party) was created in 1948 as a result of a merger between ha-Shomer ha-Za'ir and Ahdut ha-'Avodah. The ha-Shomer ha-Za'ir (Young Watchman) was founded in 1929 on Marxist-Zionist principles. Its main practical objective was Halutziut (pioneering). It produced a great number of collective settlements in strategic areas of the country. Its contribution to the attainment of independence was noteworthy, owing to its command brigade, the Palmah. The Ahdut ha-'Avodah was a left-wing faction of Mapai, from which it split away in 1944. It formed an independent political party in 1946 and in 1948 joined ha-Shomer ha-Za'ir to form Mapam.

Since Israel became an independent state, Mapam has rather consistently voiced interest in participating in the coalition Cabinet. Yet, of the fifteen Cabinets that were formed to date, the present one is only the sixth of which Mapam has been a member.[25] The basic reason for its failure to reach a proper understanding with Mapai can be found in Mapam's lack of ideological resilience. Mapam has carried the concept of revolutionary socialism, based on Marxist-Leninist doctrine, to its theoretical extreme. It had preached the inevitability of class struggle, the evil of private enterprise, and the downfall of the capitalist system. It had advocated a militant socialist policy and a national economy heavily weighted in favor of the collective segment of the population. It denounced any pact with the United States and other Western countries as a betrayal of Israel and the proletariat and, instead, strongly advocated firm ties with the Soviet Union.

Increased anti-Semitism and anti-Israel pressures behind the Iron Curtain brought confusion to Mapam circles. They led

24. For a fuller description and analysis of the merger among the three Labor parties, see author's article, "Old Problems in a New Guise," in *Midstream*, May 1968.

25. The additional four Cabinets in which Mapam participated were two during the Third Kneset and one during the Fourth Kneset (1955–1961), as well as the first coalition of the Sixth Kneset (1965–67).

to disenchantment in Mapam ranks and forced the party to re-evaluate its foreign policy stand but not before it suffered a number of crippling blows that almost catapulted it into political obscurity. In 1954 Mapam split into its two original components of which it was formed. The Ahdut ha-'Avodah, socialist but not revolutionary and not pro-Soviet, left the party whereas the ha-Shomer ha-Za'ir continued to function under the name of Mapam with its rigid ideology. Further splits occurred when two Mapam Kneset members joined the Mapai and two others allied themselves with the Communists because they were frustrated by Mapam's confused and embarrassing stand on international relations. In 1958 the party admitted that "In contradiction to the prophecies on imperialism's imminent downfall, capitalist economy still maintains relative stability," and that "The maintenance of the proletarian dictatorship in the Soviet Union during forty long years brought with it manifestations of perversion and signs of degeneration."[26] However, a slight adjustment in Mapam ideology on foreign affairs did not change the party's stand on domestic issues, leading it to further difficulties and ideological gymnastics.

Prior to the establishment of the state, Mapam was opposed to an independent Jewish state and supported the idea of a bi-national Jewish-Arab state. Under the pressure of realities it abandoned the idea, but to this day Mapam leaders claim that "We are the only Jewish-Arab party in Israel."[27]

The party continues to appeal mainly to the rural collective settler and maintains a stable electoral vote. The rapid increase of the general population in the country, in contrast to the stability of collective settlements, does not augur well for Mapam. Having maintained a representation of nine in the Third, Fourth, and Fifth Kneset, it dropped to eight in the Sixth Kneset.

Mapam emerged as the fifth strongest party in the 1965 Kneset elections. The alignments of its former sister party, the

---

26. Meir Yaari, *What Faces Our Generation* (Tel-Aviv: Mapam Party Press, 1958) p. 76.

27. Mark Segal, "Histadrut—The Election Promises," *Jerusalem Post*, September 10, 1965.

Ahdut ha-'Avodah, with Mapai, made a rapprochement with the leading party feasible. Though Mapam had substantial demands, not the least of which was "equal partnership with the Alignment parties in privileges as well as in responsibility,"[28] Mapam became a member of the coalition.

Mapam rarely wavered in its anticlerical program and policies. It has frequently demanded in its election platforms, on the Kneset floor and through its news media, separation of state and religion in Israel.

The State List

The State List sprang into existence on the eve of the Histadrut elections in August 1969. It offers the anomaly, peculiar even in political life, of a party's being created in support of an individual who chose to remain a ranking member of another party. Moshe Dayan, who joined the Government of National Unity in June 1967 as Minister of Defense, has been the object of legend and controversy. As the architect of the lightning victory in the 1956 Sinai Campaign and as the alleged man of steel in the Six Day War of 1967 he has been adulated by the young generation. As a member of the cabal that was instrumental in splitting Mapai ranks and forming the Rafi party, he has been viewed with suspicion by the Mapai Prime Minister and the ranking Ministers of the Cabinet. Even after he led Rafi back in a reunion with the mother party, Mapai suspicion of his motives did not ebb.

Dayan's popularity with his socialist colleagues did not improve when his supporters began the "Dayan for Premier" campaign. Top-ranking Mapai leaders warned the population of the dangers of "personality cult." Simultaneously, Dayan's policies in the occupied territories, aiming to promote peaceful coexistence and the maintenance of open borders with Arab lands, came under increasing fire in the Cabinet, particularly from Yigal Allon, the Deputy Premier and Dayan's main rival for the premiership.

Ex-Rafi, pragmatist rather than socialist, individualist rather than party follower, ambitious and popular, Dayan could not

---

28. *Jerusalem Post*, December 12, 1965.

expect much sympathy from his Labor Party colleagues. One of the claims of the State List was that weakening the Labor Alignment would strengthen Dayan's position in the Cabinet. Though Dayan ran on the Labor Alignment ticket, the greater the Alignment victory the stronger would be its opposition to Dayan until it succeeded in pushing him out of the Cabinet. Hence the State List has offered the Dayan supporters in Labor ranks an alternative choice of a list that would allow him sufficient latitude of operations in the Cabinet.

In the October 1969 elections the State List was headed by Ben Gurion. Its top candidates were mainly former Rafi members who refused to join the Labor Alignment. The key planks of its program were electoral reform to the Kneset and local authorities, liberal policy as propounded by Dayan regarding the occupied territories, and greater emphasis on individual intiative in a "depoliticized" economy. Strong leanings toward the nonsocialist Independent Liberal Party and Gahal are discernible in the State List's economic platform. The party won four seats in the elections to the Seventh Kneset.

The Communist Party

During the election campaign for the Sixth Kneset in November 1965, the Communist Party of Israel suffered a split in its ranks, largely along ethnic lines. Two factions developed: the "Wilner-Tubi" faction, which appealed to the Arabs, playing on their feelings of antagonism for an independent Jewish State, and the "Mikunis-Sneh" group, who declared that "the Communist Party will be the shield of Israel's existence, of Israel's independence, of Israel's security, of Israel's future."[29] The two groups campaigned independently on two separate lists. Their combined popular vote showed a sharp decrease from 4.2 per cent in 1961 to 3.4 per cent in the 1965 elections.[30] The Communist "Arab" Party wound up with three seats, the

---

29. Maurice Friedberg, "The Split in Israel's Communist Party," *Midstream*, 12, No. 2 (February 1966) : 26.
30. The percentage of election returns compare as follows: 1949: 3.5%; 1951: 4%; 1955: 4.5%; 1959: 2.8%; 1961: 4.2%; 1965: 3.4%; 1969: 4.0%.

Communist "Jewish" Party with one seat in the Kneset.[31]

The Communist "Arab" Party poses a potential danger to the state, since it offers an organizational framework to antagonistic elements who wish to see the state obliterated. Simultaneously, however, it offers the government a yardstick by which to measure the forces from within that pose a threat to its survival.

Arab Parties

Three Arab parties were represented in the Sixth Kneset. All three were localized. The Progress and Development concentrated on the Galilee in the north; the Cooperation and Fraternity drew its support from the Muslims and Druzes of the Mount Carmel area; and Agriculture and Development relied on the Arab vote in the central section of the country.

The three parties together had four representatives in the Kneset.[32] In the Seventh Kneset they coalesced into two parties, the Alignment-affiliated Arab and Druze lists, with their combined representation remaining unaltered at four.

They supported Mapai on political issues.[33] Before the Six Day Arab-Israeli War of June 1967, Arabs formed over 11 per cent of the population. Their representation in the Kneset was not limited solely to the above-mentioned parties. Mapai and the Leftist parties consistently placed Arabs on their lists in order to attract the Arab vote, bringing Arab representation in the Fifth Kneset to seven.[34]

---

31. Their combined representation in former Knesets was in 1949—4; 1951—5; 1955—6; 1959—3; 1961—5; 1965—4; 1969—4.

32. This compares with two representatives in the First Kneset; 5 in Second; 5 in Third; 5 in Fourth; 4 in Fifth and 4 in Sixth.

33. The exception to the rule is the question of absentee Arab property. While military rule was imposed on Arab inhabited territories in Israel, they opposed Mapai on that issue too.

34. *Facts about Israel 1966* (Israel: Ministry for Foreign Affairs), p. 57.

NONSOCIALIST PARTIES

Toward Formation of Gahal Party

On March 7, 1965, the Liberal Party split over the question of an alignment with the Herut Party. Rather than join forces with the right-wing Herut, a minority faction formerly called Progressives created the new Independent Liberal Party (ILP). By the end of August 1965 the agreement between the majority faction of the Liberal Party and the Herut Party was concluded. The Gahal Party was formed.

The Liberal Party

The roots of the Liberal Party, formerly known as the General Zionist Party, stretch back to the First Zionist Congress in 1897. Gradually, as political parties began forming within the Zionist movement with distinctive Marxist, collectivist, religious, expansionist, or territorialist ideologies, the General Zionists crystallized into a middle-class group. In the State of Israel it has advocated private enterprise, suspension of state support to collective institutions, and the termination of Histadrut control over the country's economy. While in other countries, like Great Britain or the United States, private enterprise is usually cautious and on guard with regard to state interference, in Israel the General Zionists prefer state control of several aspects of economy and welfare to Histadrut domination.

Other distinctive features of the party have been its advocacy of a unified system of education, contributing greatly to the abolition of the trend system in 1953, and its demand for a written constitution in order to preserve democratic freedom and civil rights. Though less outspoken than their former allies, the Progressives (now ILP), in voicing opposition, the General Zionists do not favor the inroads of religious legislation.

The General Zionists participated in two out of the four governments of the Second Kneset.[35] They were uneasy partners in the coalition, feeling strangulated by the socialist-oriented

---

35. From December 1952 to June 1955.

parties. Their strength in the Kneset has been subject to the widest fluctuations experienced by any political party in Israel. In the first four Kneset elections, their representation see-sawed from seven to a soaring twenty, dropping to thirteen and further again to eight. In the Fifth Kneset the General Zionists sat together with the Progressives under the name of Liberal Party, which was represented in the Kneset by seventeen members.

In view of future developments it may be noted that any drop in votes for the General Zionists brought a resurgence of strength for the Herut, and vice versa. It became noticeable that the two parties cater to a distinctive clientele, which may on occasion switch its votes from one to the other, depending on the pressing issues of the moment, yet remains faithful to the "bloc" as a whole. Although possibilities for a merger were explored as early as 1955, they only materialized in 1965.

The Herut (Freedom) Party

Of the parties that were in existence in January 1949, when the First Kneset was elected, only two have not participated in the government until the crisis leading to the Six Day War in June 1967: the Herut and the Communists. The Herut Party has become identified with entrenched opposition. In its pre-state form it opposed the Zionist Organization, the Jewish Agency, and the British Mandatory. Since the state came into being, it has represented the opposition to the government and to the Histadrut.

The Herut as an independent political party was formed only in 1948. Prior to it, the Herut ideology was incorporated in the Revisionist movement, which broke away from the Zionist Organization in 1935 because of radical differences in orientation. Revisionist orientation was activist, calling for immediate Jewish mass immigration to Palestine and for forceful measures and retaliation against Arab attacks. The Revisionists were strongly critical of British anti-Zionist policies in Palestine. They claimed both sides of the Jordan River for the projected Jewish state. Revisionist Party adherents were strongly nationalistic, well disciplined, and militaristic in outlook. They were impatient with everything that hindered the attainment of their goals. This included the Zionist Organization and the Jewish Agency leadership that advocated systematic, long-range colonization instead of immediate political action, and the Histadrut, which has supported measures to attain the workers' demands instead of banning strikes and accepting compulsory arbitration, so that the economy could move ahead full-steam.[36]

During World War II, the Revisionists transformed themselves into an illegal army, the major part of which, the Irgun Zvai Leumi, contributed greatly to the harassment of the British, the containment of the Arabs and, ultimately, to the establishment of the state.

The Herut Party is but the Revisionist Party under a different name, with overtones of the fighting Irgun attached to it. Under present circumstances it has abandoned the slogan of "a Jewish State on two banks of the Jordan," but only by substituting for it the claim to the historic boundaries of the Jewish People.[37] It demands an aggressive defense policy against the Arab neighbors. The party was bitterly opposed to any treaty and negotiation with the Germans. It has been both anti-British and anti-Russian in its foreign policy, having continually advocated a strong Franco-Israeli alliance.

By and large, the biggest disagreement between Herut and Mapai was, first of all, in the field of foreign affairs and, secondly, concerning the role of the Histadrut. Herut objects to Histadrut monopolies combining labor and ownership, and to the collectivist tinge the Histadrut lends to the whole economy. Instead, the Herut, like the Liberal Party, wishes to strengthen the private sector, individual initiative, and capitalist enterprise.

There is yet a third area of disagreement between the Herut

---

36. The Revisionist Party was the *enfant terrible* of the Zionist movement. Among the multitude of controversial writings regarding the Party, the interested student will find the works of Vladimir Jabotinsky, the party's founder, most rewarding. See also books by J. Schechtman.

37. "The right of the Jewish People to the Land of Israel in its historic completeness, is an eternal and inalienable right." Herut Party, *Principles and Ways of Action*, Platform for election to Fifth Kneset (Tel Aviv: E. Moses Printers, 1961), p. 5.

and the Mapai. These parties differ in their interpretation of events that are tied to names vividly remembered in Israel, like the sinking of the *Altalena* or the bombing of the King David Hotel. The rights and wrongs of the recent past, interwoven with searing personality conflicts, form a formidable wall between the two parties.

The Herut Party had done surprisingly well in the Kneset elections. In the First Kneset election in 1949, it gained a representation of fourteen, undoubtedly due to the glowing legend attached to the Irgun fighters. In subsequent elections the vote reflected more realistically the strength of the Herut Party. But that strength kept increasing continually: from eight (Second Kneset), to fifteen (Third), to seventeen (Fourth) and again seventeen (Fifth Kneset). The apparent decay of the Mapai and the leveling of differences between the Liberal Party and the Herut, offered Herut the long-awaited opportunity to take its leap for power. The means to accomplish this objective was the Gahal.

The Herut-Liberal Bloc (Gahal)

The timing for the creation of Gahal (Gush Herut-Liberalim or the Herut-Liberal Bloc) could not have been much better. Mapai was still being burdened by the Lavon Affair and was in the throes of a new crisis which resulted in the expulsion of its founder, David Ben-Gurion, and in the splitting of the party. Simultaneously, increased prosperity in the country seemed to favor the private enterprise parties. Thus, the Herut-Liberal Bloc had every reason to expect a sufficient increase in its voting strength that would enable it to create an alternative government to that proffered by Mapai.[38]

The first test of strength between the Mapai Alignment and the Gahal came in the elections to the Histadrut on September 19, 1965. Having voiced outspoken opposition to Histadrut domination of the country and to Mapai domination of His-

---

38. "The Herut Movement and the Liberal Party in Israel have decided to establish a joint parliamentary bloc to constitute a National-Liberal regime in Israel in place of the present regime." *Principles and Lines of Action: Herut-Liberal Bloc.* (Tel Aviv: Israel Printers, 1965), Preamble. English translation in *Newsletter* (May-June 1965), pp. 17-20.

tadrut, Gahal posed a serious challenge to Histadrut and Mapai hegemony. The Histadrut election provided a double surprise: the right-wing Gahal emerged with an unprecedented 16.5 percent of the vote and the Mapai Alignment managed to get a majority only by "the skin of its teeth," 50.5 percent.[39] Thus, in the first round Gahal came out victorious and it now looked forward to a triumph in the Kneset elections.

However, contrary to all expectations the tables were turned in the national parliamentary elections. Presumably, elements discontented with Mapai, who offered their protest vote to the Gahal in the Histadrut elections, became worried at the unexpected spurt in right-wing strength. In the national elections they switched back to the socialist parties. Total Gahal representation in the Sixth Kneset amounted to less than the combined representation of the Liberal Party and the Herut in the Fifth Kneset: twenty-six, as compared to thirty-four. Clearly, the outcome of the Kneset election amounted to a not inconsiderable defeat of the right wing.

In the new Gahal platform both constituent groups aimed to embody the principles dearest to them. The program carried the stamp of Herut in the clauses dealing with security and foreign affairs, and the imprint of the Liberals with regard to economic and financial matters. Concerning the administration of government, Gahal demanded that it be established and conducted "in accordance with state needs, not on the basis of party or coalition considerations" (Art. 6). They came out strongly with a demand for a written constitution (Art. 4) and for state health and unemployment insurance (Art. 10). However, on the issue of religion Gahal has somewhat ambiguously pledged both "freedom of conscience" and "the entrenchment of the eternal values of Israel's heritage in the life of the nation and in education" (Art. 5). The parties to the agreement agreed to disagree on certain major issues and to vote separately on them without prejudice to each other (Art. 12).[40]

---

39. In the 1959 Histadrut elections the Alignment parties received 74.03 percent of the vote; the General Zionists received 3.48 percent, and the Zionist Worker that is sympathetic to Gahal 5.77 percent. The Herut did not participate.

40. All the Articles mentioned and quoted are from the Herut-Liberal Bloc Agreement. See note 38.

The election results raised some doubts in the Liberal camp about the practicality of the alliance. In view of the results, it cannot be foreseen when and how, if at all, Gahal will be able to act in the capacity of a substitute government for Mapai. The threat against Mapai seems to have fizzled out. Even though in the election to the Seventh Kneset Gahal's position improved somewhat, it did not attain the strength of its constituent units in the Fifth Kneset (the last time they ran on independent lists). A circumstance that could help Gahal to power would be a peaceful and slow revolution of the type that helped the Democratic Party in Turkey to power in 1950, after 28 years of uninterrupted rule by the Republican Party. More feasible for the near future, however, is a better understanding between Mapai and Gahal that might lead to Gahal's inclusion in a coalition Cabinet. Indeed, in June 1967, in an effort to bring about a united front in face of Arab threats and an impending war, Prime Minister Eshkol invited the leader of Herut, Menahem Begin, to join the Cabinet.[41]

Free Centre

Gahal's setback in the 1965 Kneset elections sent ripples of discontent through Herut ranks. Herut's colorful leader, Menahem Begin, was being blamed for the election results that fell short of party expectations. Thereupon Begin resigned from the party chairmanship. Simultaneously, rumblings grew stronger within the party about its alleged lack of democracy, and its dominance by the party machine and the old guard. In an effort to maintain party discipline the leader of the revolt, Shmu'el Tamir, was brought to a party court and was sentenced to temporary suspension from the party. Begin was invited to resume the party chairmanship.

At this juncture Shmu'el Tamir, together with two Herut members of the Kneset, declared themselves an independent faction called the Free Centre. In May 1967, when Gahal joined

---

41. Mr. Begin's participation in the Cabinet has been viewed with some apprehension by left wingers. However, his cooperation has been impressive.

the coalition, the new party remained in opposition to the Government of National Unity.

The Free Centre advocates free enterprise, state ownership of health and social services, the constituency election system, and the preservation of the post-June 1967 boundaries. Essentially it differs very little from the Herut, though personality differences form an overwhelming obstacle to reunion. In the election to the Seventh Kneset the party lost one seat. Its parliamentary representation dropped from three to two.

Independent Liberal Party (ILP)

The Independent Liberal Party came into being on March 7, 1965, subsequent to a split in the ranks of the Liberal Party over the question of unification with the radical right-wing, Herut. Adherents of the ILP opposed such a step. The roots of the ILP stretch back to September 1948 when, after the establishment of the State of Israel, it was founded under the name "Progressive Party" as a result of a merger of three groups. Numerically the most important of the three constituent groups was the 'Aliyah Hadashah (New Immigration). It consisted mainly of Central European immigrants, with the middle-class element predominating. It had no clearly defined social policy and generally took a liberal stand on social issues. The second constituent group was the ha-'Oved ha-Zioni (Zionist Workers), a labor group with membership in the Histadrut, but unlike the two major parties in the Histdrut, the Mapai and Mapam, it was not socialist and rejected the conception of the class struggle.[42] The third constituent group was the Left wing of the General Zionist Party, which carried the designation "Group A." In contrast to "Group B" of the General Zionists, which exhibited strong conservative tendencies it was left of center, oriented toward the Histadrut, drawing its support from artisans, small farmers, and the members of the liberal professions.[43] Group A split from the General Zionist Party in August 1948. From this amalgam the Progressive Party emerged as the left-wing Center Party.

42. *Political Parties in Israel* (Israel Consulate), p. 3.
43. Joseph Dunner, *The Republic of Israel; Its History and Its Promise,* (McGraw-Hill, 1949), p. 134.

From an ideological point of view there is a well-defined dividing line between the Mapai and the Progressives (now ILP). Contrary to the Mapai, the Progressives are not socialist and are in favor of private investment. They are opposed to the strengthening of the Histadrut and favor state control, as opposed to Histadrut control of essential services and of welfare functions. From a practical point of view, however, the Progressives are intellectually sympathetic to socialist aspirations, while the Mapai leadership quietly acknowledges the indispensability of private capital and initiative. Thus, the two parties, while projecting radically different programs to the electorate, have sufficient common ground to make cooperation between them feasible. The Progressives joined every coalition until the election to the Fifth Kneset in August 1961, with one exception.[44] In 1961, on the eve of the election to the Fifth Kneset, the Progressives united with the General Zionist Party, forming the Liberal Party which remained in the opposition. In 1965 the two parties separated again and the Progressives, now known as the Independent Liberal Party, once again agreed to join the coalition.

Numerically, the Progressives have not carried great weight in the Kneset. In the seven Kneset elections they gained once six seats, twice four, and three times five seats, and once they ran on a combined list with the Liberals. Their moral influence, however, is greater than their number would indicate. For example, they were instrumental in pushing through the Cabinet the Education Bill, which abolished the strongly entrenched trend system.

The ILP is strongly secularist and is a staunch foe of religious encroachment and domination in the country.

RELIGIOUS PARTIES

The religious parties cannot be considered as a single unit. In the relationship to Cabinet politics, as well as in their social orientation, they maintain distinctive approaches. Nevertheless, the four parties that make up the "religious bloc" share certain basic characteristics.

---

44. The Third Government, formed in October 1951.

The religious parties, while claiming that they do not wish to establish a theocracy—a society where God's law or religious law is paramount—accept the basic premise that Israel can be considered a Jewish state only by virtue of its association with the Torah (Jewish religious law). Consequently, they demand that the Torah should be the fundamental law and constitution of the state. Only such constitutional laws should be added, in areas not provided for by Jewish law, that are in harmony with the Torah. It is only by virtue of the religious heritage that the ideal of the Jewish state survived the vicissitudes of Exile, claim the religious parties. The Jewish state is, therefore, indebted to the traditional way of life and the Torah for its survival. Being indebted to it, the Jewish state must respect and preserve it.

Among the laws of the Torah considered most significant for the preservation of the Jewish people are the family laws. Hence, the religious parties demand that matters of marriage and divorce, birth and death, with all the concomitant problems pertaining thereto, must be subject to religious authority. Though this demand was challenged by the secular parties, the religious parties had the weight of established practice on their side. The Mandatory power relegated matters of personal jurisdiction to religious authorities. When the state was established, the religious parties had to demand merely the preservation of the status quo in the status of religion. (Of course, the term "status quo" is in itself subject to interpretation.)

Though the program of some religious parties covers broad areas of foreign policy and economics, their main endeavor is in the field of religion. The four parties are kept separated from other parties by their aspiration to further religious objectives without which they could easily blend into moderate center-left and moderate center-right parties.

Repeated attempts made by the religious parties to unite have been unsuccessful.[45] For the election to the First Kneset

---

45. As early as in 1923 we read: "Efforts were continued to combine the Agudat Israel and the Mizrahists into one United Orthodox Party . . . but without results." *The American Jewish Yearbook 5684* 25 (Philadelphia: Jewish Publication Society of America, 1923) , p. 69.

in 1949 they formed a temporary coalition which suffered from inner tension and strain, and collapsed before the termination of the Kneset. Prior to the election to the Third Kneset in 1955, the ha-Po'el ha-Mizrahi and the Mizrahi formed the National Religious Party (NRP), and Po'alei Agudat Israel and the Agudat Israel joined in the Torah Religious Front (TRF). While each of the parties preserved its organizational structure and party machine, all indications point to an increasingly closer cooperation between the two members of the NRP, while the two members of the TRF have evidenced exactly the opposite trend.

The electoral fortunes of the religious parties seem to be quite independent of their success and failure in their efforts to amalgamate. Their total Kneset strength fluctuates little, ranging from a low of fifteen in the Second Kneset (1951) to a high of eighteen in the Fourth (1959), Fifth (1961) and Seventh (1969) Kneset. In the First Kneset (1949), Religious Bloc representation stood at sixteen, while in the Third (1955) and Sixth (1965) Kneset it was seventeen of a total Kneset membership of 120. The Kneset strength of the NRP has ranged from ten to twelve, that of the TRF from five to six. With twelve representatives in the Seventh Kneset, the NRP is the third strongest party.

National Religious Party (NRP)

The NRP became a single party as a result of a merger between ha-Po'el ha-Mizrahi and Mizrahi in 1956. Of its two constituent groups, ha-Po'el ha-Mizrahi has been the stronger, (approximately four times bigger), and Mizrahi is the older. Mizrahi is the mother party. Its organizational roots date back to the Zionist Organization, where it was organized as a separate faction in 1901. It is primarily an urban, middle-class, orthodox party, without a clear-cut economic program. Its principal activity lies in the field of religious education. Its offspring, the ha-Po'el ha-Mizrahi, was founded in 1922 in Palestine. The social composition of the ha-Po'el ha-Mizrahi has differed radically from that of the Mizrahi. The membership has consisted of workers who sought a synthesis between socialism and religion. Though it has formed a separate labor federation within the Histadrut, objecting to its secularist policies, the ha-Po'el ha-Mizrahi has cooperated rather consistently with the Mapai on labor issues. The party also founded a number of collective and cooperative settlements.

As opposed to the Agudah parties, the Mizrahi parties supported the aspirations of the Zionist Organization from the outset. The Mizrahi parties, however, had to defend themselves constantly from accusations hurled at them by the Agudah group that their support of the secular Zionist vision had been equal to blasphemy. Memories of that conflict, combined with personality differences in leadership ranks and divergent ideological views, have formed a gulf between the Mizrahi and Agudah groups that has so far not been bridged.

Organizationally, the NRP consists of a number of officially recognized factions. The "Central Bloc" headed by Interior Minister Moshe Shapiro and Benyamin Shahor gained 45 percent of the vote at the 1965 party convention. The Lamifneh faction, comprising the labor and union elements and the settlement movement, led by the Minister for Social Welfare, Josef Burg, Moshe Unna, and M. Hazani, has 30 percent. Twenty-five percent is divided among the alignment bloc that strongly opposes the party leadership, the youth faction, the farmers, and the Sephardim. Presently, Mr. Shahor controls the party machine, which is as tightly knit and dominant as that of any other Israel party.[46]

Within the NRP the stand on social issues is largely determined by the ha-Po'el ha-Mizrahi, thus facilitating full cooperation with the Mapai. The NRP and its constituent parties have been members of the coalition in every government since the foundation of the state. None of the other parties, except the Mapai, equals this record. Occasionally, influential voices within Orthodox Jewry call for abstention from participation in the government, contending that the party's identification with a secular-led government weakens its appeal and purpose, and cost it votes in the forthcoming elec-

---

46. *Jerusalem Post*, February 18, 1966, "Politics and Principles."

tion.[47] But the NRP leadership has preferred the hard bargaining of coalition politics to the ineffectuality of the opposition.

The NRP parties have brought about several government crises and have repeatedly handicapped the speedy creation of a new government because of religious issues.[48] The NRP was solely responsible for protracting for seventy days the negotiations for the creation of a government after the election to the Sixth Kneset. The NRP seemed to strike a hard bargain, but, as always in the past, it was obviously indispensable to the Mapai in the creation of a stable government in January 1966, as well as in 1969 in the wake of the election of the Seventh Kneset.

Torah Religious Front (TRF)

The TRF was formed in 1956 by the Agudat Israel and the Po'alei Agudat Israel. The Agudat Israel is the militant-Orthodox counterpart of the Mizrahi. It was founded in 1913 in German-occupied Poland, with the aim of stemming the tide of secularism in the Jewish community. Until the creation of the new state in 1948, the Agudah rejected a political solution to the Jewish quest for an independent homeland, stressing the primacy of a religious solution. Under the British Mandate, it refused to cooperate with Zionist and Jewish quasi-governmental bodies. "The reason for this has been the Agudat Israel's conviction that by cooperating closely with irreligious elements, the Party would fail in its supreme aim of imposing the absolute rule of Jewish religion upon Jewish life."[49] Its offspring, the Po'alei Agudat Israel, came into being in 1922 in Poland to further the religious goals of the organization among the Jewish workers. It has placed equal emphasis on self-help and the help of God in attaining the redemption

---

47. *Ibid.*, November 26, 1965. Statement by Rabbi Soleveitchik in the United States.

48. For example, a crisis over the education of Yemenite children brought down the Second Government and the First Kneset in 1951.

49. *Political Parties in Israel* (a pamphlet published by the Jewish Agency, November 15, 1948) , p. 4.

and independence of Israel. The outcome of their political efforts would be a theocratic state.

The two parties soon clashed over practical problems of settlement in Palestine. Wanting to establish communal rural units in Palestine, the labor Agudah wing entered into an agreement with the Jewish National Fund, from whom it acquired land for that purpose. The parent body objected to this implicit recognition accorded to a secular Zionist instrument, and a bitter conflict ensued.

With the proclamation of statehood the attitude of Agudat Israel became more positively oriented regarding Jewish independence. They even participated in the Provisional Council of State and held one seat in the Provisional Government in 1948.[50] The Po'alei Agudat Israel has cooperated with the Histadrut, though it did not join the Histadrut because of the latter's secularist outlook.

In attaining religious objectives, great hopes were attached to the formation of the Religious Bloc on the eve of elections to the First Kneset in January 1949. These hopes were frustrated. The Agudah refused to compromise on what it considered religious issues. Its adamant opposition to issues like the conscription of women into nonmilitary service, or to mixed swimming in a municipal swimming pool, and similar issues where the ha-Po'el ha-Mizrahi was ready to compromise, strained the alliance to its breaking point.

From 1956 on, the two Agudah parties endeavored to collaborate within the Torah Religious Front. How flimsy their success has been is demonstrated by the repeated participation of the Po'alei Agudat Israel in the coalition governments, whereas the Agudat Israel has allied itself with the opposition.[51] Within the TRF divided councils seem to prevail.

The likelihood is that the Po'alei Agudat Israel, which has more in common with the ha-Po'el ha-Mizrahi than with Agudat Israel, is gravitating toward the NRP, while simul-

---

50. Rabbi Yizhaq Meir Levin of Agudat Israel was Minister of Social Welfare.

51. Po'alei Agudat Israel participated in the Governments of the Fourth and Fifth Kneset and also joined the first government of the Sixth Kneset in January 1966.

taneously the Agudat Israel is paying ever greater heed to the religious zealots, the "Naturei Qarta."[52] It is doubtful, however, that the Agudat Israel would succumb to the Naturei Qarta anti-state agitation. In turn, it may serve as a useful bridge to these otherwise inaccessible elements. A formal union of the Po'alei Agudat Israel and the NRP is not beyond the realm of possibility. Nevertheless, as long as the Po'alei Agudat Israel can follow unhampered substantially the same line of policy as the NRP, without loss of power and prestige, it may decide to resist any change in status.

52. A group of ultra-Orthodox Jews who live in their self-imposed ghetto in the Mea Shearim quarters in Jerusalem. They deny the state, in accordance with their belief that a Jewish state can be the product only of God's direct and visible intervention, accompanied by the coming of the Messiah.

4

The Constitutional Basis of the Cabinet and of Religion

Israel, unlike its neighbor states in the Near and Middle East, does not have a written constitution. In this respect it resembles Great Britain. Great Britain, however, is an old, established democracy with built-in conventional safeguards. Israel, a relative newcomer in the family of nations, has not yet developed sufficiently powerful and respected conventions to safeguard its system. It has, therefore, been argued that Israel needs a written constitution.[1]

Despite repeated attempts to work out a written constitution for the state, the religious parties have successfully blocked its passage. Their claim has been that the Torah, the ancient religious law, could be the only constitution of Israel.[2] This did not preclude the passage of certain laws that were designated as "basic laws" and that received constitutional validity, i.e., would eventually form the basis of a written constitution and, in some instances, would require a qualified vote of the total Kneset membership for amendment, instead of a plain majority.

A number of "Basic Laws" were passed by the Kneset in the

---

1. E. Rackman, *Israel's Emerging Constitution, 1948–1951* (New York: Columbia University Press, 1955), p. 111.
2. *Divrei ha-Kneset,* First Kneset, 113th session, 4 (February 7, 1950): 733. Z. Warhaftig of United Religious Bloc.

first decade of its existence, among them The Basic Law (The Kneset) of February 12, 1958,[3] pertaining to the organization and functioning of the Kneset, and The State President (Tenure) Law of December 3, 1951.[4] Regarding two important institutions, however, the government (Cabinet) and religion, the parties could not agree to any change. This guaranteed their status and status quo within the constitutional framework on the basis of ordinary law and precedent. Thus, political realities in the form of party disagreements have imposed a sort of immobility on the structure of the government and religion in the state.

Only in August 1966, did Prime Minister Eshkol propose to the Kneset a Basic Law: The Government.[5] In proposing the bill, the Prime Minister hastened to emphasize that its main intent is to incorporate the *existing* regulations regarding the work of the government in a law of constitutional validity. The bill was referred to the Constitutional Committee of the Kneset for review. After a lapse of another two years it was finally approved by the Kneset on August 6, 1968.[6]

Although the status of religion has not been regulated by the ordinary process of law in Israel,[7] the state inherited a well-defined, extended body of law regarding religion, religious institutions and functionaries, and religious jurisdiction, from the British Mandatory administration. This was incorporated into the Israel constitutional system and remained unchallenged until the beginning of 1966.[8]

This chapter examines the status of Cabinet and religion

---

3. *Laws of the State of Israel,* 12:85.

4. *Ibid.,* 6:4.

5. *Divrei ha-Kneset,* Sixth Kneset, Special Session, vol. 44, (August 31, 1966), p. 2504.

6. *Ibid.,* Third Session (August 6, 1968), p. 3094, (August 13, 1968), p. 3293. Also *Sefer ha-Huqim,* no. 540 (August 21, 1968), p. 226.

7. It must be noted that specific issues of vital interest to religion have become subject to legal formulation.

8. *Jerusalem Post,* January 24, 1966. In a leading decision "the Court found that the (Religious Affairs) Ministry's right to issue regulations concerning Jewish burial societies was invalid because it ostensibly derived from the former Mandatory High Commissioner's powers concerning Kneset Israel, the organizational form of the Jewish Community in Mandatory Palestine. The Court ruled that since Kneset Israel ceased to exist, these powers had also lapsed."

in the constitutional system by inquiring into the Transition Law and its amendments. Although the section of the Transition Law regarding the Cabinet has been superseded by a Basic Law: The Government, the status and impact of the Cabinet on Israel politics become more clearly evident from an examination of the original document and its subsequent amendments. We will also investigate the legal basis of religion as expressed in various laws and institutions. Some of these, like the Rabbinical Council, the local Religious Councils and the Religious Courts, were inherited from the British Mandate. Others were formulated and became national law on a piecemeal basis. Inevitably, the constitutional structure evolved from, and was affected by, political realities. Hence, the next chapter discusses the political basis of the relations between state and religion.

The Legal Framework of the Cabinet

The legal framework of government in Israel is tersely spelled out in the Transition Law 5709-1949.[9] The Transition Law laid the legal foundation for the functioning of the Legislature (Chapter One), the President (Chapter Two), and the Government (Chapter Three).

The provisions of the law with regard to the legislature are particularly brief, pointing out that it shall be designated by the term Kneset (Article 1), that its enactments shall be called laws (Art. 2a), which shall be signed by the Prime Minister, the Minister charged with their implementation (Art. 2b) and the President (Art. 2c). The law shall then be published in the Official Gazette within ten days of its passage in the Kneset (Art. 2d).

Provisions on the formation, composition, and functioning of the government are equally terse. The government is formed by a "member of the Kneset" so entrusted by the President of the State after he has consulted with representatives of party groups within the Kneset (Art. 9). The govern-

9. *Laws of the State of Israel,* 3, (February 16, 1949), p. 3. The governments of the six Knesets were established on the basis of the regulations in the Transition Law, which is therefore examined in these pages.

ment consists of the Prime Minister and a number of Ministers "who may or may not be members of the Kneset" (Art. 10). Once formed, the government is required to obtain a "vote of confidence" upon presenting itself to the Kneset (Art. 11a). Within seven days thereafter each government member must pledge loyalty to the state and its laws, and "to comply with the decisions of the Kneset" (Art. 11b). In its functioning, "the government shall be jointly responsible for its activities to the Kneset, shall report to it on its activities, and shall hold office as long as it enjoys the confidence of the Kneset" (Art. 11c). Once it receives a vote of no-confidence from the Kneset, or it decides to resign, it is required to inform the President of the State immediately, "but it shall continue to exercise its functions pending the constitution of a new government in accordance with the provisions of this law" (Art. 11d).

Amendments to Chapter Three of the Transition Law dealing with the government do not substantially affect the relationship of the Cabinet to the Kneset from a legal standpoint. They regulate the appointment of one Deputy Minister,[10] later amended to two Deputy Ministers,[11] and the transfer of power from Minister to Minister without requiring the consent of the Kneset.[12] One amendment strengthens the position of the Prime Minister by stating that "if the Prime Minister has informed the government of his resignation, such resignation shall have the effect of a decision of the government to resign." On the other hand, it also regulates that the inclusion of an additional member in the government requires the approval of the Kneset and that the government announce in the Kneset any vacancy or change of portfolios within the Cabinet.[13]

One amendment to the Transition Law aims to enforce the rule of joint responsibility not only with regard to members of the government, but also on "the party group to which a member of the government belongs," under the threat of a forced resignation from the Cabinet."[14] Another amendment

10. *Ibid.* 5 (February 7, 1951) : 48.
11. *Ibid.* 10 (May 29, 1956) : 68.
12. *Ibid.* 6 (August 12, 1952) : 87.
13. *Ibid.* 6 (June 24, 1952) : 73.
14. *Ibid.* 16 (June 11, 1962) : 73.

sets a limit to the bargaining time in the process of forming a government by offering a maximum of forty-nine days to the Prime Minister designate to return a working coalition before his mandate expires.[15]

Following the pattern of continental European parliamentary systems, the Transition Law seems to depict an extremely powerful Kneset and a subordinate Cabinet. It places no limitations on the Kneset either in the exercise of authority or in duration.[16] While the Prime Minister, the competent Minister and the President have to countersign bills to elevate them to the status of laws, this is a purely formal act, since none has the power to veto legislation enacted by the Kneset. The Kneset cannot be dissolved by any authority except itself. The Cabinet, on the other hand, must retain the confidence of the Kneset in order to remain in office, it must comply with its decisions and give an account of its activities. The sole exception that offers the government discretion to exercise power is embodied in the Law and Administration Ordinance No. 1 with regard to a state of emergency, but that too can be revoked by the Kneset.[17]

The use of Western models is clearly evident in Israel's parliamentary system. This could be expected in view of its antecedents. The governmental setup did not spring into being at the moment of independence. It evolved out of the Zionist Organization and the Jewish Community Organization in Palestine. The former, of continental European origin, was set in the pattern of continental European state machinery which gave the legislature substantial control over the executive. The latter organization, under British Mandate, was patterned after the government of Great Britain, entrusting the executive with great power. As in most countries after the Second World War, the leaders of Israel endeavored to pro-

---

15. *Ibid.* 16 (July 30, 1962) : 97.

16. However, in the Basic Law of 1958, the Kneset limited its term to four years.

17. *Laws of the State of Israel* 1 (May 21, 1948) : 7. Soon after the Ordinance was passed, the Provisional Council declared that a state of emergency exists in Israel. The declaration has remained in force indefinitely. (See H. E. Baker, *The Legal System of Israel,* Tel Aviv: Steimatzky's Agency, 1961, p. 13.)

vide for a strong executive that would not be paralyzed by frequent crises of government, but that would nevertheless be under adequate parliamentary control. The attempt aimed at combining the noblest of the continental with the best of the British systems. The outcome was a powerful legislature in law, but not in practice, and a dominant Cabinet in practice, though not in law.

Religion in the Constitutional System

The Declaration of the Establishment of the State of Israel stated that "The State of Israel . . . will ensure complete equality of social and political rights to all its inhabitants irrespective of religion, race, or sex; it will guarantee freedom of religion, conscience, language, education and culture; it will safeguard the Holy Places of all religions."[18]

This declaration of intent was given legal expression in the Law and Administration Ordinance No. 1 of 5708-1948. The Ordinance provided that "the law which existed in Palestine on the 5th Iyar 5708 (May 14, 1948) shall remain in force insofar as there is nothing therein repugnant to this Ordinance or to the other laws which may be enacted by or on behalf of the Provisional Council of State, and subject to such modifications as may result from the establishment of the state and its authorities."[19]

The above quoted article of the Law and Administration Ordinance necessitated the fulfillment of many of the responsibilities that evolved upon the state from the British Mandate.

The Pre-State Era

Under the British Mandate, religious communities enjoyed special privileges in law and practice. Each religious community was granted internal autonomy. In matters of personal status the courts of each religious group had exclusive jurisdiction.

These in themselves were not British innovations. The Man-

---

18. *Ibid.* 1:4.
19. *Ibid.*, Chapter 4, art. 11, p. 9.

datory power simply continued the laws and conventions by which community affairs were regulated under Ottoman rule, prior to British occupation of Palestine.

The Ottoman Empire was based on the *millet* system, wherein membership in a religious group, rather than citizenship, nationality, or race, was a factor of identification. Each religious group was left locally to its own autonomous devices in matters of personal jurisdiction.[20]

The novel aspect of the British approach lay in incorporating the *millet* system (which ignores nationalism) into the legal framework of post-World War I Palestine, where nationalist feelings were growing by leaps and bounds. This system, perhaps inadvertently, fostered the identification of nationalism with religion.

In 1922, the Palestine Order in Council, which is in force to this day in the State of Israel, stated: "Each religious community shall enjoy autonomy for the internal affairs of the community subject to the provisions of any Ordinance or Order issued by the High Commissioner" (Art. 83).[21] The Order gave residuary jurisdiction to Civil Courts in matters of personal status, but the Religious Courts were confirmed in the enjoyment of their traditional jurisdiction over members who belonged to their respective communities (Art. 51-52). The Religious (or Rabbinical) Courts retained "exclusive jurisdiction in matters of marriage and divorce, alimony and confirmation of wills of members of their community" (Art. 53).[22]

The "Regulations" of December 30, 1927, that became fundamentally the Constitution of the Jewish Community, defining its internal structure and organization, reconfirmed the power of the Rabbinical Courts under the general supervision of a Rabbinical Council. In the "Regulations" the government designated the Yishuv (Jewish population) as a religious community.[23] Indeed, the section of the law dealing with the con-

---

20. Frederic M. Goadby, *International and Inter-Religious Private Law in Palestine* (Jerusalem: Hamadpis Press, 1926), p. 100.

21. *Constitutions, Electoral Laws, Treaties and States in the Near and Middle East,* Helen Miller Davis, ed. (Durham, N.C.: Duke University Press, 1953), p. 350.

22. *Ibid.*

23. J. C. Hurewitz, *The Struggle for Palestine* (New York: Norton and Co., 1950), p. 39.

stitution and powers of the Rabbinical Council was given undisguised priority.[24] Norman Bentwich, who was Attorney General of Mandatory Palestine at the time, attested to the fact that in drafting the "Regulations," the legislator had before him the Ottoman Regulations of the Jewish Community of 1865.[25]

Thus, the *millet* system, introduced into Palestine by the Ottomans, was preserved by the British and was transferred to the new State of Israel, where it offered a powerful boost to the ambitions of the religious parties in turning Israel into a religious state.

The Rabbinical Council

The Rabbinical Council is the supreme religious body in the State of Israel. Initially elected in 1921 by a gathering of Jewish community leaders and rabbis at the request of the British High Commissioner of Palestine, it was the first indigenous authority officially approved by the Mandatory government.[26] The Rabbinical Council was declared to be the only lawful authority recognized by the Palestine administration in matters pertaining to Jewish law.[27] Its power and exclusive jurisdiction was reconfirmed in the Religious Communities (Organization) Ordinance of February 1926,[28] and once again in the "Regulations" of 1927.

Until 1963, the Rabbinical Council was composed of two

24. The "Regulations" discuss first the Rabbinical Council and the local Rabbinical offices (sections 4–11) and only then do they turn to the Elected Assembly and the "General" Council, or Va'ad Leumi (sections 12–18). Although the Hebrew term, Va'ad Leumi, means "National" Council in its correct translation, throughout the English version of the "Regulations" it is rendered as "General" Council. The British were careful to preserve the appearance of the religious status of the Jewish community and did not officially fully endorse its national-secular status. R. H. Drayton, ed., *The Laws of Palestine*, "Jewish Community Rules" (London: Government of Palestine, 1939) 3:2132.

25. M. Burstein, *Self-Government of the Jews in Palestine since 1900* (Tel Aviv: ha-Po'el ha-Za'ir, 1934), p. 167.

26. "The Statutory Jewish Community," *A Survey of Palestine* (Palestine: Government Printer, 1946) 2:915.

27. Burstein, p. 176.

28. "Religious Communities Organization Ordinance of February 15, 1926," *Official Gazette of the Government of Palestine*, no. 157, p. 64.

Chief Rabbis and six Associate Rabbis, with one Chief Rabbi of Ashkenazi (Western), the other of Sephardi (Oriental) descent. They were elected for a period of five years by a specially appointed Electoral Assembly, that consisted of 42 Rabbis and 28 laymen.[29] In July 1963, on the eve of the elections to the Fifth Rabbinical Council, amendments provided for the enlargement of the Council to 12 members and of the Electoral Assembly to 125 members.[30]

The Rabbinical Council has extensive powers of supervision over local rabbinical offices, which sit as Rabbinical Courts of the First Instance. There are presently 19 such courts in the state.[31] The Rabbinical Council itself serves as the only court of appeals in matters which fall under the jurisdiction of the Rabbinical Courts.

The institution of the Rabbinical Council, and the powers with which it was invested under the Mandate, have survived to this day. Since the religious parties usually take into consideration the attitude of the Chief Rabbis on religious matters that become subjects of political debate, the Rabbinical Council exercises substantial influence in political life.

Rabbinical Courts

Under the British Mandate, Rabbinical Courts operated as organs of a voluntary religious community and not as organs of the state. The judges in the religious courts were appointed and their salaries were paid by the religious communities.

The Kneset, by legislative enactments, converted the religious courts into judicial organs of the state and their judges into state officials. According to the Dayanim Act of 1955, judges of Rabbinical Courts, like the civil judges, were to be appointed by the President upon recommendation by a special committee.[32] They have been required to make a declaration of allegiance and have been paid their salaries by the state.

---

29. "Elections of Rabbinical Officers and Rabbis of Local Communities," *Palestine Gazette* 9 (April 9, 1936, Supplement 1) : 230–34.

30. Ya'aqov Even-Hen, *Ha-Rabanut ha-Rashit l'Yisrael* (Jerusalem: Ministry of Religious Affairs, 1964), p. 30.

31. *State of Israel Government Yearbook*, 5727 (1966–67), p. 230.

32. *Laws of the State of Israel* 9 (May 16, 1955) : 74.

The Qadis Law of 1961 guaranteed the Muslim courts a status similar to that of the Rabbinical Courts.[33]

Norms of Religious Observance in National Law

Laws guaranteeing rabbinical jurisdiction, particularly in the areas of marriage and divorce, were claimed by the religious parties as their greatest accomplishment. The reason for this was that, from a religious point of view, a marriage contracted contrary to religious law excludes the interested parties from the Jewish community, and their children are prevented from marrying a Jew "to the tenth generation."

However, the religious parties attained concessions in law also in other matters. During the rule of the Provisional Government two religious-oriented ordinances were passed. The Days of Rest Ordinance provided that the Sabbath and the Jewish festivals shall be prescribed days of rest in the State of Israel, with non-Jews having the right to observe their own Sabbath and festivals as days of rest.[34] The Kosher Food for Soldiers Ordinance ensured the supply of kosher food to all Jewish soldiers of the Defense Army of Israel, placing the Ministers of Defense and of Religious Affairs in charge of implementing the Ordinance.[35]

On August 10, 1949, the Kneset passed the Jewish Religious Services Budgets Law. It provided that the expenses of the Jewish religious services "shall be borne (1) by the Government, to the extent of one third; (2) by the local authority, to the extent of two thirds." The Minister of Religious Affairs was charged with the implementation of the law through the instrumentality of local religious councils.[36]

The Compulsory Education Law, passed by the Kneset on September 12, 1949, declared as officially "recognized trends" the General and the Labor trends, as well as the religious Mizrahi and the Agudat Israel trends, thereby guaranteeing the religionists complete autonomy in the realm of education.[37]

33. *Ibid.* 15 (May 22, 1961) : 123.
34. *Ibid.* 1 (June 9, 1948) :18.
35. *Ibid.* 2 (November 26, 1948) :37.
36. *Ibid.* 3:66.
37. *Ibid.* 3:125.

The Hours of Work and Rest Law was passed by the Kneset on May 15, 1951.[38] It reiterated that the weekly day of rest in the case of a Jew shall be the Sabbath day (Part III, art. 7). However, it granted the Minister of Labor the power to "permit an employee to be employed during all or any of the hours of weekly rest, if he is satisfied that interruption of work for all or part of the weekly rest is likely to prejudice the defense of the state or the security of persons or property, or seriously to prejudice the economy, or a process of work or the supply of services which, in the opinion of the Minister of Labor, are essential to the public or part thereof" (Part IV, art. 12a). Even though in the next paragraph the law stated that "a general permit . . . shall be given only upon the decision of a committee of Ministers consisting of the Prime Minister, the Minister of Religions and the Minister of Labor," the religious feared that in its particulars the execution of the law and the implicit opportunities for official violations of the Sabbath would be in the hands of the Minister of Labor.

On June 17, 1952, the Kneset passed the Rabbinical Courts (Validation of Appointments) Law, wherein the Rabbinical Courts operating in the country were declared duly constituted valid organs.[39]

The Anatomy and Pathology Law was passed by the Kneset on August 26, 1953.[40] It specified that autopsies can be performed on a person's body only with his prior written consent, if the body remained unclaimed within the time specified by law, or by written authorization of three physicians for the purpose of ascertaining the cause of death or to use part of the body for curative treatment. Dissection may take place only at a medical school for the purpose of study or research. The Minister of Health was charged with the implementation of the law. It should be noted that religious law is opposed to dissection of the body. However, since it is a necessary concommitant of medical progress, the religious parties attempted to hedge around it so that autopsies would occur rarely, and

---

38. *Ibid.* 5:125.
39. *Ibid.* 6:62.
40. *Ibid.* 7:135.

certainly not on individuals who are religiously committed against it.

The National Service Law was passed by the Kneset on August 26, 1953.[41] It provided that religious women should be liable to national service (as opposed to defense service) for a period of 24 months, with the opportunities available "to maintain a religious way of life" (Art. 8).

On August 26, 1953, the Kneset also passed the Rabbinical Courts Jurisdiction (Marriage and Divorce) Law, making matters of marriage, divorce, and maintenance between Jews the exclusive jurisdiction of Rabbinical Courts, in compliance with Jewish religious law.[42] According to Jewish law a divorce can take place only at the husband's discretion, and a childless widow can remarry only if her husband's brother performs a ceremony called *Haliza* that sets the widow free to marry a mate of her choice. The Rabbinical Court was empowered to order the granting of a divorce or the performance of *Haliza* and to force compliance with the order by imprisonment. The Minister of Religious Affairs was charged with the implementation of the law.

The *Dayanim* Law was passed by the Kneset on May 16, 1955.[43] It declared the *dayan* (a member of a Rabbinical Court) a paid official of the state, to be appointed by the President of the State for life, upon the recommendation of an Appointments Committee under the aegis of the Minister of Religious Affairs. The Chief Rabbis are the presiding *dayanim* of the Rabbinical Grand Court. Each *dayan*, before taking his seat, shall pledge allegiance to the State of Israel.[44]

Less than a year later, the law empowered religious courts to compel witnesses who otherwise refuse to appear before it, under threat of arrest and a fine.[45]

41. *Ibid.* 7:137.
42. *Ibid.* 7:139.
43. *Ibid.* 9:74.
44. The Qadis Law passed the Kneset on May 22, 1961. It gave similar powers to Muslim judges. *Ibid.* 15:123. The Druze Religious Courts Law, of December 25, 1962, empowered Druze judges to act in their official capacity. *Ibid.* 17:27.
45. *Ibid.* 10 (March 14, 1956):34.

With the intent of safeguarding the authority of religious courts, the Religious Courts Law (Avoidance of Disturbance) empowered the court to impose a maximum penalty of 200 pounds upon anyone interfering with, or disturbing, its procedure.[46]

The Jewish Religious Services Budgets (Amendment) Law authorized the Minister of Religious Affairs to establish local Religious Councils wherever they do not exist. The membership of the Religious Council must not exceed that of the local Community Council. It is to be appointed by three authorities: 45 per cent by the Minister of Religious Affairs, 45 per cent by the local authorities and 10 per cent by the local Rabbinate. In case of disagreement concerning appointments, the matter is referred to a Ministerial committee consisting of the Ministers of Religious Affairs, Justice, and Interior. If they fail to agree, it is referred to the Cabinet as a whole.[47]

It must be noted that most of the statutory regulations favoring the implementation of, or in harmony with, religious law resulted from the particular type of Cabinet government entrenched in Israel. It has encouraged a process of bargaining between the religious minority and the secular majority on the Cabinet level, particularly in the course of forming the Cabinet. In many instances the secular majority that supported the religious parties in attaining their objectives acted from constraint and against their convictions, submitting to strict party and coalition discipline. Thus, the norms of religious law imposed upon the population were accountable to the political realities of a coalition government and the tactic of political extortionism by a minority, rather than to the desire of an interested majority.

---

46. *Sefer ha-Huqim* (Jerusalem: Government Printer, March 9, 1965) : 115.
47. *Ibid.*, July 11, 1966, p. 50.

5

The Political Basis of the Cabinet and of Religion

The State of Israel is a parliamentary democracy. As in every parliamentary democracy, the voice of the people is considered sovereign. However, in fact, the only opportunity the people have to exercise their sovereignty is at times of election.[1] Between elections, which the law prescribes every four years[2] unless the Kneset passes a law to dissolve itself prior to that,[3] the representatives of the people, in Kneset assembled, exercise the power of sovereignty in the name of the people. "The principle of the complete sovereignty of the legislative organ," which is the Kneset, is laid down in the Transition Law 5709–1949.[4] The same principle, derived from article 6 of the Declaration of the Rights of Man, is enunciated in the French Constitution of 1958: "National sovereignty belongs to the people, who exercise it through their representatives and by way of referendum."[5]

But in Israel, as in many other states, the above description

---

1. In some countries, like France, there are provisions for an occasional popular referendum.

2. Basic Law (The Kneset), enacted February 12, 1958, Art. 28. *Laws of the State of Israel* 12 (5718–1957/8) :85. Prior to 1958 the duration of the Kneset was not regulated by law.

3. *Ibid.*, Art. 34.

4. *Israel Government Yearbook* 5719 (1958), p. 15.

5. Dorothy Pickles, *The Fifth French Republic* (New York: Praeger) Appendix, Art. 3, p. 235. On referendum, see also Art. 11, p. 237.

of parliamentary democracy appears to be more a fiction than reality. For the power exercised by Parliament in the name of the sovereign people is superseded by a select body of men who are themselves representatives of the membership in Parliament. To be sure, this select body, or Cabinet, is constantly subject to parliamentary scrutiny and criticism. Ostensibly, they are also subject to parliamentary guidance and are duty-bound to fulfill the will of the representatives of the people.[6] However, the will of Parliament is the will of the majority of the representatives. In Israel the exact same majority supports the Cabinet and identifies with its policies. In addition, the Cabinet in Israel usually contains the leading personalities of the *majority* in Parliament. Hence, the Israel Cabinet is in complete control of Parliament and of the state, and is the wielder of sovereign power.

The edge of that power is perceptibly dulled by the conflicting aspirations of the Cabinet members and the parties they represent. Differences of opinion may arise on matters of interpretation of basic principles in the government program or concerning the priority of translating articles of the program into acts of law. These disagreements not only weaken the effectiveness of the government and have a damaging effect on its domestic and international prestige, but also bring about frequent and prolonged crises and changes in it.

A frequent source of turmoil in the government has been the religious parties. An innocent observer would expect that, as a major irritant, they would surely be the least desirable coalition partner. Surprisingly, the only parties besides Mapai that have had a consistent record of participation in the government are precisely the religious parties. Indeed, their presence was often found indispensable to Mapai. As a result, the religious parties have played a disproportionately greater role in Israel's coalition politics than their numbers would lead one to assume. Since the central article of their program is strengthening religious life in the state, their continual presence and advantageous position in the government keeps the religious issue in the forefront of political life.

The cooperation between the socialist Mapai and the re-

---

6. Transition Law 5709–1949, Art. 11. On the Transition Law see Chapter 4, "The Legal Framework of the Cabinet."

ligious parties within the framework of the government is one of the phenomena of the Israel political system which has deeply influenced the relations between state and religion. This development was made possible, if not unavoidable, by the tactics and the method of formation and functioning of the coalition government.

The Cabinet in the Political System

The Cabinet is the focus of power in the political system of Israel; in it each party wishes to secure a foothold and exercise influence. When its members act in concert, it has the ability to rule with nearly dictatorial power.

Although the law leads one to believe that Israel has a strong Kneset and a subordinate Cabinet, comparable to that of pre-De Gaulle France or the Weimar Republic, in practice the situation has been quite the reverse. Instead of the Kneset dictating and the Cabinet executing, the Cabinet leads the Kneset.

The Cabinet prepares, initiates, and pilots legislation in the Kneset,[7] determines the agenda of the Kneset, formulates foreign and military policy, controls the economy, budget, and finance. In general, it holds the Kneset in the tight grip of iron party discipline. As long as the Cabinet has the backing of the majority of the Kneset, it is virtually in absolute control of the country. Though it can be harassed by the tactics of the opposition, its motions of no-confidence, its often embarrassing questions and inquiries, the Cabinet remains the focus of power in the machinery of state. The power of Cabinet, however, can remain secure only if it maintains the support of a Kneset majority. Since an absolute majority for any one party has so far not been provided in the course of the national elections (not one party received 51 per cent of the votes), it has to be established in an artificial way: through a process of discussion and bargaining among the parties that gain representation in the Kneset. The result is a Cabinet coalition of several parties.

7. Asher Tsidon, in *Ha-Kneset I'Halaha Ul'Ma'aseh* (Jerusalem: Ahiasaf, 1954) remarks that any Kneset member is legally empowered to propose a bill's introduction, but that most of the laws stem in actuality from government proposals. See p. 108.

Cabinet: Scene of Party Conflicts

The parties in Israel have no illusions about the formidable power of the Cabinet in the machinery of state. It is at Cabinet level that the destiny of the country is most affected by decisions and agreements reached among its members in virtually every sphere that is subject to legislation. Every party worthy of the name aspires to gain Cabinet status. If there are parties that have not yet been represented in a Cabinet, it is not because they resigned themselves to the role of a perpetual opposition but because of ideological and other barriers that separated them from the parties in the coalition.

Since control of the Cabinet or influence exerted within its framework has a crucial effect on the development of the country, it is not surprising that everything regarding the Cabinet is subject to controversy. Proposals that would introduce any change in the structure, composition, creation, termination, or working of the Cabinet are viewed with utmost suspicion by all concerned, except by the proponents of the change. Because of this underlying element of distrust and fear that any suggested alteration of the Cabinet involves subtle manipulations to increase or diminish its power, it was difficult to crystallize the position of the Cabinet in a basic law of constitutional validity.

It is noteworthy that of the three important but scanty chapters of the Transition Law dealing with the Kneset, the President and the Government (Cabinet) respectively, two chapters have been superseded by more detailed and basic legislation with reasonable speed. The State President (Tenure) Law of December 3, 1951 replaced, for all practical purposes Chapter Two of the Transition Law regarding the President.[8] The Basic Law (The Kneset) of February 12, 1958 took the place of Chapter One of the Transition Law pertaining to the Kneset.[9] Only Chapter Three—dealing with the Government, the most sensitive area of politics in Israel—took twenty years to be replaced by a comprehensive basic law. During that time, it has been dealt with cautiously on a piecemeal basis, owing

---

8. *Laws of the State of Israel* 6:4.
9. *Ibid.* 12:85.

to the party conflict underlying any attempted change in the Cabinet.

In the words of a discerning member of the Kneset, "when amendments to the Transition Law are presented to the Kneset . . . it is a clear indication that once again something happened in the coalition Government, or that something is not in order among the coalition partners."[10] He further commented on the same issue: "With us there persists a state of emergency about everything. Daily we are reminded of the existence of a state of emergency as we are presented with laws. Only on one item—the most basic and important item—there does not seem to be a state of emergency: on the composition of the Government."[11]

Another member of the Kneset justifiably observed that "the legal aspect is less important than the political aspect" in the formulation of laws on the Cabinet.[12] When, after much delay, the Prime Minister finally presented to the Kneset a draft law on the government, he hastened to state in his introductory remarks that there is little that is new in the proposal. "The main intention of the proposed law is to gather and concentrate in a Basic Law the regulations pertaining to the work of the Government and thereby incorporate in an all-embracive fashion into a constitutional law the method of functioning of the Government of Israel, the executive arm of the State of Israel."[13]

Almost any issue involving the Cabinet is potentially explosive. Because it is the actual source of power, the focus of the machinery of state and the axis around which the parliamentary system in Israel revolves, its daily functioning is filled with tension, conflict, and the expectation of imminent crisis. Among the parties of the coalition there usually reigns an uneasy truce, which is based more on a feeling of dislike for the opposition than on mutual liking for each other. The coalition partners often stand at opposite poles on important issues. But for the sake of attaining their goals through the

---

10. *Divrei ha-Kneset,* Second Kneset, 97th session, 12 (June 23, 1952) : 2382, George Pelesh, General Zionist.

11. *Ibid.* 12:2383.

12. *Ibid.,* Israel Bar Yehuda, Mapam.

13. *Ibid.* 12 (August 31, 1966) : 2504. Levi Eshkol of Ma'arakh (Mapai) .

most powerful single organ in the state, they aspire to reach some sort of mutual accommodation.

Formation of the Cabinet

The articles of the Transition Law describing the procedure for the formation of a government are few and simple.[14] Yet, they encompass the most crucial process in the political life of the state. The process of forming a Cabinet taxes the ingenuity of the most seasoned statesmen to the utmost. When the first Prime Minister, Ben-Gurion, resigned from his office in November 1953 because of ill health, he placed the blame squarely on the arduous strain of coalition bargaining.[15]

There have been variations to the procedure of forming a government, just as there have been a variety of causes that have brought governments down. No matter how widely the approaches differed in practice, the mechanics of the Transition Law were faithfully followed.

The law has involved both the presidential and the legislative sectors in the appointment of the Prime Minister. An aspirant for the Prime Ministership requires first a presidential appointment. Although this is usually but a pro-forma step because it is assumed that the leader of the greatest party, the Mapai, would be appointed, the President may exert personal influence upon the choice of the Prime Minister and the formation of a Cabinet.[16] In practice, however, the hands of the

14. See Chapter 5 on "The Cabinet in the Political System."

15. *Davar*, November 5, 1953, p. 12.

16. Such an instance came up first in October 1950. President Weizmann, after consultation with party leaders requested the Mapai leader, Ben-Gurion, to form a government. Ben-Gurion, however, was obliged to announce that he failed in the attempt. Thereupon the President delegated the task to Pinhas Rosen, the leader of the small Progressive Party, who succeeded in constructing a new government. The curious fact was that, though Pinhas Rosen's skill brought the coalition about, he recognized Mapai's dominant role and indispensability, and immediately handed the reins of government over to the Mapai leader. [*Divrei ha-Kneset*, First Kneset, 184th session, 7 (October 30, 1950):102.] A similar instance occurred in September 1961, when the President, after Ben-Gurion returned the mandate, delegated Levi Eshkol of Mapai to form a new government. (*Jerusalem Post*, September 15, 1961.) In this case the President's choice was purely formal, since the Prime Minister designate acted solely in the capacity of the representative of Ben-Gurion. When he suc-

President are tied. As long as Mapai maintains its relative strength vis-à-vis the other parties, no matter who would succeed in forming a government, Mapai would control the rudder.

Though the President has the legal right to appoint the Prime Minister, the legislature has the prerogative to grant or refuse him and his Cabinet the seal of approval. To date, fifteen governments have been presented to the Kneset.[17] All of them received a parliamentary vote of confidence. Though the vote is only a formality, since a Prime Minister would not present a government to the Kneset unless he is certain of the majority's support, the debate preceding the vote nevertheless serves a purpose. It offers the minor coalition partner the opportunity to inform the Kneset and the electorate of inter-party agreements (usually with Mapai), that are not embodied in the Basic Principles of the Government Program. At least once it pinpointed to the prospective coalition partners sensitive areas of misunderstanding. This led to the suspension of the debate and some tense hours of bargaining before an agreement was reached and the vote of confidence granted.[18] The debate gives the official opposition the best opportunity to criticize the government and the partners of the coalition for their alleged shortcomings.

The President's calling upon the Prime Minister designate and the Kneset's vote of confidence for the final Cabinet slate and its program offer the legal stamp of approval to the most crucial undertaking in the political life of the nation, the negotiations for the establishment of a Cabinet. Yet, despite their great importance, the conduct of the negotiations themselves have not been regulated by law, except insofar as their duration is concerned.[19]

To avoid the frequent and long stretches when the nation had no executive authority having the legislature's confidence,

---

ceeded in establishing the government, it was Ben-Gurion who was heading it and who introduced it to the Kneset.

17. For the composition and duration of the governments see table in Appendix, "Governments in Office."

18. *Divrei ha-Kneset,* Second Kneset, 241st session, 14 (June 3, 1953): 1499.

19. One caretaker government lasted nine months, from January 31, 1961, to November 2, 1961.

an amendment setting the time limit for these negotiations was adopted.[20] The purpose, however, was not accomplished by the new law, since it still granted a total of ninety-one days to the parties for haggling and bargaining. This is long enough to have a demoralizing effect on a country whose average governmental life span has been slightly higher than 13 months.[21]

Besides this time limit, the only practical consideration for the formation of a government is that it consist of a coalition that would command a majority in the Kneset. This has offered an open arena for political maneuvering with an unlimited scope for bargaining. The bargaining has encompassed, in the words of a political observer, "the assignment of Kneset committee chairmanships, the election of mayors in the larger cities and towns, and, within the Government, changes in administrative jurisdiction of ministries and the allocation of Deputy Ministers to the parties."[22]

As will be clearly discernible from the examples supplied in Part III, the process of Cabinet formation consists of several stages. These are: the resignation of the government in the wake of a government crisis or other cause; consultations between party leaders and the President of the state; the appoint-

---

20. In July 1962 an amendment to the Transition Law set a limit to the time to be expended in the formation of a Cabinet. According to law, the Prime Minister designate has 28 days to his disposal to establish a Government, if he does not return the mandate to the President within three days. At the end of the 28 days the President has the prerogative to postpone the deadline by 14 days and then by an additional seven days. Thus, the Prime Minister designate has a total of 49 days to form a new government. If he fails to do so, he must return the mandate to the President who, after a second round of consultations with the representatives of all parties in the Kneset, will assign the task of forming a government to a member of Kneset. That person will have only 21 days to his disposal. Should the second Prime Minister designate also fail to round up the necessary support in time, the President may appoint a third candidate, if the leaders of the parties representing a majority of the Kneset agree. If this happens, it is a virtual certainty that the new Prime Minister designate would succeed, since he has the preliminary de facto backing of the Kneset majority. The third candidate has 21 days to his disposal to form and to present a Cabinet to the Kneset. *Laws of the State of Israel,* 16 (July 30, 1962) :97.

21. The first time the law could be tested, in November 1965, the religious parties forced Prime Minister Eshkol to apply for an extension.

22. M. Bernstein, *The Politics of Israel* (Princeton, N.J.: Princeton University Press, 1957), p. 130.

ment of a Prime Minister designate by the President; interparty negotiations between the Prime Minister designate (or his party representatives) and the potential coalition partners; distilling the results of the negotiations in a document called the Basic Principles of the Government Program which is supposed to express the united stand of the proposed coalition; presentation of the coalition to the Kneset; Kneset debate on the program and the Cabinet; and Kneset vote of confidence. On five occasions the resignation of the government was followed by a call for new Kneset elections. In such an instance there are additional intermediate stages: the election campaign; the presentation of party election platforms to the electorate; the conduct of the elections; and the re-evaluation of party positions based on the newly emerging picture of relative party strength. A minor change in the party spectrum may bring about a shift in emphasis in the bargaining process.

Basically, the parties, including the religious parties, have aspired to three main objectives in negotiating for the formation of a new government: (1) to secure the most and the best portfolios; (2) to have as many party goals embodied in the government program as possible; and (3) to secure coalition agreements that would either guarantee Mapai's support for partisan objectives, or would free the party from supporting the government on certain limited issues that the party diehards could not countenance. On these three objectives the prospective coalition parties had been capable of waging a war of attrition and a war of nerves that lasted once for a period of nine months (from January 31, 1961, to November 2, 1961), and twice for a period of over five months (from February 14, 1951 to October 8, 1951, a total of seven months and 24 days; from July 5, 1959 to December 17, 1959, a total of five months and 12 days).

Composition of the Cabinet

The architect of the Cabinet is the Prime Minister. To date four Prime Ministers have served in the Israel Government: David Ben-Gurion (May 1948–December 1953, November 1955–November 1963), Moshe Sharett (December 1953–November 1955), Levi Eshkol (November 1963–February 1969) and Golda Meir (March 1969–   ). The recent Basic Law: The Government, makes it mandatory that the Prime Minister be a member of the Kneset.[23]

The law provides for the automatic resignation of the whole government should the Prime Minister resign. He is free to hand in the resignation at his own discretion, without consultation with the Cabinet or any member of the administration.[24] Thus the Prime Minister occupies a central and superior position in the Cabinet vis-à-vis his Ministerial colleagues and could be considered, in the words of John Morley, "the keystone of the Cabinet arch."[25]

The most effective weapon a Prime Minister could apply toward his Cabinet or individual Ministers to keep them in line and to safeguard the proper functioning of the government is the threat of resignation. It has proved effective in other countries, notably Great Britain.[26] In Israel, however, this threat is more potential than real. Its effectiveness is limited by two considerations. First, the lack of alternatives available to the Prime Minister in forming an alternate government that could dispense with Ministers who chose to take an independent stand on an important issue, and, second, by the very ambition of the recalcitrant Ministers or parties to force a resignation and a possible new election.

It has been alleged that the Prime Minister is the determining factor in the choice of his coalition partners when forming a government.[27] This allegation is, at best, only partially true. The Prime Minister's choice is limited by the councils of his own party as well as by the availability of parties that are ready to strike a satisfactory bargain with him.

For example, when negotiating for the Ninth Government

---

23. *Sefer ha-Huqim*, no. 540 (August 21, 1968) p. 226, paragraph 5b.

24. *Ibid.*, paragraph 23a.

25. Sir Ivor Jennings, *Cabinet Government* (Cambridge: Cambridge University Press, 1951) , p. 160.

26. "The Prime Minister can, by a personal resignation, force a dissolution of the Government," *ibid.*, p. 74. Thus "members must take the responsibility either of supporting the government or of risking their resignation or a dissolution of Parliament." Jennings, *The British Constitution* (Cambridge: Cambridge University Press, 1961) , p. 146.

27. Asher Tsidon, *Beit ha-Nivharim* (Jerusalem: Ahiasaf, 1964) , p. 312.

in November 1959, Prime Minister designate Ben-Gurion came out in favor of a narrow coalition of Mapai, General Zionists, and Agudat Israel.[28] The leftist parties made themselves undesirable by their unwillingness to support stricter rules of Cabinet responsibility that Ben-Gurion wanted to embody into law. The Progressives had to be ruled out temporarily, since they placed themselves in direct competition with Mapai in their aspiration for the mayoralty of Tel Aviv. Ben-Gurion wished to leave out the NRP (National Religious Party), since he desired "to see religious and political matters separated in the State."[29] Mapai's "Havereinu," the supreme council of the party, however, came out in favor of a broad coalition and continued negotiations with the leftist parties.[30] Ben-Gurion had to acquiesce to the party's supreme council. The government that resulted from his continued efforts had the opposite composition of the one he originally favored. It consisted, besides Mapai, of the two leftist parties, the NRP, and the Progressives.[31]

If his own party has such a restraining effect, the attitude of the other parties has an even more decisive impact on the Prime Minister's choice of potential coalition partners. The Prime Minister's hands are tied by his inability to pick his own colleagues for the Cabinet. Ministerial candidates are chosen by the parties and they remain representatives of their respective party machines in the government. This indicates the limitations of the Prime Minister, who must satisfy, and come to terms with, a party machine instead of an individual.[32]

---

28. *Jerusalem Post*, November 17, 1959.
29. *Ibid.*, November 20, 1959, Supplement.
30. *Ibid.*, November 18, 1959.
31. Presented to Kneset on December 16, 1959.
32. The setup is a fertile breeding ground for personality problems and clashes, both within the Prime Minister's own party or outside it. An example of the former was Dov Josef of Mapai who, owing to his stature, had to become part of a reconstituted government. The Prime Minister designate, Ben-Gurion, offered him the Ministry of Communications. He refused, demanding instead the portfolio of Treasury or Trade and Industry. Since Ben-Gurion had already promised both portfolios to prospective candidates, it resulted in additional complicated maneuvers and delay of time to satisfy the unyielding Dov Josef. (*Ha-Zofeh*, December 12, 1952.) No less serious was the problem of the General Zionists who demanded two first-rank portfolios as a result of their difficulties in choos-

Cabinet Ministers fall into two broad classifications: those who are members of the Kneset and those who are nonmembers. The law does not provide that a Minister must be an elected representative of the people. This offers the Prime Minister and his party the opportunity to co-opt Ministers, either for their outstanding ability in certain fields of endeavor, or on occasion, as a political strategem. The co-optation of a Minister who is not a member of a Kneset has usually involved intricate interparty bargaining, since the minor coalition partners surmise that the Prime Minister resorts to this practice because it is of vital political significance and benefit to Mapai. It is of no small interest that the First Government of Israel fell in a crisis elicited by the Religious Bloc over the co-optation of a nonparty Minister into the Cabinet.[33] It seems that Mapai was eager to rid itself temporarily of a politically explosive portfolio that it considered valuable enough to be kept out of the hands of another party. The strategem of the nonparty Minister was thus applied. In another instance, a religious party demanded that the nonparty Minister for Religious Affairs, Rabbi Toledano, be removed from his post as a condition for joining the Ninth Government, in December 1959.[34]

Cabinet Ministers who were not members of the Kneset were rare in the first twelve governments. Their number, however, greatly increased in the Thirteenth Government, partially owing to the Mapam strategem of having their Ministers resign from the Kneset upon receiving their Cabinet appointment. This offered them additional opportunities to place party leaders in the highest echelons of governmental administration. Whether this will set a precedent, and if so, what this may do to the Cabinet and its relationship with the Kneset remains to be seen. Presently the law provides that "a member of the Government who is not simultaneously a member of the Kneset is subject to the same rules regarding the Kneset as a member of

---

ing a leader from between their two top personalities, P. Bernstein and I. Rokah. (*Al ha-Mishmar,* July 26, 1951.)

33. See chapter 9 on "Reorganization of Government."

34. *Divrei ha-Kneset,* Fourth Kneset, 10th session, 28 (December 17, 1959) :120. Z. Wahrhaftig of the NRP.

the Government who is simultaneously a member of the Kneset, except that he has no right to vote."[35]

The number of Ministers and portfolios is not prescribed by law and they have varied from government to government. (See Appendix for list of portfolios and related tables.) There has not been a direct relationship between the number of Ministers and the number of portfolios. Frequently one Minister would hold two or more portfolios, and on occasion, ministerial appointees would be left without any portfolio. The number of Ministers has varied from 12 to 21 and the number of portfolios from 15 to 22. The fluctuation in the composition of the Cabinet depends upon the relative party strength in the coalition and upon the outcome of the coalition negotiations.

In order to produce the highest quality of Cabinet Ministers, attempts have been made to lift the Cabinets above the give-and-take of coalition bargaining that often forces a Prime Minister to relinquish an important post to a second-rate Minister as the price of a party's support for the government. In the debate of the "Basic Law: The Government" in the Kneset, Shimon Peres of Rafi suggested that the number of Ministers be limited to twelve. To accomplish this, he proposed the consolidation of Ministries. Thus, the Ministries of Police, Religion, and Social Welfare should be incorporated into the Ministry of the Interior.[36]

The structure of the Israel political system encourages the distribution of portfolios and Deputy Ministerships purely on the basis of political considerations. The most bitter struggles in the formation of a government evolved around the acquisition of portfolios, since each Ministry is considered a stronghold of the party that managed to attain it.

In order to balance the composition of the Cabinet to the satisfaction of its partners and yet to maintain power and control over it, Mapai devised most ingenious techniques. These include splitting Ministries and abolishing them, shifting de-

---

35. "Basic Law (The Kneset)" enacted February 12, 1958. *Laws of the State of Israel* 12 (5718–1957/8) :85. A list of Cabinet members who were not members of the Kneset is in the Appendix.
36. *Ibid.,* Sixth Kneset, special session, 44 (August 31, 1966) :2512.

partments from one Ministry to another (depending on which party inherited a specific Ministry) and pacifying the discontented with the appointment of one or two Deputy Ministers.

Thus, in November 1961, Mapai handed over the Ministry of Labor, which it had ruled since the establishment of the state, to Ahdut ha-'Avodah, but not before removing the important Department of National Housing Administration from its jurisdiction. A new Ministry of Housing was created under a Mapai Minister.[37] Ahdut ha-'Avodah remained with an empty shell of the Labor Ministry, stripped of real power.

In December 1959, the Ministry of Development was placed under a Mapam Minister, but it would not include the District of Eilat, one of the fastest-growing Israel territories. This district was annexed to the Ministry of Commerce and Industry, in the hands of a Mapai Minister.[38]

To counteract the abuse of Ministries for coalition bargaining purposes, Meir Ya'ari of Mapam proposed that the permission of the Kneset should be necessary not only for the consolidation, division, abolition, or establishment of new Ministries as specified in the proposed "Basic Law," but also for the transfer of departments from one Ministry to another. The Kneset voices confidence in a Minister in a specific capacity which could be completely nullified by transfers of departments. Hence, he argued that transfers should require the concurrence of the Kneset.[39]

With the sole exception of the Governments of National Unity (1967), Mapai always assured itself a controlling majority of Ministries and Ministers in the composition of the Cabinet. In the aftermath of Ben-Gurion's resignation from the post of Prime Minister in January 1961 as a result of the Lavon Affair, Mapai's former coalition partners formed a "joint front" to force Mapai to relinquish its Cabinet majority.[40] This rebellion was fruitless. Mapai was represented by 11 Ministries in the new coalition, the greatest number it had in any govern-

37. *Jerusalem Post*, November 1, 1961.
38. *Ha-Zofeh*, December 10, 1959.
39. *Divrei ha-Kneset*, Sixth Kneset, special session, 44 (August 31, 1966): 2514.
40. *Davar*, September 1, 1961.

ment, although it took nine months to accomplish this feat. The first government in which Mapai had to accept parity (9 out of 18) instead of majority was established after the elections to the Sixth Kneset, in January 1966. Together with its Ma'arakh partner, however, Mapai still had a controlling Cabinet majority (12 out of 18).

Functioning of the Cabinet

Since this study is basically concerned with the politics of compromise rooted in party interrelationships, the technical operation of the Cabinet will be examined only in a general summary fashion.

The Cabinet meets weekly, unless emergencies demand otherwise, under the chairmanship of the Prime Minister; in the Prime Minister's absence, his deputy becomes chairman. The agenda is set by the Prime Minister. Decisions are reached by majority vote, provided that at least four Cabinet Ministers vote in favor of a motion.

Not all the business for which the Cabinet is responsible is transacted in full Cabinet. The Cabinet works through six standing committees on Èconomics, Security, Interior, Legislation, Foreign Affairs, and Protocol. Their decisions, unless challenged within a week in the Cabinet, are equivalent to full Cabinet decisions.[41]

Cabinet proceedings are secret. The Transition Law obligates its members to adhere to joint Cabinet responsibility, discussed later in this chapter. Absolute discretion is expected of Ministers and their parties on all issues handled by the Cabinet.

Despite the rule of joint Cabinet responsibility and a Government program agreed upon by the parties joining a coalition, the Israel Cabinet has usually lacked cohesiveness. National interests may be paramount at times of emergency, but under normal circumstances Ministers adhere to partisan loyalties and considerations. A basic feature of the Israel Cabinet is the Ministers' inclination to serve the party first, perhaps because they are convinced that by doing so they serve the nation best. Each

---

41. Asher Tsidon, *Beit ha-Nivharim*, p. 307.

Ministry is virtually an autonomous unit where the Minister dominates and dispenses favors.

Ministers occupy their respective positions mainly because of affiliation with, and service to, their specific party. When their term of service ends, they are not provided for by the state. They fall back upon the party and remain dependent upon the party machine for their future political advancement or survival. Without the good will of the party, the astutest politician will remain in political obscurity.

The party's good will has to be earned through proper services rendered to it. By virtue of their position, the Ministers render service by securing a maximum number of jobs in their Ministry for faithful party adherents and by utilizing their authority to implement party goals as opposed to government goals.

The rivalry among the coalition parties for the possession of certain portfolios substantiates the claim that Ministries are utilized for the furtherance of party objectives. The General Zionists would not enter a government without the Ministry of Trade and Industry in their possession, expecting to influence, if not control, decisively private investment objectives in the country. Similarly, Ahdut ha-'Avodah demanded the portfolios of Agriculture and Labor, Mapam the portfolio of Development, and NRP that of Religious Affairs, for the sole purpose of furthering their partisan ambitions.

Because of the great influence exerted by a party through a Ministry in its possession, the question of which Minister should be empowered to implement a specific Cabinet decision or law becomes a matter of decisive importance. For this reason, acrimony arose between Ahdut ha-'Avodah and NRP concerning a projected Sabbath Bill on whether the Labor Minister or the Minister of Religious Affairs should be in change of the bill's implementation.[42] It was clearly understood that, should the Ahdut ha-'Avodah Labor Minister, Yigal Allon, be in charge, he would take a most lenient approach in the enforcement and execution of the bill's provisions. It will be seen later on that it was during a relatively short period, when the NRP

42. *Jerusalem Post*, July 2, 1965.

relinquished its hold on the Ministry of the Interior, that the new Mapam Minister, Bar-Yehuda, passed the controversial regulations determining who is a Jew, which led to the resignation of the NRP from the government.[43]

While the significance of ruling a Ministry for the purpose of attaining ideological objectives is clearly discernible, such possession also holds other rewards in store. The report that the Mapai rank and file may have had to vacate as many as 1,500 to 2,000 positions of influence to make way for Ahdut ha-'Avodah men upon establishing the Ma'arakh may not have been exaggerated.[44]

In any country, sharing in the government means sharing in the spoils. Under the system of Israel's coalition government with its politics of compromise, sharing in the government is equated with a virtual party take-over of certain realms to the exclusion of anyone else.

A clear insight into the functioning of the Cabinet and its Ministries could be gained from a news item reported in the daily, *Ha-Arez*. The paper reported that mutual recriminations were exchanged between Moshe Shapiro, the leader of the "center faction" of the NRP, and Josef Burg, who headed the "La-Mifneh" faction of the party.

The "center faction" accused Dr. Burg of exploiting his position as Minister of Social Welfare in behalf of his La-Mifneh faction to the neglect of the party membership at large. Among the examples brought up was the transfer of a La-Mifneh leader from a minor post in another Ministry to the Assistant Directorship of Social Welfare, by-passing equally competent candidates of the "center faction," employed in the same Ministry for some time. The General Secretary of the party, Benyamin Shahor, calling upon Dr. Burg and his assistants, said, "Not in the name of La-Mifneh do you sit in the Ministry of Social Welfare, but in the name of the whole party."

Dr. Burg responded with a strong attack against Moshe Shapiro, citing cases of his partisanship in behalf of the "center faction." He further boasted of the accomplishments his Min-

---

43. See Part III, Chapter 8, "Who is a Jew?"
44. *Jerusalem Post*, February 4, 1966.

istry achieved for the party, "whose institutions and members benefit more now than they benefited when Mr. Shapiro was at the helm of Social Welfare." Dr. Burg revealed that "great sums" have been flowing to various institutions connected with the movement (the NRP), and he was even willing to produce a detailed list to that effect. He also pointed out that party members are being instructed, at his Ministry's expense, in accelerated courses to take over responsible positions. The Director of the Ministry, Dr. Kurtz, added in defense of Dr. Burg that under his leadership the Ministry of Social Welfare assumed "more and more of a party character." As an example, he cited the fact that of 60,000 pounds that were the Ministry's budgetary allocation for development, 54,000 pounds were allocated to religious institutions.[45]

It could be surmised that this instance regarding the partisan activities of a Ministry is not a singular one, though understandably parties do not relish leakage of such news.

Under these circumstances, where the government consists of ministries pulling in different directions, its functional efficiency must inevitably be marred. Minority parties, including the religious parties, are virtually free to exploit the authority placed in their hands, often to the detriment of the majority. The situation needs changing. A change in the functioning of the Cabinet would, however, demand an alteration of the structure and mechanics of the politics of compromise.

Collective Cabinet Responsibility

Crucial to the functioning of a Cabinet government is the matter of joint Cabinet responsibility. A Cabinet could not survive without it, either in a two-party or in a multiple-party system. Essentially the term "collective responsibility" means that the Cabinet as a body is responsible for the act of every one of its Ministers and that each Minister is responsible for the act of the whole Cabinet or any of its members. A characteristic feature of the Israel Cabinet system has been continual breakdown, or threat of breakdown, of joint Cabinet responsi-

---

45. *Ha-Arez*, February 14, 1961.

bility. A corollary of it has been the strenuous effort to embody the principle of Cabinet discipline first into the Government program and later into law.

The principle of joint Cabinet responsibility finds expression in the Transition Law, as well as in Article One of the government programs that were presented to the Kneset. The government programs of March 8, 1949, October 7, 1951, and November 3, 1955, state that "The Government will be established on a basis of collective responsibility of all its members and all the Parties which form part of it. The collective responsibility applies to the agreed program of the Government and its decisions."[46] The First Government Program added that "It does not withhold from Members of the Kneset freedom to discuss any proposal under consideration or freedom to criticize the Government, should it deviate from the principles determined for it by the Kneset or the coalition."[47] Since the members and the parties abused this freedom, the proviso was dropped from future programs.

Upon joining the government, parties often tried to establish a precondition allowing them to disagree with, abstain from, or vote against certain motions of the government without the act being considered a breach of joint Cabinet responsibility. On a number of occasions, the religious parties stipulated that they must have a free hand to vote according to the dictate of their conscience on matters affecting religion. Thus, in the negotiations for the Third Government (October 1951), Rabbi I. M. Levin of Agudat Israel stipulated, and Mapai agreed, that if no satisfactory solution is found to the problem of conscription for religious women, he will resign and vote on the issue against the government.

In the negotiations for the same government, an agreement between ha-Po'el ha-Mizrahi and Mapai stated that if "the ha-Po'el ha-Mizrahi will not concur with the new program (of national education) it shall be free to leave the coalition without this being considered a breach of the coalition agreement.[48]

46. *State of Israel Government Yearbook* 5712 (1951–52), 1; *ibid.* 5717 (1956):25.
47. *Ibid.* 5711 (1950):50.
48. *Ha-Zofeh*, December 16, 1952.

The government established in December 1959 agreed that the "NRP members have a right to abstain from voting for reasons of religion and conscience and to explain the reasons for their abstention."[49] In the 1959 government, the Progressives also requested a free hand in religious issues, but from motivations that were the exact opposite of those of the religious parties.

On other occasions, parties demanded a free vote on such issues as a change in the electoral system, the matter of stricter enforcement of collective responsibility, and questions of wages and strikes by civil servants. In the First Government, the Progressives made a stipulation to be free to vote against the trend system, should the Cabinet support it.[50] In the negotiations for the Fourth Government (December 1952), the Progressives were given the right to vote against the government on an election law amendment.[51] In the Fifth Government crisis, the Progressives reserved the right to withdraw from the government should the so-called "exclusion clause" be approved by the Cabinet.[52] In the Ninth Government (December 1959), every party had agreements to disagree with Mapai on various issues.[53]

The demands and stipulations of the parties were always addressed to the Prime Minister who negotiated as a representative of his party. Since all four Prime Ministers to date were leaders of Mapai, that party became identified with the government. It may be bordering on the trite to state that Mapai alone, as the "Government Party," cared about adherence to the principle of collective responsibility.

The attitude of the other parties seemed to differ from Mapai's attitude regarding their interpretation of joint Cabinet responsibility. The General Zionists felt free to criticize their coalition partner on the floor of the Kneset. Apparently, they may have preferred a parliamentary system in which the government could be voted down without endangering its existence,

---

49. *Ibid.*, December 15, 1959.
50. *Divrei ha-Kneset,* First Kneset, 12th session, 1,2 (March 10, 1949) :119.
51. *Davar*, December 22, 1952.
52. *Ibid.*, February 2, 1954.
53. See Chapter 13.

and where only specifically designated issues would be considered for a vote of confidence in the government. Upon entering the coalition, a General Zionist member of the Kneset stated, "We did not change in any manner, neither did Mapai change. We united only for a joint effort, but the debate between us will continue."[54]

Mapai was undoubtedly ready to accept the challenge of continued debate between the two parties, but it expected to confine it to the Cabinet framework. Political realities made it imperative that any rift between coalition partners be healed in the privacy of the Cabinet setting, in order not to endanger its existence. The General Zionist approach would have strengthened the Kneset vis-à-vis the Executive (Cabinet). It would have increased the influence of an individual member within the Kneset and encouraged relaxation of party discipline.

Mapai, with its dominant position within the Cabinet, desired to preserve a powerful government, buttressed by disciplined party groups in the Kneset. It also wanted to prevent the opposition from asserting itself through obstructionist tactics.

The parties diverged, therefore, not only in their economic and social programs, but also in some basic attitudes to strategy of government action and their desire to preserve a strong government.

The first serious threat of a breach of Cabinet responsibility came from the Religious Bloc in February 1950, resulting in a Cabinet crisis. In order to force the fulfillment of their demands regarding religious education, three Religious Bloc Ministers boycotted sessions of the Cabinet. Prime Minister Ben-Gurion warned them that this is tantamount to a breach of collective Cabinet responsibility. Since they refused to return he laid before the Kneset a decision adopted by the Cabinet. It stated

1. that any Minister willfully absent from Cabinet meetings or declining to implement Cabinet decisions shall be regarded as having resigned and his portfolios and authority

---

54. *Divrei ha-Kneset*, Second Kneset, 156th session, 13 (December 22, 1952) :300.

shall pass to the Prime Minister pending the appointment of a successor:

2. that the Prime Minister shall report the incident to the next meeting of the Kneset and, if the House does not pass a vote of no-confidence, the Government shall remain in power without the recalcitrant Minister.[55]

The Prime Minister's firm stand brought the two-week-old government crisis to an end. But almost a year later the Second Government resigned over a vote of no-confidence wherein the Religious Bloc voted against the government of which it was a member.[56]

When the principle of joint Cabinet responsibility is fully operative in Israel, there is no possibility of a government losing control between elections. Joint responsibility can be enforced, however, only by a threat of resignation coming from the Prime Minister, which means the automatic resignation of the whole government. Since the act of resignation is occasionally the objective of a recalcitrant coalition partner, it is not a reliable weapon in coalition politics. Therefore, potential dissidence is an ever-present danger in the Cabinet system of Israel. The only successful means to ward off disruptive government crises is through hard bargaining, resulting in compromise formulas.

The principle of collective responsibility is of paramount importance to the functioning of the Cabinet. It brings out clearly some relevant features of the politics of compromise and the exploitation of the government by the religious minority. For these reasons, several chapters are dedicated to the crises resulting from its breach.[57] However, the reader may be forewarned that the strenuous efforts to tighten Cabinet discipline have not met with resounding success. The situation may have somewhat improved, due to the imperceptible relaxation of ideological-doctrinaire warfare among the parties. But a solution to the problem, which may demand a complete political reorientation, is yet to be found.

---

55. *Divrei ha-Kneset,* First Kneset, 118th session, 4 (February 21, 1950): 830.

56. *Ibid.,* First Kneset, 227th session, 8 (February 14, 1951):1109.

57. See Part III.

Termination of the Cabinet

A Cabinet may terminate under any of the following circumstances: (1) expiration of the Kneset's four-year term; (2) a vote of no confidence by the Kneset; (3) resignation of the Prime Minister; (4) resignation of the Cabinet, or a substantial segment of it; and (5) breach of collective Cabinet responsibility.

The only natural method of terminating a Cabinet is the conclusion of a full Kneset term. All the other ways cut short a Cabinet's normal life span and are the result of a crisis within the Cabinet. Although resignations of Prime Ministers may on occasion be motivated by purely personal considerations, to date every such resignation was tied in with unfavorable political circumstances.

Of the fifteen governments in Israel until the election of the Seventh Kneset (November 1969), only one, the Fifteenth, came to a natural end by living out its full span of years. It is true that, from a legal point of view, the Sixth Government formed toward the end of the Second Kneset (August, 1955) and the Twelfth Government at the end of the Fifth Kneset (November 1965), enjoyed parliamentary confidence to the very end. Yet the Sixth Government, which ruled one month and eighteen days, acknowledged that its role was purely that of caretaker for the forthcoming elections. The Twelfth Government, with a life span of ten months and ten days, was, similarly, not a viable entity in a period of confused and bitter party struggle, political realignments, party splits and fusions and feverish preparation for new Kneset elections.

Four governments terminated as a result of the resignation of the Prime Minister. Ben-Gurion resigned for the first time in December 1953 for reasons of poor health, resulting from the excessive strain of coalition bargaining. His second resignation came in January 1961, in protest against a decision of the majority of his Cabinet on the Lavon Affair. He resigned for the third time in June 1963 for what was termed personal reasons which, in fact, resulted from bitter clashes within Mapai between Ben-Gurion and his young Mapai adherents on the one hand and the old guard of the party on the other. The fourth Prime Ministerial resignation came from Levi Eshkol in December 1964 over Mapai interparty differences on Lavon.

Only one government fell as a result of a Kneset vote of no-confidence. In February 1951, on the question of religious education in immigrant camps, the Religious Bloc coalition partners voted with the opposition against the Cabinet of which they were members.

Breach of collective Cabinet responsibility brought down three governments. In June 1955 the General Zionist coalition partner abstained in the Kneset from a vote of confidence on the Kastner case. Prime Minister Moshe Sharett chose to view this as a breach of joint Cabinet responsibility and, when the General Zionists refused to resign, he handed in the resignation of the Fifth Government. In December 1957 the Seventh Government came to an end when the Ahdut ha-'Avodah coalition partner refused to resign after it leaked confidential Cabinet information to the public. The Eighth Government was terminated by a breach of Cabinet responsibility when, in July 1959, the Ahdut ha-'Avodah and Mapam voted against the government on a no-confidence motion over the sales of arms to Germany and yet refused to resign from the Cabinet. The action of the two leftist parties was classified as a breach of collective Cabinet responsibility and not as a vote of no-confidence, since the motion of no-confidence was defeated and the government could have continued functioning.

Two governments terminated as a result of the resignations of religious parties, leaving the government short of a majority in the Kneset and with no other recourse but to resign. The First Government was brought down by the Religious Bloc in February 1950, allegedly protesting the co-optation of a non-party Minister into the Cabinet. The Third Government was brought down in December 1952, when the religious parties resigned over the question of the conscription of women, leaving the government with a precarious majority.

It emerges clearly that virtually all the Cabinets of Israel terminated in a state of crisis, as a result of internal upheaval among the Ministers and disagreements among the coalition partners.

Not all coalition crises, however, have resulted in changes of government. Ministers may resign and parties may leave the Cabinet, or they may contravene the regulation of collective responsibility, without provoking an actual change of government. Such things have happened frequently and there have been innumerable coalition crises. Nevertheless many a Cabinet crisis was patched up, and the Cabinet survived despite the seriousness of the issue involved in the crisis. For example, the crisis elicited by the religious parties over the question of "Who is a Jew?" (July 1958), or the one brought about by the General Zionists on the issue of the Red Flag (May 1953), or the resignation of Lavon from, and the return of Ben-Gurion to, the Ministry of Defense (February 1954) did not cause the government to fall. These were matters of utmost seriousness that affected party relations and political developments perhaps more than some of the crises that led to a government change-over. Yet they did not force the Prime Minister to submit a new Cabinet slate to the Kneset.

The curious fact is that, whatever the reason for the termination of a government, the minority (religious) parties have always managed to take advantage of it for their own benefit.

RELIGION IN THE POLITICAL SYSTEM

The religious element in Israel has been asserting itself in the political life of the nation through the medium of the Ministry of Religious Affairs, the statutorily recognized religious institutions, and the religious political parties.

The Ministry of Religious Affairs

Immediately upon the inception of the state in May 1948, the Va'ad Le'umi (National Council) declared the creation of the Ministry of Religious Affairs. This Ministry took over the legal powers formerly held by the British High Commissioner in connection with religious sects, jurisdiction of religious courts, and registration of marriages and divorces.[58] It has organized the religious services for all denominations in Israel

---

58. *State of Israel Government Yearbook* 5711 (1950) :188.

and has supervised the post-primary religious education that is not within the purview of the Ministry of Education and Culture.[59] The Ministry of Religious Affairs was deemed essential since three world religions have vested interests in the country and their rights had to be safeguarded for domestic as well as international reasons. It was the first instrument established by the state to carry out major functions of religious life on a governmental level.

Prior to the Proclamation of Independence, religious sects enjoyed special privileges under the British Mandate. These privileges are now protected by the Ministry in the name of the state. Thus, the Ministry has special departments for Muslim and Druze Religious Affairs, as well as for Christian Communities. There are also departments for religious councils, the Rabbinate and Rabbinical Courts, and Jewish Religious Affairs.

Through the Religious Councils, the Ministry provides for the religious needs of the Jewish population on a local basis. There are 188 such councils, whose members are nominated by the Minister, the local authority, and the local rabbinate. The state, through the Ministry, covers a third of the council's budget.[60]

The Ministry works together with the rabbinate on the supervision of *Kashrut* in the army hospitals and the import of meat. It takes care of all administrative and financial matters relating to Rabbinical Courts. It is also in charge of the registration of marriages and divorces and pays the salaries of the rabbis.

The Ministry's Department for Jewish Religious Affairs is concerned with the organization of religious life in immigrant settlements and with the supervision and the needs of the Yeshivot (higher religious institutions of learning). It promotes scientific research seeking solutions to the proper implementation of religious law in a technical society and provides for the building of ritual baths and synagogues. It further seeks to maintain and preserve historical monuments and sites sacred to any of the religious groups. It is the province of the

---

59. *Ibid.* 5726 (1965–66) :270.
60. *Sefer Ha-Huqim* (July 11, 1966) , p. 50.

Ministry to promulgate regulations for the conduct and procedure of the Religious Courts and for the elections to the Chief Rabbinate and to the Religious Councils.

The religious minority is an area of concern to the Ministry of Religious Affairs. The Karaites and the Samaritans, the Muslims, the Druzes, and the Christians fall within its purview. Their religious personnel are paid by the state through the Ministry. Their autonomy is carefully safeguarded.[61]

The Ministry of Religious Affairs has been under constant attack from representatives of secular parties who clamor for its complete abolishment and the absorption of its useful functions into the Ministry of the Interior.[62]

Religious Institutions

All the statutorily recognized religious institutions have legal ties with the Ministry of Religious Affairs. The budgetary allocations, payment of salaries, regulations concerning nominations, elections, appointments and tenure, and even institutional policies are directed or channeled through the Ministry. This, however, ought not be taken as an indication that the Rabbinical Council, the *Dayanim* (Religious Courts), or the local Religious Councils are subordinate to the Ministry. They are recognized as autonomous organizations with their own sphere of action. Their existence lends an aura of "religious presence" to the state and affects its political climate.

Political Clashes Within the Religious Establishment

The most serious clash has occurred between the Ministry of Religious Affairs and the Chief Rabbinate concerning the election regulations for a Chief Rabbi. Rabbi Herzog, the Ashkenazi Chief Rabbi of Israel, died in 1959. Coincidentally,

---

61. Joseph Badi, *Religion in Israel Today* (New York: Bookman Associates, 1959) , p. 30. Also Dr. P. Colbi, "The Ministry of Religious Affairs in the State of Israel," *Iggeret la-Golah* (April-May 1954) , p. 30. Also, "Review by the Minister of Religious Affairs on the Work of His Ministry," *Divrei ha-Kneset*, Sixth Kneset session, 44 (May 31, 1966) :1559.

62. See above, Chapter 5, note 36; below, in Chapter 15, "Politization of Religion and Crisis of Faith."

his death came in the wake of the resignation of the NRP from the Cabinet as a result of the controversy over "who is a Jew."[63] When the NRP resigned, Prime Minister Ben-Gurion appointed the nonparty Rabbi Toledano to fill the position of Minister of Religious Affairs vacated by the NRP.

The death of Chief Rabbi Herzog necessitated the election of a new Ashkenazi Chief Rabbi. The initiative to that effect was in the hands of the Minister of Religious Affairs who inherited this authority from the Va'ad Le'umi (National Council) of the Mandatory period. Accordingly, Rabbi Toledano issued a set of new regulations that differed in some respects from the regulations applied in the four former elections for the Chief Rabbinate. The three basic changes, introduced in the form of amendments, were the following: Instead of an Elections Committee of eight, four of whom were appointed by the Chief Rabbinate and four by the Minister of Religious Affairs, who then chose their chairman from among themselves, there would be a committee of nine, the ninth person serving as chairman of the committee and appointed by the Minister of Religious Affairs; whereas until now there was no age limit for candidates, the new regulation would provide for retirement at age 75, making someone past 71 ineligible for candidacy to a four-year elected office; whereas in the past there were no residency requirements for the office, the new regulations would make it available only to an Israeli citizen.[64]

The motive of the three amendments was to strengthen the Ministry of Religious Affairs vis-à-vis the Chief Rabbinate. A concurrent motive was the assurance of the election of a Chief Rabbi who would be progressive, forward-looking, and sympathetic to the needs of the maturing Israeli generation and to requirements imposed by a technical society upon a modern state machinery.

Ben-Gurion was eager to gain the appointment of Rabbi Shlomo Goren as Chief Rabbi of Israel. The Prime Minister made his acquaintance as Minister of Defense, when Shlomo Goren was serving in the capacity of Chaplain to the Israel Defense Forces. Indeed, Shlomo Goren was proposed as a can-

---

63. See chapter in Part III of same title.
64. *Ha-Zofeh*, December 4, 1959.

didate, but he had two formidable candidates opposing him: Rabbi Unterman, who was then Chief Rabbi of Tel Aviv, aged 71, and Rabbi Soloveitschik, an outstanding leader of Orthodox Jewry in the United States, a citizen of the United States. Finding himself in agreement with Ben-Gurion's motivations, Rabbi Toledano produced regulations that would have made Goren's election a virtual certainty. They would have excluded Rabbi Unterman because of the age limit and Rabbi Solovetschik because of his American citizenship.[65]

Protests from Orthodox circles were instantaneous. The Rabbinical Council refused to appoint its four representatives to the Elections Committee. Demonstrations were held and the issue was brought to the High Court of Israel and to the Kneset repeatedly.[66]

As early as December 1959, at a meeting with NRP leaders, Rabbi Toledano agreed to shelve the regulations that would automatically exclude the candidates favored by the NRP.[67] Nevertheless, the raging controversy prevented the conduct of elections for Chief Rabbi until April 1964. Rabbi Unterman was elected.

The NRP and the conservative religious forces scored another triumph. The authority and autonomy of the Chief Rabbinate, the ultra-Orthodox stronghold, was increased. The aspirations of the NRP to control the Chief Rabbinate as well as the Ministry of Religious Affairs for political purposes were greatly facilitated, despite Ben-Gurion's attempts to raise them above party politics. Although in the Ninth Government, formed in December 1959, Ben-Gurion valiantly resisted NRP pressures to relinquish to them the Ministry of Religious Affairs, by November 1961 the religious party was in control of the Ministry. Once again it was utilized as a tool for interparty political bargaining. With the NRP in firm control of the Ministry of Religious Affairs and in its position as savior of the Chief Rabbinate, religious life and religious objectives became strongly identified with the religious political party.

65. Ma'ariv, December 11, 1959, p. 3.
66. Ya-aqov Even Hen, Ha-Rabanut ha-Rashit l'Israel. (Ministry for Religious Affairs, 1964) , p. 29.
67. Jerusalem Post, December 10, 1959.

Religious Parties in the Political System

The political parties are treated elsewhere in this study. Of direct concern at this stage is the powerful impact of the religious parties on the political life of the nation. It is a virtual certainty that without a political organization, the religious element in Israel could not have realized its present accomplishments.

The influence and control exercised by the religious elements in the constitutional, legal, and practical spheres of the state have been mainly due to the circumstances of coalition government. As was already pointed out, democratic government at its best necessitates compromises. This holds true all the more for a multiple-party system with a coalition government as exemplified in the State of Israel. The religious militants, through the medium of their political parties, managed to take advantage of the system of coalition government by extracting concessions in their behalf on sensitive issues, though supported by only 15 percent of the voting population. The religious parties became a force in the political arena of the state with which both their friends and foes must reckon.

The religious leaders, particularly the leaders of the NRP, have become consummate tacticians of coalition politics. The next section of the paper is intended to demonstrate, in several case studies, how they have operated to attain their objectives.

Part III
The Formation of Coalitions

The case studies in this section intend to demonstrate the practical impact of the trends and principles discussed in the former section on the political life of the state. Each case study deals with a government crisis and its resolution. Between these two points the characteristic features of Israel's coalition government come to light. Political parties are directly involved at every stage in the formation and functioning of coalition government. Their main, if not sole, motivation is to utilize every step between the two points of terminating and creating a Cabinet for the purpose of gaining the most advantageous position for their party.

Mapai is no exception. Similar in this respect to other parties, it, too, seeks to extract the greatest profit from the workings of the government. Without Mapai, however, Israel could not have a government. Though other parties strived for power that would enable them to wrest the initiative from Mapai in the formation of a coalition, they did not succeed. Even in the one instance when a Cabinet was actually formed by a Progressive Party leader, the Prime Ministership and control of the Cabinet had to be transferred immediately to Mapai hands.

Mapai was quick to benefit from its power. If the minor parties had their price for participation in a Mapai-controlled coalition, so did Mapai set its price for accepting them. While not averse to bargaining in order to overcome an impasse, in some areas Mapai would not yield an inch. In this category belongs the matter of portfolio distribution. Mapai was never ready to relinquish the portfolios of foreign affairs, finance, education, police, and agriculture. On occasion, however, Mapai found it politically prudent to exchange a portfolio for the prospect of a greater return. In the Fourth and Fifth Government Mapai turned over to the General Zionists the portfolio of Trade and Industry in the hope of accomplishing with their help a change in the electoral system, which would have established Mapai as the majority party in the state. Starting with the Tenth Government, Mapai relinquished the portfolio of Labor to Ahdut ha-'Avodah, balancing the loss of an influential Ministry to another party with the prospect of bringing about an early merger with that party. In the Fourteenth Government, Mapai Prime Minister Levi Eshkol placed the Defense Ministry into the hands of Rafi's Moshe Dayan under the most unusual circumstances leading up to the Six Day War. While the loss of the Defense portfolio seemed to have come about against Mapai's will, it was not a coincidence that it was followed up by merger negotiations with the Rafi Party.

Taking advantage of its plurality of electoral votes, of its power in the economic sector, and of its tight grip on the administration, Mapai proceeded with the task of forming coalitions, keeping the interests of the party uppermost in mind. Time was usually on Mapai's side. Until a new government could be formed, the preceding government with its Mapai majority continued to rule in a caretaker capacity. Thus Mapai had little to lose, although its public image could be marred by a protracted paralysis in coalition negotiations and by the inability to pass controversial legislation in the Kneset.

Besides Mapai, the religious parties were the only ones who were involved in each of the thirteen governments (with the "Governments of National Unity" of June 1967 and March 1969 fifteen governments) in the state's history. They, therefore, offer the best example for comprehensive case studies of a minority party's influence on coalition politics. The main objective of the religious parties has been the enhancement of religious law and life in Israel in the face of a resisting secular majority. Hence, a study of their tactics and strategy also offers perhaps the clearest available picture of the relation of state and religion in Israel.

In order to see this relation clearly, it is necessary to view the struggle between Mapai and the religious parties in the light of the coalition activity involving other parties. Only by examining the partnership of Mapai and the NRP within the broad framework of possible coalition configurations could one reach any conclusions regarding the efficacy of the coalition government in Israel and the resolution of its religious problem.

The religious parties managed to gain results by using political tactics available to minority parties in a coalition government. This study examines the parties in instances when their efforts to extract religious concessions actually produced a complete breakdown of the Cabinet. It will show their skill and power to advance their cause in cases where Mapai was aligned with either the right (General Zionists), or the left (Mapam and Ahdut ha-'Avodah), and where the religious parties seemingly played only a secondary role. We will also scrutinize their technique and accomplishments in cases that did not lead to a breakdown in the government.

The emerging picture should demonstrate: (1) the tactics of Mapai in face of a coalition crisis, (2) the technique of interparty bargaining, (3) the dependence of Mapai on the religious parties, (4) the inability of the secular parties to combine forces in face of a religious challenge, (5) the skill of the religious parties in exploiting every avenue in behalf of the advancement of institutionalized religion, (6) the politization of religion through its exploitation for political ends, and (7) the secret of the success of the religious establishment, which derives from the particular mold of Israel's coalition government.

6

Rivalry for the Voters of the Future

The establishment of the State of Israel brought in its wake a wave of mass immigration on an unprecedented scale. The new arrivals were placed in hastily constructed immigrant camps. There the government tried to provide them with essential services, including the education of the young.

The type of education the immigrant children were to receive led to the first serious government crisis and to the downfall of the Second Government.

CRISIS OVER RELIGIOUS EDUCATION: ACT ONE

Ten months after the First Government of the State of Israel was approved by the Kneset, a crisis erupted that threatened its downfall. The issue in question was the religious education of the children in immigrant camps.

In most Western countries a unitary system of education, free from political influence and party affiliation is provided for by law. In contrast, at its inception the State of Israel adopted a decentralized educational system supported by public funds, with autonomous branches (called "trends") controlled by doctrinaire political parties.

According to the Compulsory Education Law of September 1949, parents were given the right to choose a school for their children from one of four recognized trends: General, Labor, Mizrahi, and Agudat Israel.[1] The rivalry among the parties to attract children to their specific trend became intense, since the party with the greatest success stood to benefit most in the country's political future. It was expected that competition would become especially keen in the new immigrant camps where the great mass of immigrants could have changed the political complexion of the nation.

Because the government wanted to prevent the introduction of trend divisiveness into the camps and because of the big turnover of children and the temporary setup of the schools, the government decided to preserve there a unified school system. Optional classes in religion were available for those who desired it. The system was placed under the Director of the Cultural Department, rather than directly under the Ministry of Education, and was kept separated from the trend network. Soon this arrangement broke down.[2]

Early in January 1950, the religious parties charged that inquisitorial methods were used by educational authorities against religious families in the immigrant camps, forcing them to give their children a strictly secular education. They were assumedly threatened with unemployment, withholding of housing, and various economic sanctions if they did not comply.[3]

At an extraordinary session on January 9, 1950, the Executive of ha-Po'el ha-Mizrahi, with its Cabinet Ministers and Jewish Agency representatives participating, decided that if no improvement was introduced in the religious education of children in immigrant camps, the party's representatives would leave both the government and the Jewish Agency Executive. The Religious Bloc unanimously adopted the same position.[4] They demanded that: 1) all pressures and coercion applied on religious parents in immigrant camps and settlements to send their children to nonreligious classes should be discontinued; 2) opportunities of religious education should be of-

---

1. *Laws of the State of Israel* 3 (September 12, 1949) :125.
2. *Davar*, January 11, 1950.
3. *Jewish Agency Digest* 2 (January 29, 1950) :752.
4. *Ha-Zofeh*, January 10, 1950.

fered to all children; and 3) the autonomy of the religious trend should be fully safeguarded.[5]

At its regular weekly meeting on January 10, the Cabinet took the matter of religious education in immigrant camps under consideration.[6] A week later, the Cabinet appointed a Ministerial Committee of five to work out a settlement on the issue.[7]

Since the religious parties did not receive satisfaction on their demands, the Ministers representing them repeatedly renewed their threat of resignation. They refused to attend Cabinet meetings and declared their intention of staying away until religious control of education in the immigrant camps was assured.[8] On February 18, the Prime Minister warned the three Religious Bloc Ministers that if they stayed away from the next Cabinet session he would consider it an act of resignation and would inform the Kneset about it.[9] The Ministers failed to attend an extraordinary Cabinet meeting on February 21. Although they informed the Prime Minister of their intention to attend the next regular Cabinet meeting, Ben-Gurion immediately proceeded to bring the situation to the Kneset's attention. He asserted that the action of the Religious Bloc Ministers was tantamount to a breach of collective responsibility; he laid before the Kneset a decision adopted by the Cabinet earlier in the day on that matter. It stated that any Minister who refuses to attend meetings or declines to implement the decisions of the Cabinet should be considered as having resigned. Unless the Kneset passes a vote of no-confidence, the government continues in power without the recalcitrant Minister.[10]

On February 21, the two-week-old government crisis came to an end. The next day the Religious Ministers terminated their boycott and attended a Cabinet meeting where it was decided to hold a referendum in the immigrant camps, offer-

---

5. *Ibid.*, January 12, 1950.
6. *Ibid.*, January 11, 1950.
7. *Davar*, January 18, 1950.
8. *Ibid.*, February 14, 1950.
9. *Ibid.*, February 20, 1950.
10. *Divrei ha-Kneset*, First Kneset, 118th session, 4 (February 21, 1950) : 830.

ing the parents a choice of the type of school they wanted their children to attend.[11]

Negotiations continued, aiming at a satisfactory solution of the problem. After a delay of three weeks, the plan calling for a referendum was abandoned. Instead, leaders of the Mapai and the Religious Bloc arrived at a compromise formula that was presented to the Kneset on March 14. The agreement of March 14, 1950, provided that in immigrant camps with a predominantly Yemeni population, education would be religious and supervised by a committee of four Orthodox persons representing the four trends. In the other immigrant camps religious and nonreligious schools would be set up. The whole system was placed under the direct supervision and responsibility of the Ministry of Education.[12] The Kneset approved the formula as an amendment to the Compulsory Education Law.[13]

In its broader ramifications the crisis offered an opportunity to re-examine the whole principle of "trend" versus "united" school system. Six parties—the Herut, Wizo, Fighters, General Zionists, as well as two members of the Coalition, the Progressives and the Sefardim—pressed for unification of the school system, taking a stand against the accepted position of the government. The Mapam and the Religious Bloc fought for the preservation of the trends, but for diametrically opposed reasons. The Mapam wanted to preserve a trend in which the values of a socialist society could be inculcated in the young generation. The Religious Bloc feared absorption into a general system where the attitude of the secular majority would prevail.[14] The Mapai was divided on the issue, but for coalition purposes it enforced strict discipline among its members of the Kneset to vote for the trend system in favor of the Religious Bloc. When the opposition demanded a roll call on the question, Mapai fought bitterly against it, with all procedural tricks to its disposal. It wished to avoid embarrassment to the

11. *Davar,* February 23, 1950.
12. *Davar,* March 15, 1950.
13. *Divrei ha-Kneset,* First Kneset, 126th session, 4 (March 14, 1950) : 1015.
14. *Ibid.,* pp. 1010–21.

majority of its members, who on principle wanted a unified system of education. The Kneset member who requested a roll call was I. Cohen of the Progressive Party, a partner of the Coalition.[15]

The trend system temporarily survived a severe challenge of its opponents, and the Cabinet weathered its first crisis which was precipitated by the Religious Bloc on the question of education.

Timing and Motives of the Boycott

The Religious Bloc claimed that the sole objective of its Cabinet boycott was to "save the souls of our children." Any education other than religious for the immigrant children was compared by them to nothing less than "conversion" away from Judaism.[16]

Despite these allegations, there were indications that the crisis was precipitated by them in order to forestall Ben-Gurion's attempt to push them out of the Coalition, or at best, make them a minor partner. Thus, what could have been an insignificant episode, a routine request to provide for religious needs in immigrant camps, was turned into a real threat when Mapai chose to enter into negotiations with Mapam and the General Zionists for the purpose of including them into the Coalition.[17] An impartial observer claimed that the Religious Bloc decided to make an issue of religious education in the immigrant camps for the tactical purpose of introducing a wedge between Mapai and Mapam and removing the chances of Mapam joining the Coalition.[18]

On the other hand, Mapai could not permit a pressure group with partisan interests, even of the size of the Religious Bloc, to succeed in deciding policy that may have radically affected the country's future. Mapai claimed that the goal of the Religious Bloc was "a monopoly for the Mizrahi trend over all the children."[19] In order to accomplish that, it precipi-

---

15. *Ibid.*, First Kneset, 129th session, 4 (March 21, 1950) :1081.
16. *Ha-Zofeh,* January 9, 1950.
17. *Ha-Boqer,* January 12, 1950.
18. *Ha-Arez,* February 17, 1950, editorial.
19. *Davar,* January 11, 1950.

tated a Cabinet crisis, creating "an absurd situation that had no parallel in any other country." The Ministers held their position in the Cabinet and yet preserved their independence of it and even flaunted it.[20]

Since the pressures of religious partisan interests were constant and threatening and challenged the basic postulate of collective Cabinet responsibility, Mapai had no choice but to try to broaden the Coalition. However, Mapai's efforts proved fruitless and only contributed to an increase in bargaining strength of the Religious Bloc who saw themselves as the sole major party on whom Mapai could rely.

The first threat to the government of the State of Israel was heatedly debated in the Kneset. It was not resolved by the House, where many members had to vote against their personal convictions, following the dictates of party interests on the subject of education. The solution to the problem was found in the caucus room, where party leaders conducted the negotiations.

Except for Mapam, which saw in the agreement on education in the immigrant camps a betrayal of labor through the elimination of the labor trend, the other parties felt that they had attained at least part of their objective. Herut and the center parties recognized it as the beginning of a unified school system which may soon be applied to the whole country. Mapai managed to preserve secular education in the camps. And the Religious Bloc received far-reaching concessions in religious education.

CRISIS OVER RELIGIOUS EDUCATION: ACT TWO

The first threat to the survival of the government subsided on February 21, 1950, when the religious Ministers terminated their boycott and returned to the Cabinet. On October 15 of the same year the Cabinet fell on the issue of government reorganization that was protested by the Religious Bloc.[21] On October 30 the Second Government was reconstituted by the same parties on the same basic principles as the former government.

---

20. *Ibid.*, February 20, 1950.
21. See Chapter 9.

Despite statements pledging cooperation between the Mapai and the Religious Bloc less than a month after the new government was established, tensions began to mount in the political arena.

Dissatisfaction with the condition of religious education burst into the open once again in the Kneset on December 11, 1950. Religious Bloc speakers utilized a report by the Labor Minister concerning plans for the improvement of conditions in immigrant camps to denounce the abuses of Mapai in restricting and oppressing religious education in the camps.[22] They accused Mapai of breach of trust for not implementing the agreement of March 14, 1950, which provided that immigrant children from religious families should automatically receive religious schooling.

Since the agreement many of the immigrants had been transferred from "camps" (*mahanot*) to "settlements" (*ma'abarot*), their possible permanent location. In the settlements the government introduced the system of education prevalent throughout the country. Hence, parents were offered the choice of the four existing trends. As a result, thousands of children had been transferred from religious to other school systems. The Religious Bloc protested against the setup. It demanded that the original agreement should apply equally to the *mahanot* and *ma'abarot*, since the families, not yet acclimated to the country, were still subject to partisan pressures. Mapai remained unconvinced.

Two weeks later, the Religious Bloc embarrassed the government by voting with the opposition in the Kneset for a full debate on the charge that civil servants were selected on the basis of neither merit nor need, but mainly by partisan considerations.[23] This was followed by another embarrassing moment when, on January 3, 1951, Rabbi Maimon, Minister of Religious Affairs, walked out of a Cabinet session threatening to resign if no satisfactory solution were found to the education problem without further delay.[24]

---

22. *Divrei ha-Kneset*, First Kneset, 198th session, 7 (December 11, 1950): 411.

23. *Divrei ha-Kneset*, First Kneset, 206th session, 7 (December 27, 1950):610.

24. *Davar*, January 5, 1951.

Tensions mounted to crisis proportions with the publication of the recommendations of the Ministerial Committee on Education on February 1, 1951.[25] They were approved by the majority of the Cabinet, but opposed by the Religious Bloc. The recommendations included provisions for the immediate establishment of religious schools for children in all Yemeni camps and in all religious settlements where no religious schools existed; the participation of a religious representative in the process of registration in all immigrant camps; and the establishment of a committee of three, composed of the Prime Minister, the Minister of Education, and the Minister of Religious Affairs, to be charged with the implementation of the recommendations.[26]

The Religious Bloc objected mainly to the provision which called for the establishment of religious schools in all settlements where no such schools existed. It charged that this provision dealt a blow to the very foundations of the religious trend, since it did not specifically designate the Mizrahi and Agudah schools as the sole religious educational institutions concerned in the matter. On the contrary: from preliminary discussions it became clear that the disputed provision implicitly recognized the recently organized Histadrut schools that were labeled "religious." The religious parties protested that neither the teachers nor the curriculum of the Histadrut schools were religious and that the religious subjects were introduced only as a camouflage. They claimed that Mapai was putting up a veneer of support for religious education, whereas in fact it had hastened to establish Histadrut "religious" schools in dozens of settlements in order to eliminate the possibility of creating authentic religious schools in these communities.[27]

Three days after the Cabinet accepted the recommendations of the Ministerial Committee, the Religious Bloc officially rejected them. It pledged to fight them in public, in the Kneset, and the government. It labeled Mapai's action, striving for

---

25. *Davar,* January 18, 1950. In the middle of January 1950 a Ministerial Committee of five was appointed by the Cabinet to work out a settlement on the issue.
26. *Davar,* February 2, 1951.
27. *Ha-Zofeh,* February 2, 1951 and February 4, 1951, editorials.

official recognition of the religious labor schools, a deception.[28]

The Mapai objected to the demands of the Religious Bloc to impose the same educational system on the *ma'abarot* that were applied in the *mahanot*. Its reasoning ran as follows: One could possibly accept that upon arrival to the country the new immigrants were unable to choose between two or more trends. But when they became acclimated and were consequently moved to their permanent settlements, they should be entitled to all the benefits of full-fledged citizenship, including freedom of choice in education. Such freedom of choice may have entailed a choice not only between religious and secular schools, but also between different types of religious schools. "The Religious Bloc wishes to declare as unfit the religious education of the Labor trend. Indeed, these schools, their teachers, supervisors and curricula are religious, though they lack the approval of the four religious parties represented in the Kneset, who even condemn each other as religiously unfit. . . . They condemn each other to such an extent, that two factions of the Religious Bloc cannot even combine into one religious trend in education." It emerged clearly, claimed Mapai, that all the maneuvers of the Religious Bloc were purely political tactics, exploiting religious values for political ends.[29]

As Mapai and the Religious Bloc were preparing for a showdown on the issue of education in the immigrant settlements, both the right and left wings of the political spectrum supported Mapai in principle. The left wing called upon Ben-Gurion not to yield to religious blackmail.[30] Right-wing opinion argued against the use of children's education as a vicious instrument in the hands of politicians who have future voters in mind.[31] Nevertheless, when the statement of the Minister of Education wherein he presented the Committee's recommendations to the Kneset[32] was brought to a vote, it was rejected 49 to 42 by a combined vote of the opposition and the Religious Bloc with only the Sephardim supporting Mapai, and the

28. *Ibid.*, February 5, 1951.
29. *Davar*, February 4, 1951, editorial.
30. *'Al ha-Mishmar*, February 7, 1951.
31. *Jerusalem Post*, February 8, 1951.
32. *Divrei ha-Kneset*, First Kneset, 222nd session, 8 (February 5, 1951): 980.

Progressives and Wizo abstaining.[33] Opposition to Mapai triumphed once again over principles and placed into one camp the extreme left (Communists) and extreme right (Herut), a fraternal labor party (Mapam), and the strongest advocate of reform in the educational system, the General Zionists. Ironically, all these supported the Religious Bloc, whose goals all major parties violently opposed.

After the adverse vote, Ben-Gurion announced the government's resignation.[34]

Mapai's Stand Toward the Religious Bloc

The stand of the Religious Bloc elicited a sharp attack from Ben Gurion on the floor of the Kneset. He denounced it for striving to establish a monopoly over religious education and the Jewish religion. He said that

> A person is permitted to be a religious Jew without resorting to a visa from the Mizrahi or the Agudah. A religious Jew who does not want to be in the Mizrahi party does not cease being a religious Jew. We did not and we shall not recognize, and no Government can be forced to recognize, the monopoly of a party that calls itself religious, over religious Jews; similarly, we did not and we shall not recognize—at least not this Government—the monopoly of the Mizrahi and the Agudah over religion. . . Religious parties do not represent Judaism. . . And I do not believe that anyone represents basic and traditional Judaism only by belonging to the Religious Bloc.[35]

He further stated that the Law of Compulsory Education provided for four trends but did not determine that only one of the trends could be religious, or secular, or pioneering. As a matter of fact, the religious trends did not abstain from teaching pioneering values in religious kibbutzim. Similarly, the labor trend need not abstain from teaching religious values in its schools. The labor (Histadrut) supervised religious schools are as legitimate and competent as are the religiously supervised pioneering schools.

---

33. *Ibid.,* 227th session, 8 (February 14, 1951) :1109.
34. *Ibid.*
35. *Ibid.,* p. 1099.

Ben-Gurion then continued to reveal his true feelings about the trend system.

> I will not betray a secret to you if I say that I see in the trend system a miserable system. Already thirty years ago, at its very start, I considered it a poisoned root. But it is not the only miserable inheritance that we received from the period preceding the state. And I regret that the greatest party in the country, of which I have the honor of being a member, did not as yet examine this question in the light of the new reality, after the emergence of the state. . . . Even if the system of trends was justified in its time—and I dare to think that even in its time it was not justified and was a mistake—the problem needs to be examined anew. As far as I know, there are only a few men in our party who think that the trend system should still be maintained. . . . I hope the conclusion will be reached that education must be freed from the rule of parties and handed over to the Government.[36]

This was in contradiction to Ben-Gurion's stand in the Kneset on other occasions when he defended the trend system, in the name of his party, obviously as a concession to the Religious Bloc.[37] Ben-Gurion must have felt, however, that the distrust and aggressiveness of the religious parties warranted an open and clear-cut stand on the issue of school trends, as well as on the position of religious parties in the state, both of which he denounced heatedly and without reservations.

The Kneset's vote of no-confidence in the government also brought forth a sharp reaction from the Central Committee of Mapai, which issued a statement condemning the Religious Bloc.

> The Religious Bloc had constantly exploited its balance of power in the Government coalition to press demands that were not commensurate with its political strength. . . . Mapai, which headed the Government, could not submit to political extortionism under the mantle of religion—extortion whose end was not yet in sight—and could not tolerate

---

36. *Ibid.*, p. 1101.
37. *Divrei ha-Kneset*, First Kneset, 11th session, 1–2 (March 10, 1949): 136.

the repeated dislocation of working routine resulting from the incessant pressure on the part of the Religious Bloc.[38]

All indications pointed to Mapai's unwillingness to carry on with the government as presently constituted, even if a solution could be found to the prevailing impasse. On February 25, 1951, President Weizmann appealed to Ben-Gurion to form a new government within the framework of the First Kneset. Ben-Gurion rejected the President's request. He made it clear that attempts at cooperation with the Religious Bloc had proven consistently futile. On March 5, Weizmann informed the Kneset about Ben-Gurion's refusal to form a new government. He requested the outgoing Cabinet to stay in office until a new government was formed following the elections.[39]

Under the Caretaker Government

The resignation of the Cabinet and Ben-Gurion's refusal to form a new government served as a signal to the parties to prepare for a probable election campaign. The Kneset became a platform for party maneuvers calculated to get the greatest advantage for the forthcoming elections.

Within the Cabinet Mapai shed all pretense of cooperation with the Religious Bloc. Overriding religious objections it approved an amendment to the Compulsory Service Law, requiring women who object to military service on religious grounds to serve the nation in immigrant settlements, agricultural or governmental institutions for two years. The amendment was presented to, and passed by, the Kneset over the united opposition of the Religious Bloc, General Zionists and Herut.[40] The passage of the bill was preceded by a protracted debate wherein the Religious Bloc charged that Ben-Gurion was motivated to produce the amendment not by the merits of the case, but by a desire "to punish the Religious Bloc."[41]

---

38. Statement of the Central Committee of Mapai, February 15, 1951.
39. *Divrei ha-Kneset*, First Kneset, 233rd session, 8 (March 5, 1951): 1233.
40. *Ibid.*, 234th session, 8 (March 6, 1951):1294.
41. *Ibid.*, 233rd session, 8 (March 5, 1951):1247, Rabbi Levin of the Religious Bloc.

Even the parties who on principle agreed with Mapai on the issue accused it of "playing politics,"[42] of attempting to take revenge on the Religious Bloc for breaking up the coalition,[43] or of being motivated by political considerations.[44]

Simultaneously, the Religious Bloc joined with the opposition in the Kneset to inflict a historic first defeat on a government bill at its first reading. The bill, in the form of an amendment to the Transition Law, would have permitted the Prime Minister to dismiss Ministers without obtaining prior Kneset approval. The Progressive Mr. Rosen, the Minister of Justice, explained that the bill was his, that it was essential for good government, and, having been drafted two months before, it had nothing to do with the present government crisis. Despite his appeal, the opposition defeated the government motion.[45] They feared that the bill, if passed into law, would enable Ben-Gurion to dismiss all non-Mapai Ministers from the caretaker government and organize new elections with a Cabinet composed of Mapai Ministers alone.

The women's party, the Wizo, hoping to benefit by the rift between the Religious Bloc and Mapai, introduced a Private Member's Bill in the Kneset designed to establish equality before the law between marriage partners with regard to matters of personal status, such as marriage, divorce, custody of children, property, inheritance and alimony.[46] By a vote of 51 to 13, overriding objections from the Religious Bloc, the Kneset voted to request the Cabinet to return, by a fixed deadline, with a draft for an Equal Rights Bill. The bill was duly tabled in the Kneset on June 18. During the ensuing debate, Rabbi Levin, Minister of Social Welfare, criticized the Cabinet and the Kneset for drawing up legislation that was "contrary to the letter and spirit of the Torah . . . which is the only binding agent that unites the Jewish people."[47] On the other hand,

---

42. *Ibid.*, 234th session, 8 (March 6, 1951):1257, Esther Raziel-Naor of Herut.
43. *Ibid.*, p. 1275, Arieh ben-Eliezer of Herut.
44. *Ibid.*, 233rd session, 8 (March 5, 1951):1251, Yizhaq ben-Aharon of Mapam.
45. *Ibid.*, p. 1243.
46. *Ibid.*, 243rd session, 8 (March 27, 1951):1456.
47. *Ibid.*, 267th session, 9 (June 26, 1951):2090.

Miss Ada Maimon of Mapai insisted that equality for women could be achieved within the legitimate bounds of rabbinical interpretation.[48] On July 17, in extraordinary session called almost on the eve of the elections, the Kneset approved the Women's Equal Rights Bill.[49]

Another controversial bill, the Hours of Rest Bill, opposed by the Religious Bloc, was passed by the Kneset on May 15. The Religious Bloc wished to give the Minister of Religious Affairs discretionary powers with regard to the execution of the bill's provisions. As passed, however, the Kneset gave these powers to the Minister of Labor.[50]

The pre-election period was climaxed by the discovery of a plot of religious zealots to carry out acts of sabotage within the Kneset. The arson attempt was attributed to religious opposition to the conscription of women.[51] The press warned that the religious leaders have become "associated in the public mind with saboteurs who do not stop short of raising arms against the State of Israel."[52] During the Kneset debate of the armed plot, the stormiest debate in its brief history, Mr. Sharett declared that the existence of terrorist groups attempting to enforce religious observance by burning cars and by similar illegal means was beyond dispute.[53]

In such a stormy and tense atmosphere the country was approaching the elections to the Second Kneset. In the beginning of April the Kneset passed the Second Kneset Elections Law, which designated July 30 as the date for the national elections.[54]

The Election Campaign

For the election to the Second Kneset, twenty lists attempted to register with the Election Board. Of these, sixteen were accepted and four were voided. Besides the four "acknowledged"

48. *Ibid.*, p. 2092.
49. *Ibid.*, p. 2165, passed clause by clause.
50. *Ibid.*, 252nd session, 9 (May 15, 1951) :1750.
51. *Ma'ariv*, May 14, 1951.
52. *Jerusalem Post*, May 16, 1951.
53. *Divrei ha-Kneset*, First Kneset, 255th session, 9 (May 22, 1951): 1822.
54. *Ibid.*, 250th session, 9 (April 12, 1951) :1697.

religious parties, religious groups called "Kneset Israel,"
"Yeshurun," and the "List of Rabbi Toledano," applied for
a place on the slate. When Rabbi Toledano was asked why he
was running for office on a private religious list instead of
supporting a genuine religious party, he justified himself by
saying, "In other countries rabbis have been representatives
in Parliament."[55]

The election campaign developed into a battle between the
moderate right and left-wing parties. Substantial gains by the
General Zionists at the recent Municipal Elections held out
high hopes to that right-wing party for similar gains in the
Kneset and were a source of grave concern to leftist Mapai.
The General Zionists spared no effort in an attempt to terminate Mapai supremacy and to lift themselves "from opposition to government."

The General Zionists accused Mapai of bringing ruination
to the country's economy and proclaimed that "the government
of Mapai is a government of terror and coercion."[56] In return,
Mapai mocked the General Zionists for their promises of "para-
dise on earth," abundance without rationing and controls, and
a cure-all for all economic ills through "free initiative."[57]

But the election was not a clear-cut fight of right against left.
If anything was clear about Israel's second national election,
it was that each party tried to snatch votes from those closest in
the party spectrum and was looking out strictly for its own
partisan interest. In that spirit, the General Zionists accused
their former colleagues, the Progressives, of belonging heart
and soul to Mapai, but since they are "snobs," they hold on to
their own party organization instead of joining the "plebs."[58]
Mapam deduced, from the platform of Mapai, its Histadrut
partner, that "its road is closer to the road of the bourgeois,
clerical, anti-worker parties than it is to the United Workers
Party."[59] Even the Religious Bloc was shattered as the religious
parties parted ways amidst mutual recriminations, as a result

55. A. Sha'anan, "Elections and Election Strife," *Davar*, July 6, 1951.
56. *Ha-Boqer*, July 8, 1951.
57. *Davar*, July 24, 1951.
58. A. Rambah, "Last Days of the First Kneset," *Ha-Boqer*, July 8, 1951.
59. M. Oren, "Decisive Majority—For whom and for What?" *'Al ha-Mishmar*, July 27, 1951.

of personality frictions and on the question of distribution of mandates in the forthcoming government.[60]

The election platforms themselves contained, besides the projection of party ideology on contemporary problems, a surprising amount of invective aimed at other parties. Thus, Mapai's platform accused the General Zionist, the Herut, and even part of the Religious Bloc, of aiming to accomplish their goals through unbridled freedom of speculation and profiteering at the expense of the masses, while the Mapam and the Communists continually subordinate themselves to the alien interests of the Cominform.[61] Herut's platform warned the voters that the choice is not between a coalition of Mapai and the Religious Bloc, or Mapai and the General Zionists, but rather between a "Government of class egoism, of dictatorial oppression . . . and a Government of honest national service and civil liberty; the choice is between a free State of Israel and a subjugated State of Mapai." In the spirit of guilt by association, it projected Mapai's degeneration onto its "partners," the General Zionists, Mizrahi, ha-Po'el ha-Mizrahi, and others.[62]

It turned out to be the bitterest campaign to date on record in Israel's history.

Election Platforms of the Parties

The party platforms for the election to the Second Kneset differed only slightly in substance from the election platforms of the First Kneset. In both instances they were a logical outgrowth of party ideology. The relevant surprise elements could be summed up briefly.

In Mapai's platform the realization of socialism was omitted as a goal, with the party obviously inching toward a more solid center position. Besides the platitudes of "freedom of conscience and religion"[63] that reverberated also in the platforms of other

---

60. "On the Breakdown of the Religious Bloc," *Ha-Zofeh,* July 10, 1951.
61. *Davar,* July 16, 1951, p. 1; "Mapai Platform for Elections to 2nd Kneset."
62. *The Herut Movement:* Working Platform for the Second Kneset, 1951.
63. *Davar,* July 17, 1951, p. 1 (art. 46).

parties, a special section was dedicated to the issue of religion and religious parties. "The existence of parties on the basis of religion—for or against religion—is a pervision of public truth. Religion does not demand a united stand on political and social questions that arise within the framework of the state and are debated in the Kneset. Turning religion into a political and party tool sows the seeds of discord in Israel and inflicts blemish upon the honor of Judaism."[64] Mapai struck out unequivocally against the religious parties, its major source of crisis and yet its only eager partner in the government. It also took a stand against the Chief Rabbinate, which has claimed to be the only authoritative interpreter of Jewish law and tradition, by stating that "The whole people is equally entitled to the spiritual possession of former generations and every group and trend is permitted to find in it spiritual nourishment according to its particular spiritual needs."[65]

Mapam's program became more doctrinaire and unbending than ever before. It aspired for speedy socialization at home and strict "neutrality" abroad, under the aegis of a united front of Labor parties. Its manifesto concluded with the ringing declaration: "We are not inclined to move an inch from our program."[66] Mapam's price for participating in the government was nothing less than full acceptance of its platform.

The General Zionists stepped up their demands for freedom of initiative, encouragement of private capital investment, a unitary system of national education, state control of labor exchanges and medical and social services. They also clamored for abrogation of controls in the economy and the discontinuance of rationing. In foreign affairs the General Zionists leaned toward the west, since the Western countries facilitated contact with world Jewry, whereas the Eastern countries put obstacles in its way.[67]

The Progressives were plagued, as during the First Kneset election, by the problem of providing the voter with a clear-cut

64. *Davar*, July 26, 1951, p. 4 (art. 24).
65. *Ibid.*
66. *Al ha-Mishmar*, July 13, 1951, p. 3.
67. *Party Platforms* (State of Israel Government Press Division, July 29, 1951), p. 6.

distinction between themselves and the General Zionists. Although they marked themselves as "a left center" party, as opposed to the General Zionists who were "right center," the distinction did not come across in the program. Perhaps the only tangible difference between the two parties was the insistence of the General Zionists to drop controls in the economy, whereas the Progressives advocated control and "planning for the sake of freedom."[68]

The religious parties, having dissolved the Religious Bloc, came out with individual platforms that maintained the underlying principle of the sovereignty of Torah. Accordingly, they demanded legislation to provide for Sabbath observance and the preservation of the sanctity of family life by adherence to rabbinic jurisdiction. Women must not be mobilized in the army. The Ministry of Religious Affairs must be maintained.[69]

The Herut toned down somewhat its demands for the conquest of historic Palestine. This demand was at once its most attractive feature in the eyes of the militants, and its greatest obstacle to success before those who preferred peace in a small land to war in a large one. Of course, the goal "to void the artificial partition of the eternal Jewish homeland" was still a central feature of its platform, but the party was taking its first steps toward grappling seriously with problems of socioeconomic import.[70]

The programs of the Communists and the Arab parties did not differ in substance from their earlier platforms. The Communists, however, emphasized their anti-Western and pro-Russian orientation more clearly. In addition the Arab parties were emboldened to ask complete equality for the Arabs, including equal citizenship, restitution of property and abolition of military government in Arab areas.[71]

All major parties agreed on the need to safeguard the security of the state and to further immigration, development, and economic progress. They all differed from Herut on the issue

68. *Ibid.*

69. *Ibid.*, pp. 1–3.

70. *The Herut Movement:* Working Platform for the Second Kneset, Herut Office, Israel, 1951.

71. *Party Platforms* (State of Israel Gov't, Press Division, 1951), pp. 7–8.

of legitimate boundaries, Herut being the sole party that openly declared its desire to enlarge the state. They parted ways with Mapam and the Communists, who were the only ones favoring the Eastern as opposed to the Western countries. The major parties disagreed with the General Zionists and the Herut, who wanted to abrogate government controls on the economy. They differed from Mapam and the religious parties, who wished to safeguard the trends in education. They all differed from the religious parties in the objection to any attempt to impose a religious way of life on the population. Although there were enough unifying elements to keep the parties working together in the interest of the state, the differences were substantial enough to forecast protracted troubles for the new coalition government.

Toward Creation of Government: Post-Election Bargaining

Elections to the Second Kneset were held on July 30, 1951, with 695,007 voters participating. The mandates were distributed as follows: Mapai—45 members; General Zionists—20; Mapam—15; ha-Po'el ha-Mizrahi—8; Herut—8; Communists—5; Progressives—4; Agudat Israel—3; Arab Democrats—3; Mizrahi—2; Po'ale Agudat Israel—2; Sephardim—2;[72] Yemenites—1; Progress and Labor (Arab) —1; Agriculture and Development (Arab) —1.[73]

Immediately upon the publication of the official election results, President Weizmann began conferring with party leaders concerning the creation of a new government.[74] On August 15 he entrusted Ben-Gurion with the task of forming it.

Bargaining for Power: Mapai Standpoint

Mapai's hopes of emerging as a solid majority party from the elections to the Second Kneset did not materialize. However, it did emerge with an impressive plurality of 45 representatives in the Kneset, as compared to 20 General Zionists, who ranked

---

72. Later affiliated with the General Zionists.
73. *Israel Government Yearbook 5713/1952*, p. 51.
74. *Davar*, August 10, 1951.

next in order of party size. This led Mapai to the following deductions: None of the parties could assume the responsibilities of government by itself; no government could be established without the Mapai at its center; aside from Mapai, none of the other parties could have a right to dictate the conditions under which the government would be created.[75]

The first of these deductions was an admission of failure on the part of Mapai, since it was the only party that aspired for a clear majority in the elections. The second deduction was a fact that none would care to dispute, since the opposition was hopelessly fragmented. Although the General Zionists offered their services to President Weizmann, should they be requested to form a government, this was but an empty gesture. It remained obvious that Mapai's leadership in forming a government was imperative. The third deduction expressed Mapai's hope and confidence that its indispensability to the proper functioning of government would be recognized. In the words of Ben-Gurion, "No Government could arise that would go contrary to the foreign policy and to the order we conducted till now. If they (the other parties) would accept the democratic decision of the people, they would join the Government on the basis of the Mapai platform."[76]

After the election Mapai hoped to create a broad coalition on the basis of the following guiding lines: No change in foreign policy; planned economy with controls; broadening of mass immigration; and satisfaction of religious needs without any compulsion. In consonance with these guiding lines Mapai was ready to enter into coalition with any party except Herut and the Communists.[77]

The Prime Minister designate, David Ben-Gurion, held 55 meetings with various party representatives in an effort to frame a joint program.[78] The possibility of establishing a broad coalition, instead of the narrow coalition of the former government, depended on two conditions: Mapam would have to

---

75. *Divrei ha-Kneset*, Second Kneset, 12th session, 10 (October 7, 1951): 198 (Ben-Gurion).
76. *Davar*, August 9, 1951.
77. *Ibid.*, August 12, 1951.
78. *Divrei ha-Kneset*, Second Kneset, 12th session, 10 (October 7, 1951): 198.

agree to the principles of the acting government in foreign affairs and the General Zionists would have to accept the basic outlines of the present economic policy.[79]

Negotiations were first opened with Mapam. Mapam proposed to Mapai a 34-point program, 29 points of which were found mutually acceptable, two were not acceptable, and on three a satisfactory compromise could be reached. The main point of fundamental disagreement was foreign policy. Despite repeated assurances by Mapai that it would not join any Western power bloc, and despite ample proofs that Israel often voted against the United States in the international arena, Mapai's recent support of American policy in Korea was viewed by Mapam as sufficient cause to break off negotiations.[80]

Additional difficulties in the negotiations with Mapam arose with regard to the composition of the government. Although Mapai aspired for a broad coalition, Mapam desired a narrow coalition of two parties, the "Labor Front." It evidently did not realize that, although the Labor Front is embodied in the Histadrut, it must not be embodied in the government.[81]

Mapai claimed that it was sincerely interested in having Mapam in the coalition. It warned Mapam that if negotiations broke down, the basic cause would not be disagreement over the conditions of partnership, but rather the "nonexistence of a will to join" that seems to be pervading Mapam circles.[82] On September 11 Mapam, in convention assembled, voted against continued negotiations with Mapai. The discussion and vote revealed a factional split, with the minority Ahdut ha-'Avodah desiring further negotiations and renouncing any responsibility for the majority decision.[83]

The negotiations with the General Zionists were long and tedious. On several occasions they seemed to be on the verge of a successful conclusion, only to be bogged down once again on a detail that brooked no compromise.

Just as Mapam preferred a narrow coalition of the workers

79. *Davar*, August 14, 1951.
80. *Divrei ha-Kneset*, Second Kneset, 12th session, 10 (October 7, 1951): 206, Meir Argov of Mapai.
81. *Ibid.*, 13th session, 10 (October 8, 1951):250 (Ben-Gurion).
82. *Davar*, August 24, 1951, Yona Yagul, "The Will to Join."
83. *Ibid.*, September 11, 1951.

parties (the Labor Front), so did the General Zionists aspire for a government consisting solely of them and Mapai. They did not want Mapam and the Religious Bloc. They did not even want their former colleagues, the Progressives. Mr. Bernstein, leader of the General Zionists, tried to convince Ben-Gurion that, "according to the (party) key there is no place for them in the government, since they do not even have six representatives."[84]

Mapai claimed that what destroyed the possibility of a coalition between them and the General Zionists was the arrogant attitude of the latter to the effect that they are the only ones who know anything about economy and that they alone could save the country from certain disaster with their own particular economic approach. However, following the elections, the General Zionists were ready to subscribe to a government program that incorporated Mapai's economic platform, including government control of major industries. "The consent of the General Zionists to all that was proposed to them in opposition to their own beliefs, disturbed us," stated a Mapai representative.[85] It soon became clear from the pronouncement of a General Zionist leader, that, in their view, the program was unimportant. The control of portfolios was important. Therefore, the danger began looming large that, with the economic portfolios in the hands of General Zionists, there would be two governments within the coalition that would clash day in and day out. It was the recognition of this danger, of the willingness of General Zionists to accept the government program only to boycott it once they possessed the key ministries, that eventually led to the breakdown in negotiations.[86]

On this basis it is understandable that the consideration of portfolios was more important than the government program or the composition of government. The General Zionists demanded the portfolios of Treasury, Trade and Industry, Education, and Agriculture, or Communications.[87] Later on they

---

84. *Divrei ha-Kneset*, Second Kneset, 13th session, 10 (October 8, 1951): 249 (Ben-Gurion).

85. *Ibid.*, p. 233 Yisrael Guri of Mapai.

86. *Ibid.*, p. 224. Akiva Guvrin of Mapai.

87. *Davar*, September 18, 1951.

were willing to renounce their demand for the Treasury in exchange for the portfolios of Development, the Deputy Ministership of the Treasury, or the Deputy Prime Ministership. They also requested that the Office of Supply and Rationing be handed to them as part of the Ministry of Trade.[88] Recognizing that Mapai would not renounce its absolute control of the purse, the General Zionists gave up all their demands for the Treasury and finally settled for Trade and Industry (including Supply and Rationing), Interior, Education (including all the institutions now under Social Welfare), and Development and Communications.[89]

Mapai reached an agreement with the General Zionists according to which educational trends would be replaced in six months by a national unitary system of education, with sufficient guarantees for religious education for religious children. On the basis of this agreement, the portfolio of Education could have ceased to be a controversial one. The General Zionists, however, insisted on attaching to the Ministry institutions that were previously under Social Welfare. This smacked of subterfuge and aroused suspicions that the General Zionists, when in possession of the Ministry, would attempt to attain their goal of nationalizing social welfare agencies, like health and unemployment offices.

But the biggest bone of contention was the portfolio of Trade and Industry. Mapai was ready to offer the General Zionists the portfolio of Industry, but Trade, including Supply and Rationing, was out of the question. It could not be forgotten that the General Zionists made criticism of the economic structure, of supply and rationing, and of incentives for free enterprise, the cornerstone of their earlier opposition to Mapai. As Ben-Gurion said, "there is no possibility to hand this particular portfolio over to the General Zionists, since Mapai has obligations towards its voters in the matter of supply and rationing," and in the conduct of the economy.[90] On September 25, negotiations broke off because of the half-portfolio of Trade.

---

88. *Ibid.*, September 28, 1951.
89. *Ha-Boqer*, September 28, 1951 or *Davar*, October 4, 1951.
90. *Davar*, September 28, 1951.

Mapai was left with two alternatives; to establish a narrow coalition or to return the mandate to the President. It chose the first.

The Progressives informed Ben-Gurion that they would not participate in the government without the General Zionists. In case a narrow coalition could be established, however, they would not vote against it.

The only hope rested in satisfactory negotiations with the religious parties, and particularly with the ha-Po'el ha-Mizrahi, which commanded eight of the fifteen religious party votes. The demands of the religious parties were mainly in the religious sphere. None were novel. They dealt with supervision of *kashrut,* a Sabbath observance law, rabbinic jurisdiction, and conscription of women, aiming mainly for the preservation of the status quo. Mapai and ha-Po'el ha-Mizrahi reached an understanding on most issues. The issue of education, however, again became a sensitive point. Mapai proposed that the four trends be reduced to two trends, religious and secular, in a unified national education system under the direct control of the Ministry of Education. The ha-Po'el ha-Mizrahi was ready to consent to two educational trends but demanded autonomy for the religious trend instead of a unified system of supervision. At one point, Mapai felt that the demands of ha-Po'el ha-Mizrahi sounded like an ultimatum. They were, therefore, rejected, and negotiations were broken off temporarily.

The only serious demand, aside from religious issues, came from the Po'alei Agudat Israel, which desired a portfolio in the government, making it a condition for participation.[91] In view of the offer to ha-Po'el ha-Mizrahi of two portfolios and to Mizrahi and Agudat Israel of one each, the aspirations of Po'alei Agudat Israel were understandable. Regretfully, however, Mapai could not spare a fifth portfolio, and the religious party eventually gave up its demand.[92]

Having assured itself of the expected support of five Arab votes in the Kneset, Ben-Gurion presented his new government to the House on October 8, 1951.

---

91. *Davar,* October 4, 1951.
92. *Ibid.,* October 5, 1951.

Bargaining for Power: Standpoint of Mapam

Mapam, faithful to the position it took in its election platform, was ready to participate in a government headed by a united front of workers' parties, on the basis of a jointly agreed program.[93] It maintained that the two parties must work together, bearing in mind that, "Mapai does not have a majority; the workers' parties have a majority."[94]

Mapai, however, was not interested in a jointly agreed program. It pressed for the acceptance of its own unilateral platform. This Mapam could not countenance. "Let it be clear: if the program of Mapai is the basis, it means no partnership; it means rejecting the establishment of a United Worker's Front."[95]

Mapam endeavored to assure the state economic and political independence, absolute neutrality, and progressive socialist government, with civil and racial equality. Nevertheless, Mapai refused to establish a responsible partnership.[96]

The two workers' parties clashed violently in their approach to foreign and domestic policy. Mapam consistently pursued its neutralist approach in foreign affairs, in opposition to Mapai's pro-Western orientation. Ben-Gurion refused to commit himself on the issue of neutrality. On domestic issues, Mapam could not compromise with the economic and political independence of the state. It aimed to accomplish its economic goal through the mobilization of the available working power in the state and through more systematic taxation of wealth, instead of through reliance on foreign aid. This was the way to stop inflation, to bring the black market and speculation to an end, to proceed with the orderly absorption of immigrants and to raise the standard of living. The differences between the two approaches could not be bridged and the negotiations broke down.

At the national convention of Mapam, where the vote with

93. *'Al ha-Mishmar,* August 14, 1951.
94. *Ibid.,* August 1, 1951.
95. *Ibid.,* August 15, 1951.
96. *Divrei ha-Kneset,* Second Kneset, 12th session, 10 (October 7, 1951) : 204. Meir Ya'ari of Mapam.

regard to joining the coalition was taken, the negotiators reported that the party's demands on foreign affairs and on some domestic issues were rejected by Ben-Gurion.[97] It was also revealed that "Ben-Gurion did not consent to Mapam's demands concerning secularization of the state and said that one must respect the sentiments of the people and guard the tradition."[98] The majority voted against continued negotiations. A minority was ready to make additional compromises in order to enter the government. It found Mapam's participation in the government imperative for the purpose of saving the country from ruin.[99] Without Mapam, the government would be completely at the mercy of the General Zionists. However, despite a vocal minority, the left-wing party claimed that negotiations had to be terminated due to Mapai's recalcitrant and insincere attitude and her refusal to subscribe to a minimum program.[100]

Bargaining for Power: Standpoint of General Zionists

A week prior to the publication of the final election results, when President Weizmann began conferring with party leaders, the General Zionists announced that they were willing to enter into a government coalition with all parties except Mapam and the Communists.[101]

Despite their willingness to become part of a governing coalition that would be initiated by Ben-Gurion, the General Zionists had their reservations about Mapai. They suspected that, since Mapai failed to gain the imposition of her policy and outlook on the state by winning a sweeping majority in the elections, she would try to accomplish this through negotiations.

The General Zionists were fully aware that Mapai could not, because of prestige, and would not, because of principles, accept their economic platform. Therefore, they presented only a minimum program. Mapai, however, presented a maximum

97. *Davar*, September 10, 1951.
98. *Ha-Zofeh*, September 10, 1951 (quoting Ya'aqov Hazzan of Mapam).
99. *Divrei ha-Kneset*, Second Kneset, 13th session, 10 (October 8, 1951):
229 Y. Ben-Yehuda of Mapam.
100. *'Al ha-Mishmar*, September 12, 1951.
101. *Davar*, August 1, 1951.

program, simultaneously demanding greater concessions of the General Zionists than Mapai herself was willing to consider.[102] Mapai initiated negotiations with the religious parties "as a softening action against the General Zionists," forcing them to renounce even their minimum demands.[103]

The General Zionists stipulated five conditions for joining the government: national unitary system of education, within whose framework there shall be opportunity for religious education, but without political trends and party supervision; national employment offices; national medical and social security; depolitization of the government administration, i.e., the party affiliation of the Minister shall not be the decisive factor in the formation of the administration; and free economy with transitional stages aiming for the realization of this goal.[104]

Even before the start of the negotiations, there were strong objections within Mapai to a coalition with the right-wing General Zionists.[105] Apparently, objections were stilled by the hope that Mapai and Mapam could jointly counteract right-wing pressure within the government. Indeed, satisfactory progress was made in the negotiations, as long as prospects of partnership with Mapam were also favorable. When, however, Mapam announced her withdrawal from the bargaining table, Mapai underwent a change in attitude.

After the withdrawal of Mapam, objections to a coalition with the General Zionists grew stronger, and Mapai ranks split on the question.[106] Henceforth, Mapai tried to raise, instead of overcome, obstacles to a satisfactory conclusion of the negotiations. It was becoming increasingly obvious that, without Mapam at its side, Mapai was reluctant to enter into coalition with the General Zionists.

After two-thirds of the negotiations were concluded, with Mapai having raised no objection to the General Zionist request for the Ministry of Trade and Industry, Ben-Gurion suddenly discovered that it would be too much for one Minister to

102. *Ha-Boqer*, September 18, 1951, editorial.
103. *Ibid.*, September 27, 1951.
104. *Davar*, August 12, 1951.
105. *Ha-Zofeh*, August 6, 1951.
106. *Ibid.*, September 12, 1951.

handle, and the portfolio would have to be divided in two.[107]
He wanted to create a new portfolio for the General Zionists,
that of Industry and Development, in place of the existing one
of Trade and Industry. Even the portfolio of Development
Mapai was ready to hand over to the General Zionists in a
truncated form only. It would leave it with the supervision
over fuel supplies, mining, and tourism but remove actual
participation on planning and development. The General
Zionists were ready to make far-reaching concessions with regard to portfolios, provided the Ministry of Trade and Industry
would be given to them intact. They claimed, "The public
that put their confidence in them expects them to exert influence upon economic problems."[108] Mapai remained unbending,
bringing about the collapse of the negotiations and the entrance
of the General Zionists into the ranks of the opposition.

Bargaining for Power: Standpoint of the Progressives

In two former governments, the Progressives were identified
with the left-of-center policies of the Mapai-controlled coalition. The hopes of the Progressive Party for survival and
growth rested in the hands of the voter who considered himself
a "liberal" and who was in sympathy with labor aspirations
but whose economic interests kept him somewhat right of
center. The Progressives were determined, therefore, not to
enter a coalition without the right-wing General Zionists. Their
main demand was that the new government be a broad coalition.[109]

By Progressive definition, a broad coalition would be one
that consisted of the Mapai, the General Zionists, and themselves. Among their other demands were a national unified
system of education, with provisions for religious and secular
trends, but without the participation of political parties, a

107. *Divrei ha-Kneset*, Second Kneset, 12th session, 10 (October 7, 1951) :
201. P. Bernstein of General Zionists.
108. *Ha-Boqer*, September 28, 1951.
109. *Davar*, August 14, 1951. It should be noted that the loss of one
seat in the Kneset, where Progressive representation diminished from five
to four, was also attributed to a blurred image of the Progressive Party
as a possible extension-in-caricature of Mapai.

guarantee of no discrimination between the private and the collective economic sector, and depolitization of the administration.[110]

When negotiations between the Mapai and the General Zionists began to falter, the Progressives repeatedly stepped in, attempting to bridge the differences between the two parties.[111] Their efforts brought no results. The General Zionists suspected that the Progressives were acting as Mapai's emissaries, attempting to influence them so they would lessen their demands.[112]

When the broad coalition fell through and a narrow coalition was established, the Progressives announced their decision not to participate in it, but also not to vote against it in the Kneset.[113]

Bargaining for Power: Standpoint of the Religious Parties

When President Weizmann invited party opinions concerning the creation of a new government, he was told by representatives of ha-Po'el ha-Mizrahi that, in view of the economic situation, a broad coalition would be preferable. They would, however, also be willing to join a narrow coalition.[114] In the protracted negotiations, the ha-Po'el ha-Mizrahi reversed its stand. Although still not opposed to a broad coalition, they showed preference for a narrow one.[115] In a narrow coalition, the religious parties would not be exposed to the relentless pressure of the General Zionists' attempts to abolish the trend system in education. They would carry greater weight vis-à-vis Mapai and would receive a greater number of portfolios.

Among the conditions of the ha-Po'el ha-Mizrahi for participation in the government was: removal of obstacles that brought about the former government crisis by solving the problem of religious education in the immigrant camp. The ha-Po'el ha-Mizrahi was inclined to accept two, instead of four,

110. *Davar*, September 18, 1951.
111. *Ha-Zofeh*, September 30, 1951.
112. *Ha-Boqer*, September 18, 1951.
113. *Davar*, October 3, 1951.
114. *Ha-Zofeh*, August 14, 1951.
115. *Ha-Boqer*, October 2, 1951.

trends, provided one of the trends were religious and would have complete autonomy under a religious supervisor. Other conditions were: continuation of the Ministry of Religious Affairs; passage of a Sabbath Observance Law; establishment of religious military units and enforcement of *Kashrut* in the army; settling the problem of kosher meat import; and guaranteeing religious life in the state.[116] A month later party representatives added demands for the preservation of status quo in rabbinic jurisdiction, laws of personal status and conscription of religious women, as well as a request for assurance of governmental stability.[117]

The other religious parties did not differ with ha-Po'el ha-Mizrahi on substantive issues. They all agreed, that their basic condition for support of the coalition was that "every Jew must be given the opportunity to educate his children according to his will and his beliefs. . . . Every religious and traditional Jew must be given the opportunity to live by his faith."[118]

The religious parties were taken by surprise when the presentation of their demands was met by a Mapai claim that this was equivalent to an ultimatum. The ha-Po'el ha-Mizrahi representatives denied that this was their objective. "The truth is that the ha-Po'el ha-Mizrahi reached the limit of the permissible and possible concessions on its demands."[119] This alone was made clear to Mapai, but without any ultimatum. A coalition government must be based on "concessions up to a certain limit. From that point on every demand for a concession is a demand for self-denial," a demand that parties concede themselves out of existence. The religious parties could not renounce their elementary request that a religious Jew should have the opportunity to live by his faith and his child be guaranteed religious education. Such an approach by Mapai would block the creation of a government and, when eventually established, cooperation within it.[120]

---

116. *Ha-Zofeh*, August 6, 1951.
117. *Davar*, September 10, 1951.
118. *Ha-Zofeh*, September 18, 1951.
119. *Ibid.*
120. *Ibid.*, p. 2, editorial.

It became obvious to the religious leaders that Mapai lacked good will in its negotiations with them. The succession of events proved that Mapai prepared a program for the establishment of a coalition with the General Zionists and Progressives alone.[121] The religious parties were evidently not welcome partners in the coalition. They were Mapai's last choice and, fortunately for the religious parties, Mapai was left with no other recourse.

Bargaining for Power: Standpoint of other Parties

The Arab Democratic List offered full support to the new government. However, it demanded the guarantee of full equality for the Arabs, as stated in the program. Beyond the program, it requested a revision of the law concerning Arab lands in Israel, the return of their property to the Arabs living in Israel, the raising of standards in Arab schools, the usage of the Arabic language in official correspondence with the Arab population, the abolition of military government in areas where it was not essential to the security of the state, concern for economic development of the Arab population, and the leaving of "Vakf" (sacred properties to Islam) under Muslim administration. They also requested that the government provide identification papers to those Arabs who were reunited with their families by crossing the border illegally prior to the election to the Second Kneset.[122]

In contrast to the support of the Arab Democratic List, the Yemenis opposed the coalition, since the Mapai did not deserve to be maintained in power by the religious parties. Besides, the "so-called religious parties," with their participation in this government, were acting unethically, utilizing religion as a political weapon to attain their objectives of propaganda and power. There were also other religious parties, like the Yemenis and the Sephardim, and large religious groups, notably among the General Zionists, who considered the so-called religious

---

121. *Ha-Boqer,* September 25, 1951.
122. *Divrei ha-Kneset,* Second Kneset, 13th session, 10 (October 8, 1951) : 233 Alzebi Sif-Aldin Mahmad Seid of the Arab Democratic List.

parties' claim for monopoly on religion as unjustified as Mapai's claim for monopoly on power.[123]

The Herut Party made no pretense about its entrenchment in the Opposition camp. It claimed that the government program was unrealistic and could not be fulfilled. The blame for economic failure was unjustifiably placed on the new immigrants, whereas in fact, they have created an expanded market and brought sufficient private wealth along for basic support. The blame was with the government which could not elicit confidence.[124] The extreme right-wing party further condemned the government for its negotiations with Germany for blood money (compensation for Nazi atrocities) and products, and for its lack of planning to cope with the border problems and infiltration.[125]

In addition to the criticisms voiced by the other opposition parties, the Communist Party emphasized the lack of equality in the country with regard to the Arab minority, in whose territory military rule has been enforced. This has been the result of support given by the government to imperialist interests within the country and without. The Communists demanded that the government take a clear-cut stand in behalf of peace by supporting Stalin's plan for atomic disarmament, and by opposing the rearmament of Germany and the reestablishment of a Nazi army.[126]

The Government and its Program

On October 7, 1951, the Prime Minister presented the new government and its program to the Kneset.[127] The government consisted of a narrow coalition of Mapai and the religious parties with thirteen members. The portfolios were distributed

---

123. *Ibid.*, p. 240. Sh. Geridi of the Yemenis.
124. *Ibid.*, Second Kneset, 12th session, 10 (October 7, 1951) :208. B. Avniel of Herut.
125. *Ibid.*, 13th session, 10 (October 8, 1951) :241. Aryeh ben-Eliezer of Herut.
126. *Ibid.*, 12th session, 10 (October 7, 1951) :216. Sh. Mikunis of the Communist Party.
127. *Ibid.*, p. 198.

as follows: Mapai—9; ha-Po'el ha-Mizrahi—2; Mizrahi—1; Agudat Israel—1. Po'alei Agudat Israel promised its support of
the coalition without the granting of a portfolio.

Basic Principles of the Government Program

One of the most troublesome features of former governments
was the lack of joint responsibility among its members. As in
the past, therefore, this program also started out with a declaration of a procedural principle, aiming to enforce collective
responsibility of the members of government and their parties.
This applied to the agreed government program and to decisions of the Cabinet (Art. 1).

The government aspired for the preservation of a democratic
system of government by guaranteeing full equality of rights
without distinction of sex, race, party, religion and nationality,
as well as freedom of religion and conscience. The powers and
rights of public servants were to be determined, as well as
the liberties of individuals and associations. These guarantees,
in the form of fundamental laws, would be incorporated into
the basic Constitution of the State (Art. 2).

In foreign affairs the government will promote peace and
friendship with every peace-loving country (Art. 3). Concern
for the security of the state, ingathering and integration of the
exiles and speedy development of the natural resources of the
land will be in the forefront of activities (Art. 4, 5).

In cooperation with the Zionist Organization, the government would strive for economic independence through greater
production in agriculture and industry, expansion of communications and construction and the development of under-
developed areas (Art. 6, 7). The government will encourage
sound economic initiative in the form of private and collective
enterprise, will make every effort to attract both private and
public capital, and will avoid any discrimination whatsoever
between the private and cooperative economic sectors (Art. 8,
9).

Increase in the productivity of labor will be rewarded. Development projects vital to the state will be offered relief from
taxation and customs duty. The government will make certain

of its influence in the electricity and Dead Sea concessions, and in the Negev mines (Art. 10). It will further devote itself to the orderly distribution of raw materials and vital necessities (Art. 11).

Strictest supervision of just distribution in rationing will be maintained, as long as there shall be a need for rationing. To the extent that efforts to expand production will succeed, rationing will be progressively reduced (Art. 12). An Economic Council, composed of representatives of the private and economic sectors in all branches of economy, will be established. Invested with advisory powers, it will be to the disposal of the Prime Minister (Art. 13).

The tax burden will be equitably distributed (Art. 14). Compulsory national insurance—old-age hospitalization, sickness, disability, unemployment, and other—will be introduced for all inhabitants (Art. 16). In the war against inflation, the government will attempt to balance the budget and to fight relentlessly against the black market (Art. 17, 18).

A government committee will prepare a curriculum to institute state education in all elementary schools, with a minimum requirement for all schools. The right of parents in choosing an educational trend will be recognized. Religious education will be guaranteed for all children whose parents desire it (Art. 20).

The government will guarantee to the Arab and other minorities full equality of rights and obligations. The rights of ownership and property of Arabs who are lawfully in the state will be settled according to law (Art. 24).

Freedom of conscience and religion will be a guiding light of government activities. The State will scrupulously satisfy the communal religious needs of its inhabitants and will not tolerate any coercion in matters of religion, from whatever side or in whatever direction (Art. 25).

The government will endeavor to assure full employment, economic security, proper working conditions, freedom of association, collective bargaining and freedom of strike (Art. 26). A law governing conditions of work (privileges and duties) of civil servants, will be presented to the Kneset, guaranteeing appointment according to personal qualification, on the basis

of examinations and without any regard for party affiliation
(Art. 27) .[128]

Debate on the government program proceeded immediately
after its presentation to the Kneset. It took two days before
the final vote was taken that secured the establishment of the
government by a narrow margin of 56 to 40, with four abstentions.[129]

Analysis of Discord and Compromise

From its inception, on October 30, 1950, the Second Government was a crisis government, not because of external threats
of aggression but because of internal stress and disagreements
between two partners of the coalition. The Religious Bloc kept
making demands that religious law be respected. It accused
Mapai of abuses, but Mapai insisted that it maintained the
religious status quo as agreed upon by the members of the
coalition. The pro forma cause for the breakdown of the government was the religious education issue. In reality this was
only part of a broader religious problem which consisted of an
attempt by the religious community to gain recognition, acceptance, and greater control in the state.

The process that led to the downfall of the government, as
well as the negotiations that led to the establishment of its successor, indicated that the major opposition parties were separated from Mapai by a deeper chasm than from the Religious
Bloc. In the no-confidence vote, the Mapam and the General
Zionists voted with the Religious Bloc and against Mapai on
a religious issue. In subsequent negotiations, they considered
specific policy differences greater obstacles to cooperation with
Mapai than the differences separating the secular from the
Religious Bloc.

Although Mapam was militantly anti-religious and wanted
to destroy religious influence in the state, it forced Mapai into

128. English translation in *Israel Government Yearbook* 5712 (1951/2).
"Basic Outline of the Policy of the Government as Presented to the
Kneset by the Prime Minister, Mr. David Ben-Gurion." (October 7, 1951):
pp. L–LII.

129. *Divrei ha-Kneset,* Second Kneset, 13th session, 10 (October 8, 1951):
270.

the arms of the religionists by its unwillingness to consider a reorientation in its foreign policy. Mapam was also running the risk of a de-socialized economy if Mapai reached a working agreement with the General Zionists.

Mapam's action was difficult to understand, especially in view of a drop in its Kneset representation, a strong and vocal minority within its ranks that wished to join the government, and Mapai's eagerness to have her as a coalition partner. It would appear, however, that Mapam simply did not take Mapai's invitation seriously. Mapam suspected that Ben-Gurion was compelled to turn to it in order to prove to the Religious Bloc Mapai's independence of the religious parties. Accordingly, Mapam felt that Mapai was only playing a tactical game. Without wanting her in the government, it utilized the negotiations with Mapam to de-escalate the demands of the ha-Po'el ha-Mizrahi to the level where it would become an acceptable partner in a narrow coalition. Simultaneously Mapam was convinced that Mapai was forced to turn to it under substantial working class pressures. Thus, Mapam's attitude reflected disbelief that Mapai would really wish to accept her as a partner in the government.[130] Hence, convinced that it had nothing to lose, Mapam retained its foreign policy approach which, for all appearances, became the main reason for discord between the two workers parties. This disagreement prevented a mutually satisfactory coalition agrement.

Actually, Mapai was ready to cooperate with Mapam on all substantial points, except for switching from the Western powers to the Eastern, in order to get her into the government. With Mapam at its side, Mapai would have felt strong enough to accept the General Zionists into the coalition. It was no coincidence that Mapam's refusal to join the government led to a toughening of Mapai's attitude in its negotiations with the General Zionists.

Curiously enough, just as Mapam revealed strong suspicion and traces of an inferiority complex in relation to Mapai, so did Mapai reveal similar tendencies toward the General Zionists. Ben-Gurion intimated that the General Zionists felt su-

---

130. See *'Al ha-Mishmar*, August 22, 1951, and August 24, 1951, editorial.

perior to the workers. This attitude, he claimed, carried over from the Zionist Congresses. "Would we have negotiated on the composition of the Government as equals with equals, it is possible that a wide coalition would have been established."[131] With Mapam at its side, Mapai may have felt the equal of the General Zionists. Without Mapam, Mapai felt inexplicably inferior to them and a coalition between the two parties became a practical impossibility.

These real causes of friction between Mapai and the General Zionists, however, never came to the surface. Instead, their feelings of distrust and inferiority were covered by a veneer of doctrinaire differences over control of the economy. In practical terms, they appeared as a dispute over who should rightfully possess the half portfolio of Supply and Rationing. The General Zionists seemed to be ready to bend even in matters most crucial to them—economic policy—but no amount of bending could help when Mapai realized that a coalition with the General Zionists and without Mapam would have projected an image of her as a centrist, nonsocialist party, an image Mapai tried hard to avoid. There was some irony in a situation where Mapai incorporated most of the crucial demands of the General Zionists in the government program but kept the General Zionists themselves out of the government.

Once Mapam rejected Mapai's offer of partnership, and Mapai determined to reject the General Zionists, the only recourse left to Ben-Gurion was to negotiate with the religious parties. This was both distasteful and humiliating to Mapai. It was the Religious Bloc that caused the downfall of the two preceding governments. Between the Mapai and the religious parties, relations had become very strained. Mapai leaders wanted to avoid a partnership with the religionists who were a continual threat to a balanced coalition. Mapai's election platform clearly indicated its repugnance to deal with the religious parties. There was strong opposition in Mapai circles to a narrow coalition with the religionists, since such a coalition was considered as only a temporary expedient.[132]

---

131. *Divrei ha-Kneset,* Second Kneset, 13th session, 10 (October 8, 1951): 252.

132. *Ha-Boqer,* October 5, 1951.

On the positive side, the religious parties were a more pliable partner in a coalition than the Mapam and posed less of a threat to Mapai's psychological equilibrium than the General Zionists. The issues they used to challenge Mapai were less threatening than those projected by Mapam (foreign policy), or by the General Zionists (economic policy). Many in Mapai's ranks, while not actually religious, were willing, for sentimental reasons, to cooperate with the religionists to maintain the Jewish faith and law. Having a religious party in the coalition would also have shown the Jewish world that Mapai could come to terms with religious circles. If the specific religious party could be the ha-Po'el ha-Mizrahi, it would give Mapai at least one workers' party in the coalition. Thus, even though many of its followers would have liked to stop negotiating with the religious parties once and for all, after the breakdown of negotiations with Mapam, Mapai began to consider ha-Po'el ha-Mizrahi's conditions for joining the government.[133]

The keenest critic of the government, the Herut, was quick to observe that the Religious Bloc considered the functioning of the Histadrut religious schools in camps sufficient cause for breaking up the government and for taking the people to the polls. Yet, it accepted these objectionable institutions in the new coalition agreement. Simultaneously, Mapai, which wanted the mobilization of religious women, promised under the new coalition agreement, to give up this patriotic objective. Both parties retreated from their basic principles of religion and patriotism proving themselves unprincipled opportunists.[134]

Leaders of both parties did not deny that the negotiations consisted of a frank give-and-take. Ben-Gurion declared, "We are not ashamed of making compromises if there is a need for them and they do not touch on essentials."[135] A religious leader stated:

> I emphasize, that the program is without doubt the fruit of compromise. We do not scoff at compromise, since we

133. *Ibid.*, September 20, 1951.
134. *Divrei ha-Kneset,* Second Kneset, 12th session, 10 (October 7, 1951): 209. B. Avniel of Herut.
135. *Divrei ha-Kneset,* Second Kneset, 131st session, 13 (November 3, 1952):12.

contend that there is no other possibility in Israel, except a Government that is built on it. Therefore we claim that this coalition is not so accidental. She has really been operating for twenty years, first in the Zionist Organization and now in the Government, since there have been matters of common interest between us and Mapai.[136]

The ha-Po'el ha-Mizrahi agreed with Mapai's claim that basic changes in the system of education were needed, but it wanted these changes introduced in the course of two years rather than a few months. Mapai consented.[137] What this amounted to in fact was, that a moratorium was placed on the issue for a specified period of one year. This gave the ha-Po'el ha-Mizrahi a semblance of victory. However, at the expiration of one year the religious party would be obligated to support Mapai in the educational reforms.

A similar arrangement was made between the two parties concerning the conscription of religious women, as well as Rabbinic jurisdiction. A Mizrahi leader reported to the Kneset:

We were facing the danger that a blemish would be inflicted, heaven forbid, on the most precious thing or on one of the most precious things in the fabric of the people of Israel—in the Jewish family. I am glad to point out that from this Government—to the best of my knowledge—there shall be no danger of amending the law of civil marriage, and that marriage, divorce and alimony will be under Rabbinic jurisdiction.[138]

The political situation two months after the election was not perceptibly different from what it was two months before the election. This does not mean, however, that the government crisis was meaningless. It permitted the planting of the seeds of change, that would ripen and bloom a year later.

---

136. *Ibid.*, Second Kneset, 12th session, 10 (October 7, 1951):213. Z. Warhaftig of ha-Po'el ha-Mizrahi.

137. *Ibid.*, Second Kneset, 13th session, 10 (October 8, 1951):223. M. Una of ha-Po'el ha-Mizrahi.

138. *Ibid.*, p. 248. David-Zvi Pinkas of Mizrahi.

7

Expiration of Moratorium: Conscription of Women and Trends in Education

When the Third Government was established on October 8, 1951, an agreement was entered into by Mapai and the religious parties that placed a one year moratorium on two controversial issues: the conscription of religious women and the unification of educational trends into a national system of education. As the government was approaching its first anniversary, tremors of conflict became palpable again. Some of the religious parties were getting ready to utilize the expiration of the moratorium to extract further concessions on religious issues.

Conscription of Women

The Israel Defense Service Law regulated among others the conscription of women for military service.[1] Women were to enlist for a twelve-month period, only a fraction of which would be spent in the army. The law offered exemption to those women who objected to military service on conscientious or religious grounds.

---

1. *Sefer ha-Huqim,* September 15, 1949, p. 271.

Due to the security problem facing the state and the shortage of manpower, Ben-Gurion, in his capacity as Minister of Defense, urged that women be included under compulsory service for noncombat duties. By contrast, religious leaders declared military service for women contradictory to the laws of the Torah.[2] However, since the religious women were offered exemption, religious protest was raised only on principle.

Four months later, in the face of an ever-growing shortage of manpower, Ben-Gurion reintroduced the issue of conscription of women into the Kneset. He requested that their period of service be extended from twelve months to two years: one year of basic training and agricultural work and a second year of army and noncombat duties. The religious parties opposed the measure. The bill nevertheless passed the Kneset.[3] Opposition to the bill was motivated by concern for the morals of the girls and their alienation from Jewish practices during a protracted stay in the army.

Soon, however, a different problem presented itself. The wording of the law provided a convenient loophole for those women who wished to escape military service. All they had to do was to claim exemption on religious grounds. In order to counteract the substantial dropout of girls on religious pretext, the government proposed to the Kneset the consideration of measures for the conscription of religious girls as well. However, they would be called to national rather than military service, replacing personnel in offices, hospitals, or kitchens. On February 27, 1951, Chief Rabbis Herzog and Uziel issued a strong protest against such a measure. "With regard to the amendment to the Compulsory Service Law now before the Kneset, we, after studying the situation, proclaim the opinion of the Torah that the recruiting of women—even unmarried ones—into any form of military organization is expressly prohibited. . . ."[4] Nevertheless, Ben-Gurion was determined to terminate the abuse to which the law was subjected. The ensuing debate was conducted in an atmosphere of acrimony, in

2. *Divrei ha-Kneset*, First Kneset, 72nd session, 1 (August 29, 1949): 1446. Rabbi Levin (Minister of Social Welfare) of Agudat Israel.

3. *Ibid.*, First Kneset, 114th session, 4 (February 8, 1950):752. The General Zionists supported the religious group in their opposition to the bill.

4. *Ha-Zofeh*, February 28, 1951.

the midst of a crisis that was brought about by the Religious Bloc.

The religious parties themselves were split on the issue. The ha-Po'el ha-Mizrahi favored some sort of national service for women, while the ultra-Orthodox were staging public protests against it in order to save "the purity of the Jewish family." The passions aroused by the issue could be understood best by considering that they produced the first attempt by a religious fanatic to bomb the Kneset.

On March 6, 1951, an amendment requiring religious women previously exempt from military service to participate in national service passed its first reading in the Kneset by a vote of 62 to 28.[5] It never proceeded, however, to its second reading.

On February 26, 1952, the Kneset passed an amendment requiring religious objectors to provide proof from a competent authority as to the veracity of their claim.[6] It was soon voted into law.[7] Ben-Gurion simultaneously promised the introduction of a bill that would provide for national service by religious women, but he refused to specify a deadline for the contemplated measure.

The double standard, rooted in the exemption from the existing law, was a major irritant to the population. It was considered discriminatory in nature by hindering full equality of participation to the religiously oriented women and by imposing certain hardships on others who were not religious. There was no solution to the problem in sight, since it was rooted in the complexities of coalition bargaining where it served as a strategically crucial pawn in the agreements between partners.

With the termination of the one year moratorium on the issue, it remained to be seen whether the Mapai would take any drastic step to implement the conscription of religious women. Such action would erase a source of abuse and strengthen the nation militarily. But it would be a reversal

---

5. *Divrei ha-Kneset,* First Kneset, 234th session, 8 (March 6, 1951): 1284.

6. *Ibid.,* Second Kneset, 60th session, 11 (February 26, 1952) p. 1453.

7. *Ibid.,* Second Kneset, 65th session, 11 (March 6, 1952), p. 1564.

of Mapai's established policy of compromise toward its religious partner in all former coalitions.

Unification of Trends in Education

Since the controversy revolving around education has been explored in the two preceding chapters, only the bare outlines of the problem will be presented here.

It emerged clearly that only two parties were in favor of preserving the four trends provided for in the Compulsory Education Law of September 1949.[8] They were the Mapam and the Religious Bloc, together commanding less than a quarter of the Kneset's voting strength.

The trend system imposed a situation on the country that subordinated economy, efficiency, and high standards in education to the party struggle and to interparty bargaining. To cite but one example, in the town of Rishon L'Zion one school had one hundred students with four teachers, the nearby Mizrahi school had nine students with one teacher and the Agudat Israel school, located less than half a mile away, had forty to fifty students with four teachers. A similar situation prevailed in numerous places in the country. "Is this concern for religion or destruction of the state?" asked the Minister of Education, Benzion Dinur.[9]

Yet the trend system managed to survive and was thriving after four and a half years of statehood. It became obvious that the system of education, just as the compulsory service for women, was used as a pawn in the coalition bargaining between Mapai and the Religious Bloc. Mapai upheld the trend system, just as it withheld a law requiring compulsory service of religious women, in return for religious support of a Mapai dominated coalition.

However, internal pressures within Mapai to unify the educational system and to remove it from the partisan hands of political parties were growing stronger. Simultaneously, the General Zionists and Progressives made the abolition of trends

8. *Laws of the State of Israel* 3:125.
9. *Divrei ha-Kneset,* Second Kneset, 156th session, 13 (December 22, 1952) :313.

a condition for joining the government. Indeed, the new government that emerged from the impending crisis stated in Article 20 of its program the aspiration for a national unified school system, with full guarantees to those desiring religious education.[10]

As far as the religious parties were concerned, they were not particularly adamant about safeguarding the trends. However, they did voice their insistence on complete and exclusive religious control of the schools encompassing religious objectives. While fulfilling the minimal requirements as programed by the Ministry of Education, they wished to preserve the autonomy of the religious schools.

Shakeup in the Government

On September 17, 1952, newspapers reported that a meeting took place recently between the Mapai Prime Minister and General Zionist leaders concerning the broadening of the coalition. Although Mapai claimed that the initiative for the meeting came from the General Zionists,[11] and the General Zionists maintained that they were approached by the Prime Minister,[12] there was no doubt that the meeting resulted from a disagreement among the partners of the existing coalition. The purpose of these negotiations could have been twofold: to remind a party in the Cabinet that it was not indispensable since other parties could take its place and, simultaneously, to secure adequate support, should an impending ministerial resignation occur.

Indeed, it soon became evident that differences of opinion in the coalition on the issues of religious education and conscription of religious women threatened a government crisis.[13] Even though Mapai spokesmen denied that there was any connection between their negotiations with the General Zionists and a threatening religious crisis,[14] their concomitant appearance was hardly coincidental.

---

10. *Ibid.*, Second Kneset, 12th session, 10 (October 7, 1951) :200.
11. *Davar*, September 17, 1952.
12. *Ha-Zofeh*, September 17, 1952.
13. *Ibid.*, September 18, 1952.
14. *Davar*, September 18, 1952.

On September 18, Agudat Israel and Po'alei Agudat Israel announced their withdrawal from the government in view of the fact that their religious demands were not fulfilled. In his letter of resignation, the Minister of Social Welfare, Rabbi Levin of Agudat Israel claimed that Ben-Gurion agreed to maintain the status quo for at least a year with regard to military service for girls and the trends in education. "In my view, changes in the status quo occurred before the year agreed between us expired. . . Our religious demands were, in fact, of the minimum, and our sharing in the collective responsibility was given in exchange for very little. Profoundly I regret that even this minimum has not been granted, but was continuously whittled down." Ben-Gurion in his reply stated that according to agreement orthodox girls would be enlisted for national service (not the army) a year after the government was formed. He therefore saw no adequate cause for resignation.[15]

The shakeup in government occurred during parliamentary recess. When the Kneset reconvened on November 3, Ben-Gurion announced the resignation of Rabbi Levin and the simultaneous co-optation of Rabbi Nurok of the Mizrahi into the government to head the newly created Ministry of Posts. The resignation of Rabbi Kahana of Po'alei Agudat Israel as Deputy Minister of Education was also announced. Despite the defection of the two Agudah parties, an opposition motion for a vote of no-confidence in the Kneset was defeated 56 to 36.[16]

Technically speaking, the prevailing situation did not create a government crisis. Ben-Gurion could have divided the portfolios vacated by the resignations among the functioning Ministries, or he could have co-opted new Ministers. However, the base of the coalition was narrowed to sixty members in the Kneset, exactly half its total membership. Consequently, Ben-Gurion decided to broaden the parliamentary basis of the government.

---

15. *Jewish Agency Digest* 5, no. 1 (Jerusalem: Information Department of the Jewish Agency, October 3, 1952) :6.
16. *Divrei ha-Kneset*, Second Kneset, 131st session, 13 (November 3, 1952) :8.

Attitude of Coalition Partners to the Impending Crisis

Mapai. Once again, for the third time in a row, the government was brought to the brink of a crisis as a result of excessive demands by one or more religious parties.

For eleven months the coalition that was formed in October 1951 functioned well on the basis of the guaranteed one-year moratorium on conscription of religious women and religious education. It was understood when the original agreement was made that conscription of women and the abolition of educational trends is a necessity for the security and welfare of the country. Mapai consented to a one year delay, despite an urgent need for clear-cut laws in the specified areas, only to work out an approach that would be equitable and satisfactory to all concerned.

As the year was drawing to an end, the Agudah parties began applying pressures to extend the moratorium.[17] Their action was militantly encouraged by Orthodox spokesmen abroad.[18] It became obvious to Mapai that the religious parties never seriously considered the possibility of working out a satisfactory solution to the problem. The moratorium was used by them strictly as a delaying tactic to perpetuate the status quo. Failing in this endeavor, they decided to resign.

Without the Agudah parties, Mapai still had the support of half of the Kneset. Yet it could no longer fully rely on its Mizrahi and ha-Po'el ha-Mizrahi partners in the coalition who might occasionally be divided in their loyalties between the government and the dissident religious groups. Under the circumstances, Mapai felt obliged to enter into exploratory negotiations with the General Zionists about the possibility of their joining the coalition.

Religious Parties. The Agudah parties felt it would be a betrayal of their voters to associate with a government that contemplated introducing conscription for religious women,

---

17. *Davar,* September 18, 1952.
18. *Ibid.,* September 22, 1952, quoting a religious spokesman from England: "Conscription of women in the army can be compared to immorality, spilling of the blood and idolatry." These are three cardinal sins of Judaism.

an act which they interpreted as contradictory to the laws of the Torah. Therefore, when the moratorium was about to expire and Mapai remained adamant in its stand favoring conscription, the Agudah parties had no choice but to resign from the government.

The ha-Po'el ha-Mizrahi expressed its regrets at the action of its sister parties. Neither the Mizrahi nor the ha-Po'el ha-Mizrahi were opposed to national service for religious girls, but they were concerned about public pressures from ultra-religious circles that might be applied against them as a result of the Agudah resignations.[19] Ha-Po'el ha-Mizrahi reasoned that, even though the government did not fulfill all its promises, much was accomplished in the religious field because of religious participation in the Cabinet.[20] After the withdrawal of the Agudah parties in order to avoid sharp criticism from the religious electorate, ha-Po'el ha-Mizrahi felt it might be forced to take a more radical stand on religious issues. The party feared this would weaken its position within the coalition and lessen its effectiveness in the councils of government.

The Mizrahi parties resented Mapai's entering into negotiations with the General Zionists without first consulting them. This resentment grew into antagonism when Mapai, during the negotiations, promised to the General Zionists Cabinet posts still held by the religious parties.[21] This added insult to injury and stiffened the position of the religious parties vis-à-vis Mapai.

Bargaining for Power: Mapai Standpoint

The failure of the Mapai-General Zionist negotiations for the previous government (October 8, 1951) was mainly attributed to Mapai's suspicions of General Zionist aspirations to undermine the collective sector of the economy from within the government. Therefore, in a letter to the General Zionist leader, Peretz Bernstein, Ben-Gurion made it clear that the two parties could work side by side only if the General Zionists

19. *Ibid.*, September 19, 1952.
20. *Ibid.*, September 23, 1952.
21. *Ha-Zofeh*, December 16, 1952, p. 2, editorial.

would acknowledge and accept the constructive contribution of the socialist sector, just as Mapai has welcomed the contribution of the private sector. "The state could not at this time be exclusively capitalist or exclusively socialist." Only when these basic attitudes to the economic goals of the state were clarified, would it be worthwhile to discuss concrete proposals regarding the allocation of Ministries. Participation in the government cannot consist in "readiness to accept a certain number of portfolios." Such allocation must be a direct result of a jointly agreed government program. This, in turn, would require justifiable compromises on matters that could tolerate compromises.[22]

Mapai welcomed a statement by Bernstein that his party "explicitly recognized the right of every citizen of the state to conduct his economic activities in any social or organizational form pleasing to him. . . From our side we did not object to the prevailing situation in Histadrut enterprises."[23]

After two months of procrastination, Mapai and the General Zionists approved a joint agreement.

Mapai–General Zionist Agreement

The main points of the Mapai–General Zionist agreement were as follows:[24] Both parties undertook to preserve the coalition till the end of the Second Kneset. An amendment to the election law would be introduced, requiring ten percent minimum of the total vote for party representation in the Kneset. This article had an escape clause attached, offering the possibility, if jointly agreed, to determine a different method of amending the election law provided it would attain the principal objective. Municipal elections would be postponed for two years and made to coincide with national elections.

In the realm of education, the trends would be abolished and a unitary system of state education introduced within a year.

The Civil Service Law would be amended in order to de-

22. *Davar*, October 6, 1952.
23. *Ibid.*, October 5, 1952.
24. *Ibid.*, December 16, 1952.

termine the categories of civil servants who would be forbidden to participate in political activities, to guarantee collective bargaining between the state and the representatives of the civil servants, and to guarantee the position of the Histadrut in those articles of the law that make negotiations with workers obligatory.

In the area of economic controls, as long as full supplies to the entire population could not be guaranteed, the control of essential products would be maintained. All unnecessary and ineffective controls would be abolished and steps would be taken to stabilize prices and the currency of the country.

Budget expenditures would be tightened and the budget balanced. The income-tax system would be reexamined in order to distribute the burden more equitably to all the citizens of the state. Activities would be initiated to attract capital from abroad and to create suitable condition for such capital in the country. A permanent committee would be established to examine complaints and claims of diverse economic sectors.

In addition to the above agreement reached in writing, an understanding was reached to create a coalition committee to work toward the improvement of procedure in the Kneset.

Bargaining for Power: Standpoint of the General Zionists

The General Zionists, concerned with the difficult economic situation in the country, wished to engage actively in the responsibilities of government.[25] They could not, however, participate responsibly in the coalition without being offered a field of activity where their influence would be felt. Therefore they demanded portfolios of important economic ministries. Similarly, they requested that their basic conditions with regard to taxes, controls and private enterprise be met by Mapai, so that the new government should carry some of the traits characteristic of the General Zionist outlook.

Mapai was ready to offer four portfolios to the General Zionists. It also made numerous concessions to them, specifically in the field of education where it agreed to the abolition of trends

---

25. *Ha-Boqer*, December 12, 1952.

and the institution of a unified national school system. Regarding municipal government, Mapai consented to the postponement of new elections for two years in a period when the General Zionists controlled many municipalities. Mapai agreed that Civil Service would be lifted above and freed from party contention. With regard to the economy, a new orientation would be adopted toward taxation, currency, controls and import.[26] Consequently, the General Zionists declared themselves ready to enter the government.

The General Zionists were eager to emphasize that there was no intention to reach an agreement with Mapai at the expense of the religious parties. "It must be made clear immediately that this agreement is not a 'conspiracy' either at the expense of religion, or at the expense of other values. The religious parties could occupy their rightful place in this Government. . . . But since every party in the Government is obligated to dispense with its party aspirations that disrupt collective strength, it is required of all who wish to join it, that they cease the sterile bickering for places and positions that they do not deserve according to the democratic distribution of power."[27]

The Executive of the General Zionists was eager to incorporate the religious parties into the first government in which they were about to participate, in order to make it a "Government of National Unity."[28] They were also ready to accommodate the Progressives in their objection to a change in the electoral law. They were willing to accept a compromise on the article which would require 10 percent of the votes for representation in the Kneset by lowering the minimum to five or 6 percent.[29] This would have pacified the Progressives.

Bargaining for Power: Standpoint of the Religious Parties

The religious parties were eager to remain in the government. To achieve this, they were ready to renounce aspirations

---

26. *Ibid.*, December 17, 1952.
27. *Ibid.*, editorial.
28. *Ibid.*, December 18, 1952.
29. *Ibid.*

for additional concessions in religious matters. In turn, however, they demanded assurances that the religious status quo would be preserved. The Central Committee of the Agudat Israel demanded an unconditional declaration by Mapai that the status quo on the issue of conscription of women would not be changed.[30] They warned that full autonomy for religious trends should be granted. Otherwise "the outcry resulting from the destruction of traditional Toraitic education would be so great, that it would be heard everywhere in the world where Jews could be found."[31] They requested facilities for religious men in the army to safeguard a religious life for them and the prohibition of pork breeding in the land. They insisted on provisions for a Sabbath rest law, as well as curtailment of Christian missions.

Within the Po'alei Agudat Israel, which substantially agreed with the Agudah demands, internal squabbles broke out on the conditions of reentering the government. The Council of the party, dominated by laymen, determined, by a two-thirds majority, to join a new coalition. The rabbinic leaders, however, reversed the decision of the Council purportedly under pressure from the Agudah and an ultimatum by the Assembly of the Sages of the Torah.[32] One Po'alei Agudat Israel settlement, representing popular sentiment within the party, demanded, in turn, that all ties with the Agudat Israel be cut and that recognition be denied to the Assembly of the Sages because of their interference with the party's decisions.[33] After heated debates, the conservative wing in the party triumphed. Po'alei Agudat Israel did not enter the government, nor did it break relations with the Agudah.

The two Mizrahi parties, contrary to the Agudah parties, were not opposed to the conscription of women for civilian, as opposed to military, service under conditions that Mapai seemed to be ready to meet. They did remain adamant in their demand for status quo in the field of education (Miz-

30. *Davar,* October 17, 1952.
31. *Divrei ha-Kneset,* Second Kneset, 156th session, 13 (December 22, 1952) :304. Rabbi Levin of Agudat Israel.
32. *Ha-Zofeh,* December 10, 1952, quoting the Po'alei Agudat Israel newspaper *Shearim.*
33. *Ibid.,* December 14, 1952.

rahi), or for guarantees for complete autonomy of religious education (ha-Po'el ha-Mizrahi). These demands were motivated by fear that an irreligious person may be put into a position of responsibility to determine the extent and the content of religious education.[34] The ha-Po'el ha-Mizrahi flatly denied the contention of Mapai that they agreed unconditionally to a national unitary system of education since it was incorporated in Article 20 of the outgoing government's program. In fact, the leaders of the religious party stated that they always demanded two trends, a religious and a secular, with religious supervision for the religious trend. Since Ben-Gurion did not agree to this condition, it was decided to establish a committee to examine the question. The agreement between the two parties explicitly stated: "If at the conclusion the ha-Po'el ha-Mizrahi will not concur with the new program (of national education), it shall be free to leave the coalition, without this being considered a breach of the coalition agreement."[35]

The Mizrahi parties further demanded a law that would give full authority to the Rabbinate in matters of personal status. Mapai was ready to promote such a law that would guarantee rabbis the power over marriage and divorce, but not alimony.

Eventually, but only after the formal presentation of the new government to the Kneset, a satisfactory understanding was reached on the issue of religious education. Mapai consented to the establishment of a supreme authority consisting of fourteen persons headed by a religious individual, to supervise and control the religious staff and curriculum in the religious state schools. The Committee would be appointed by the Minister of Education with the consent of the government. Half of its members would be taken from a list drawn up by the Minister of Religious Affairs, while the rest would be equally divided among the religious members of the Council of Education and the Organization of Religious Teachers.[36]

As for conscription of religious women, Mapai agreed that

---

34. *Ibid.*, December 16, 1952.
35. *Ibid.*, December 18, 1952.
36. *Ibid.*, December 25, 1952.

they be utilized for civilian duties in religious settlements preferably close to their homes. However, Mapai insisted that the implementation of the law be in the hands of the Minister of Labor.

Satisfied with these arrangements, the Mizrahi parties joined the coalition.

Bargaining for Power: Standpoint of the Progressive Party

The Progressive Party welcomed the possibility of the formation of a broad coalition. It declined to join the last government for the sole reason that it was constructed on a narrow basis. With the General Zionists in the government, the Progressives were ready to join it.[37] They were also willing to subscribe to the Mapai-General Zionist agreement. Only one point in the agreement, the reference to the amendment of the Election Law, disrupted the progress of the negotiations. A demand for a 10 percent minimum vote as a prerequisite for representation in the Kneset would have eliminated the Progressive Party from the political stage quickly and decisively. Since the party drew only four percent of the popular vote in the last elections, acquiescence to the ten percent minimum clause would have amounted to political suicide.

Facing strenuous objections by the Progressives, Mapai's Council determined that appropriate concessions would be made for their benefit. Mapai suggested that the article dealing with elections in the government program should not specify percentages. It would only generally state that "the government will present to the Kneset amendments to the Election Law" with the intent of avoiding continual splintering of the population and to safeguard a democratic and stable regime. A coalition committee would be established to search for alternative solutions agreeable to all partners, and in case no joint version could be agreed upon, the Progressive Party "will be free to decide on its stand."[38] This was interpreted as giving the Progressives the right to disagree and vote against the government on this one issue or to withdraw from the govern-

37. *Ha-Boqer,* December 12, 1952.
38. *Davar,* December 22, 1952.

ment completely, in case of basic disagreement concerning the election law. Armed with this assurance, the Progressive Party joined the government.

The Government and its Program

When Prime Minister Ben-Gurion presented the new government to the Kneset on December 22, 1952, it consisted of nine Mapai, one Progressive, and four General Zionist Ministers. Two Ministries were left vacant, however, in case the ha-Po'el ha-Mizrahi decided to be in the government.[39] Three days later, armed with adequate assurances of religious autonomy in education and of special treatment for orthodox girls, the ha-Po'el ha-Mizrahi and the Mizrahi joined the government.[40]

Basic Principles of the Government Program

The government program which was presented to the Kneset on December 22, 1952, followed the main principles of the former government that were presented to the legislature on October 7, 1951.[41] The main distinctions dealt with education, taxation and the electoral system.

Concerning education, Article 8 stated: "A Government committee will prepare, in the course of the year, a program for a national system of education in all elementary schools, which will be implemented not later than the begining of the next school year. The program will be based on the following fundamentals: The abolition of school trends based on parties and organizations; the determination of minimum obligatory requirements for all schools; guarantee of religious education to all children whose parents desire it; recognition of parents' rights to a specific direction in education under the supervision of the Ministry of Education, provided the minimum requirements are adhered to." This article on education agreed in substance with its famed predecessor, Article 20, that was incor-

39. *Ibid.*, December 23, 1952.
40. *Ibid.*, December 25, 1952.
41. See Chapter 6, "Crisis over Religious Education: Act Two."

porated in the October 1951 program, except for the stipulation of a specific time limit which allowed no postponement.

On taxation the program conceded that the method of taxing income would be placed under immediate scrutiny, in order to establish it on an equitable and just basis (Art. 12).

Concerning the electoral system, the program declared that the government will bring proposals to the Kneset with the intent of amending the electoral law in order to avoid further fragmentization of the nation's political spectrum (Art. 20).[42]

The government and its program was accepted in the Kneset by a vote of 63 to 24.[43]

The Position of the Religious Parties in the Aftermath of the Crisis

This was the first time in the history of the state that the Prime Minister entered into interparty negotiations to establish a new government *prior* to the resignation of the functioning Cabinet, which at the time happened to enjoy the confidence of the majority of the Kneset. Although this procedure was not prohibited by law, it nevertheless created difficulties with Mapai's religious coalition partners who were not consulted by Mapai during its negotiations with the General Zionists.

Mapai's attitude to the religious parties remained ambiguous. On one hand, Mapai was continually handicapped by the demands of the religious parties that, for the third time in a row, brought about a political crisis and a change in government. On the other hand, Mapai could not find a suitable alternate partner. As one of its representatives stated, turning to the religious parties in the Kneset: "Our partnership was not a faithful one. . . You exploited every difficult hour of this Government by coming forth with requests and demands that hastened its breakdown."[44] Yet the same speaker said in the very same speech: "One cannot deny the contribution of our partners in the two previous Governments."[45] While Mapai appreciated

---

42. *Divrei ha-Kneset*, Second Kneset, 156th session, 13 (December 22, 1952) :287.

43. *Ibid.*, 157th session, 13 (December 23, 1952).

44. *Ibid.*, p. 317. Yona Kese of Mapai.

45. *Ibid.*

the religious parties' giving it a virtually free hand in economic and foreign policy, it was also weary of them for pushing too hard and against the will of the majority in the direction of a theocratic state.

The dilemma facing Mapai was whether it could rely on an agreement with the General Zionists and disregard its former religious partners. At first Mapai was inclined to do so. Hence it did not consult the religious parties about the ongoing negotiations. It did not even issue a preliminary warning to them when their portfolios were utilized as an object of bargaining. This high-handed and, to the religious parties, somewhat humiliating approach no doubt resulted from Mapai's desire and determination to break off contact with them.

However, the agreement with the General Zionists was obviously not to Mapai's liking. The General Zionists exacted heavy payment in return for their support of the government in the realm of economics and civil service. Only on one particular point, with regard to a change in the electoral system, did Mapai manage to propose an innovation to its liking, and that too did not materialize. It is true that the proposed abolition of the trend system in education could not have come about without the new coalition. Yet, while Mapai wanted it, it was exploited by the General Zionists to underscore their victory. Thus, in the balance, the new government brought little comfort to Mapai and was considered a signal triumph by the General Zionists. Mapai therefore changed its approach to the religious parties. Instead of emphasizing the disruptive tactics of the religionists in former governments, it began showering praises upon them, endeavoring to preserve them as the alternative for the formation of a new government.

All this was rather incongruous, since hardly a year earlier, the Prime Minister and the Central Committee of Mapai made separate statements, condemning the pressure tactics employed by the religious parties.[46] Evidently, the politics of compromise demands contradictions, sometimes turning an enemy of yesterday into a friend of today and a supposed threat to survival into a welcome phenomenon.

---

46. See Chapter 6, "Crisis over Religious Education: Act Two."

In none of the former government crises or elections was Mapai equally complimentary to the religious parties. Ben-Gurion praised them for their four years of cooperation with Mapai within the government, though neither side found it easy to work out a compromise, and expressed his hope that this collaboration will continue.[47] One of the important Mapai leaders, the Minister of Labor Golda Meir, said: "There is place, there must be place, for cooperation with religious circles, and I see no reason why the ha-Po'el ha-Mizrahi should not enter this new government. I wish to say to the members of the ha-Po'el ha-Mizrahi: You have no right to remain on the outside. . . I do not ask you to enter the government in order to guard the faith; I am convinced that this government will extend its protection to the same matters that would be protected whether you take your place within its ranks or not, but there is no desire to rend asunder a partnership of many years standing—there is no reason for it and there is no basis for it."[48]

Repeated assurances were given to the religionists that Mapai did not wish to exclude them from the coalition.[49] "Mapai was especially desirous to continue with the joint responsibility and work between the workers' movement and religious circles, particularly the religious workers."[50] And again, "even if the religionists would remain outside the Government—and we do not want that—religious interests would not be neglected in the least, just as if they were within the Government."[51]

Since the last government was undermined by the withdrawal of two religious parties less than three months earlier, and since Mapai party leaders had in the past condemned the religious parties, this complimentary approach was astounding. Mapai strongly desired the presence of the ha-Po'el ha-Mizrahi and Mizrahi, though they were only minor partners in the new coalition in comparison to the General Zionists.

47. *Davar*, October 6, 1952.
48. *Divrei ha-Kneset*, Second Kneset, 156th session, 13 (December 22, 1952) :309.
49. *Ha-Boqer*, December 12, 1952.
50. *Davar*, December 25, 1952, editorial.
51. *Divrei ha-Kneset*, Second Kneset, 156th session, 13 (December 22, 1952) :298. M. Argov of Mapai.

In the government program and in the written agreement between Mapai and the General Zionists religious susceptibilities were not reflected strongly. On the basis of the two documents, Mapam may have been justified in its interpretation that they mirror Mapai's capitulation to the General Zionists, the sacrifice of the workers' trend in education, and the acceptance of a capitalist economic policy.[52] Similarly, from the opposite point of view, Herut may have correctly noted that the General Zionists sold themselves to Mapai by offering their twenty-three votes in the Kneset for four worthless portfolios.[53] In practice, however, religious susceptibilities continued to be a main concern to Mapai, more so than the fulfillment of its promises to the General Zionists, even though the latter were in written form.

Contrary to expectation, Mapai's ability to establish a government based on a firm majority in the Kneset without dependence on religious support, did not lead to the overthrow or even the weakening of the religious establishment. The Ministry of Religious Affairs and the Rabbinical Council, with all its concomitant rabbinic jurisdiction, survived unscathed. Areas of religious concern were treated with respect and substantially all the major demands of the religious parties received guarantees of Mapai support.

---

52. *Ibid.*, p. 291. Meir Ya'ari of Mapam.
53. *Ibid.*, p. 292.

8

Who is a Jew?

The crisis that led to the resignation of the National Religious Party (NRP) Ministers, Moshe Shapiro and Joseph Burg, from the coalition on June 22, 1958, was significant for several reasons: It evolved from an interdepartmental conflict between two Ministries. It led to the absence of the religious parties from a coalition for the first and only time. Though the religious leaders were forced to resign from the government, indicating a secularist victory over the disputed issue, in the end Mapai capitulated to the demands of the religionists completely.

Interdepartmental Conflict

On March 10, 1958, the Minister of the Interior, Israel Bar-Yehuda, issued instructions to registration officials with the aim of introducing some order in their inconsistent registration practices. Henceforth, the registration official was to record the information supplied by the registrant concerning his nationality without obligation to investigate the truth of the statement.[1] Thus, "Any person declaring in good faith that he is a Jew, shall be registered as a Jew and no additional proof shall be required." Further, "If both members of a married couple declare that their child is Jewish, this declaration shall be regarded as though it were the legal declaration of the child itself. . . . The registering official need not be concerned over

1. *Davar*, March 12, 1958.

178

the fact that according to the law of the Torah (in case one of the parents is non-Jewish) the child has the same status as its mother. . . . The parents' declaration that their child is Jewish suffices to register him as Jewish."[2]

The Minister was obviously aware that his instructions were at variance with Jewish religious law, but he acted under the impression that an administrative order issued by a governmental arm for the sake of greater efficiency need not be hampered by and confused with religious law. According to his view, the realm of the government and the realm of religion were distinct, as were the realms of nationality and religion. If Jewish religious law considers a child Jewish only when born of a Jewish mother or of a woman who converted to Judaism prior to the child's birth, so let it be for any religious purpose. But for the purposes of state registration and the issuance of identity cards, the individual's personal conviction and declaration as to his nationality should be the relevant guiding factor. Further, if somebody wishes to declare himself by nationality Jewish, though by religion he is not (he could be a domiciled Christian or Muslim or a Jewish-born confirmed atheist), he should have a right to do so.

In issuing his instruction, the Minister of the Interior relied on three things: first, that he only repeated and clarified orders that were issued by four Ministers of the Interior who presided over the Ministry prior to his assumption of that position;[3] second, that in 1950, when Moshe Shapiro of the Religious Bloc was Minister of the Interior, the Chief Rabbinate instructed all rabbis authorized to perform marriages and execute divorces not to accept the identity card as sufficient evidence and to investigate it thoroughly before the solemnization of a marriage;[4] and third, he was fortified by a statement of the Attorney General that served as the legal basis for the regulations. The Attorney General's statement read as follows:

There are religious rulings which differ in content and na-

2. Eliezer Goldman, *Religious Issues in Israel's Political Life* (Jerusalem: Religious Party Press, 1964), p. 67.
3. *Divrei ha-Kneset*, Third Kneset, 488th session, 24 (July 8, 1958): 2236.
4. *Ibid.*

ture from the secular; the fact that according to the "Law
of Moses and of Israel" a man is considered non-Jewish does
not prevent that man from being considered a Jew as re-
gards the law of the state and vice-versa; there is no contradiction between the two.

Even the fact that, according to the Law of Moses and of
Israel, a woman is married does not prevent the law from
regarding her as though she were a divorcee.

The inherent difficulties likely to arise do so owing to the
dichotomy between the religious and general courts; as long
as this dichotomy exists we have to accept them regardless
of the difficulties into which we may be led.[5]

Two days after the Minister of the Interior issued his instructions, the Deputy Minister of Religious Affairs, Dr. Zerah
Wahrhaftig, gave the first official indication of an impending
crisis. While presenting the budget of his Ministry, he stated
in a conspicuous aside that ascertaining the religious affiliation
of an individual registering for an identity card is an important
matter. A Jew cannot be defined on a haphazard and free-for-
all basis. Jewish law has long since determined who could be
considered a Jew and who could not. This was not a task for
a secular Jew to perform. Jewish law has made it clear that the
Jewish nation and the Jewish religion are one. "One cannot
be a Jew by nationality while adhering to a different faith."[6]

Soon religious elements openly attacked "the antireligious
attitude of the Ministry of the Interior, accusing the Minister
of having treated religion and the Religious Councils with con-
tempt and of having deprived them of their elementary needs."[7]

The lines were clearly drawn. Two Ministers collided and
the Cabinet was in the midst of a new crisis.

The Practical Significance of the Crisis

It must be noted that the issue that brought about the crisis
was hardly of any practical consequence. The only instances

5. *Jerusalem Post*, March 12, 1958.
6. *Divrei ha-Kneset*, Third Kneset, 433rd session, 23 (March 13, 1958):
1296.
7. *Ha-Zofeh*, March 25, 1958.

when the determination of one's Jewish status are of crucial concern are the solemnization of marriage and the burial service. In the State of Israel, in accordance with Jewish law and in conformity with the *millet* system inherited from the Ottoman period, a person is permitted to marry only within his faith. Hence, it is important to determine what religion one belongs to officially. In Jewish religious law a child follows the faith of its mother, whereas the father's faith is of no consequence. Therefore, at the time of marriage the question of one's parentage becomes significant. A non-Jewish mother blocks her child from marrying a Jewish partner, even if the child received a thoroughly Jewish upbringing and was unaware of the mother's background. People who have considered themselves loyal Jews may suddenly find out that they are not Jewish at all. They may well resent any suggestion at a form of conversion and are "more likely to leave Israel in anger and despair or to remain as embittered and obstructive second-class citizens." They or their children would not be permitted to marry a Jew, even a non-religious or anti-religious one in Israel.[8] A formal conversion could, of course, remedy the situation. Without it, though the individual be a professing Jew, the union with a Jewish mate would be called an intermarriage, which is considered a serious infringement upon Jewish law. In the eyes of a religious Jew it is equivalent to sabotage against the existence and survival of the Jewish people. Cases are known where a family would perform the necessary rites of mourning for the dead upon finding out that one of their members had intermarried. Similarly, if at the time of a funeral it is discovered that a deceased was not legally of Jewish descent, the burial could not take place in consecrated Jewish cemetery ground. However, though in case of marriage, as well as of burial, one's Jewish status had to be determined in order to abide by those aspects of the religious law that were incorporated into the legal system of the state, this was accomplished by the rabbinic authorities without reliance on any information supplied by the identity card.[9] Why then was the Minister of Religious Affairs, the Chief Rab-

8. *Jerusalem Post,* March 14, 1958.
9. *Davar,* March 12, 1958.

binate and the religious community in such an uproar? After tracing the crisis to its end, we shall attempt to answer this question.

Resignation of Religious Ministers from the Coalition

At the request of the two religious Ministers, the Cabinet began discussions on March 30 regarding the controversial directive issued by the Minister of the Interior. The religious Ministers formally requested that the instructions of the Minister of the Interior be discarded since they introduced changes in the status quo, and they would destroy the unity of the Jewish people.[10] The Cabinet appointed a Ministerial Committee of Three, consisting of the Minister of the Interior, Mr. Ben-Yehuda (Ahdut ha-Avodah), the Minister of Religious Affairs, Mr. Shapiro (NRP), and the Minister of Justice, Mr. Rosen (Progressives) to study the legal aspects of the question and to report back to the Cabinet with their findings.

On June 22 the Cabinet received and discussed the committee's report and reached the decision that " (1) The entry 'Jewish' will be made in the identity card of any person who declares in good faith that (a) he is a Jew, and (b) he does not profess any other religion. (2) The entry 'Jewish' will be made in the identity card of any child both of whose parents declare that he is Jewish."[11]

The Cabinet decision was substantially in accord with the instructions issued by the Minister of the Interior to the registration officials. The only noteworthy difference consisted of the qualification that the person who declares himself of Jewish nationality must also declare that he does not profess any other religion. Apparently, there were instances where individuals claimed to be Jews while professing another religion.

The religious leaders were unhappy with the decision of the Cabinet. Their concern was not ameliorated by the utterances of a government spokesman at a news conference following the Cabinet session. To the question, "If a person born of a Jewish father and a non-Jewish mother declares that he is

10. *Ha-Zofeh*, March 31, 1958.
11. *The Israel Digest* 1, no. 6 (July 11, 1958) :3.

a Jew, will that be considered (a declaration) 'in good faith'?" the reply was, "I assume so." This was directly contrary to religious law. When the government spokesman was asked whether a child would be registered as Jewish if its parents, both Christians, declared that he was Jewish, he replied in the affirmative. He reiterated, however, that the data in the identity card would not be binding on any court.[12]

Two days later the two N.R.P. Ministers informed Ben-Gurion that their party could not accept responsibility for the decision of the Cabinet and that they were thus forced to resign. Dr. Wahrhaftig depicted the Cabinet's action as "a fateful decision, liable to destroy the Jewish people."[13]

Attitude of the Coalition Partners to the Crisis

Mapai. Although the withdrawal of the N.R.P. from the coalition still left the government in control of a 69-vote majority, every attempt was made by Ben-Gurion to heal the breach. A three-man committee of Mapai conducted prolonged negotiations with N.R.P. leaders to work out a satisfactory compromise and to persuade them to rejoin the Government. Ben-Gurion, addressing himself to the veteran religious leader, Rabbi Maimon, stated that

> the Government had no intention of laying down Religious Law, and it does not consider itself authorized to do so. On the contrary, in the decision adopted by the Government it was expressly stated that the Government decision is not binding on the Rabbis in matters of marriage and divorce in regard of which they must act according to Religious Law.
> In the Declaration of Independence, however, we announced freedom of religion and conscience and we did not decide that the Jewish State should be governed by Religious Law, and that the rabbis should rule it. On the contrary, we proclaimed that it would not be a theocratic state. (In our country there is equality of rights for women together with men, which I believe is contrary to Religious Law).
> . . . The Government did not consider itself authorized to

12. *Jerusalem Post,* June 23, 1958.
13. *Ha-Zofeh,* June 25, 1958.

decide who is a religious Jew. The question it had to consider was: "Who is a Jew by nationality?" I know that there is an opinion—which I am not at all disputing—that there is no such thing as a Jew without religion, but to our regret there are many Jews who are not religious, both in Israel and in the Diaspora. . . . Many believe themselves to belong to the Jewish people, although they do not observe Religious Law. It has often been stated that this country is governed by the Rule of Law and not by Religious Law, (but the law does not interfere in religious matters with regard to those who strictly observe Religious Law).

. . . I see danger both in a war against religion and in a war for religion. In the Declaration of Independence and in the Basic Principles of all the various Governments (all of which included representatives of the religious parties) we promised freedom of conscience and religion. I assume that you do not believe that freedom of conscience and religion should be guaranteed to one party alone.[14]

It need not be assumed that all in Mapai stood solidly united on the issue of Jewish nationality. At least one Mapai Kneset member took a position similar to the N.R.P., although he charged the religious parties were trying to make political capital of the crisis out of purely partisan motives.[15]

Religious Parties. The religious parties were unimpressed by the Prime Minister's appeal. At the initiative of Benyamin Mintz, the leader of Po'alei Agudat Israel, they decided to form a "united front" in order to combat more effectively the decision of the government regarding registration.[16] They pledged, "to fight for values of general Jewish concern, without consideration of any practical results."[17] The Agudah Party issued a statement that "the directives for registration adopted by the Cabinet shake the very foundations of Judaism and destroy the unity of the Jewish people."[18] Chief Rabbi Herzog came out with an official proclamation that declared: "The

14. *Jerusalem Post,* July 3, 1958.
15. *Divrei ha-Kneset,* Third Kneset, 491st session, 24 (July 14, 1958): 2270. Y. Yeshayahu-Sharabi.
16. *'Al ha-Mishmar,* July 1, 1958.
17. *Ha-Zofeh,* June 27, 1958, editorial.
18. *Jerusalem Post,* June 30, 1958.

child born of a gentile mother is subject to the same law as the mother. He is a gentile from any point of view and no earthly authority can change this gentile seed into a Jew, save by means of lawful and judicial conversion."[19] To top it all, the N.R.P. called upon Jews all over the globe, with special emphasis on England, the United States, and Switzerland, to protest the action of the Israel government.[20]

Despite their militant stand, the religious parties were taken by surprise when Ben-Gurion announced to the Kneset on July 1 that the Ministers and Deputy Ministers belonging to the N.R.P. had resigned due to the Cabinet decision taken on June 22 on the matter of registering the nationality of the country's permanent residents.[21] The other religious parties were hopeful that the crisis would be resolved by the Cabinet's adoption of one of the following alternatives: either a return to the status quo ante, i.e., before the March directives were issued by the Ministry of the Interior, or a resolution that a child of a non-Jewish mother be registered as Jewish only if he is converted, although the mother need not be.[22]

Leftist Parties. The Ahdut ha-'Avodah and Mapam were determined to support the stand taken by the government and demanded that it should not back down from its present position.[23] They insisted that nationality is a matter for the state and not for the Rabbinate to determine and accused the religious parties of wanting "to impose the Rabbinic law on the Jewish identity of the citizen by means of pressure exercised through government crises and threats of propaganda crusades. . . . It is therefore the religious parties who split the people by contesting the issue of 'Who is a Jew.' "[24] A Mapam repre-

---

19. *Ha-Zofeh*, July 9, 1958.
20. *Ibid.*, July 10, 1958.
21. *Ibid.*, July 2, 1958.
22. The question of conversion was the central topic of conversation in the negotiations between Mapai and religious leaders. "As was disclosed, in hundreds of cases the rabbis refused to convert children of Christian mothers if the mother herself would not convert, in line with the halaha that the child goes after the mother in religious persuasion. . . . It would seem that the main objective of the refusal was to force the mothers to convert." *'Al ha-Mishmar*, July 1, 1958.
23. *Ibid.*, July 4, 1958.
24. *Ibid.*

sentative in the Kneset stated that he was for an honorable coexistence between the religious and the secular public, "but, if you continue to put pressure on the secular public . . . I tell you that you will put our tolerance to too severe a test."[25] Mapam threatened that if the government repealed its decision, the party might resign from the Cabinet.[26]

Progressives. The Progressive Party also lent its full support to the decision of the government. Its leader, Pinhas Rosen, the current Minister of Justice, agreed with the Minister of Interior that his instructions were not any more extreme than those of his predecessors.[27] However, in order to save the country from the strain of a *Kulturkampf* (literally, cultural struggle; in the Israel context, religious conflict), he endeavored to act as an intermediary between the two opposing groups. He proposed a compromise suggestion that the identity card should contain one bracket for "Religion and Nationality" and another one for "Nationality" alone. This would permit those who wish to identify with the Jewish religion to sign up in the first bracket. Those who are by persuasion of the Jewish faith but not in the eyes of religious law, or those who consider themselves national but not religious Jews could utilize the second bracket. The religious parties refused Rosen's proposal, since according to religious law, the second bracket, nationality independent of religion, does not exist for Jews.[28]

Real Meaning of the Crisis

Two facts seemed to be established: first, that the disputed identity cards had been discounted as evidence in matters under Rabbinic jurisdiction for at least three and possibly eight years and, second, that the new instructions of the Minister of the Interior were not drastically different from those of his predecessors on the matter. Why, then, the crisis and what was its real meaning?

---

25. *Divrei ha-Kneset,* Third Kneset, 433rd session, 23 (March 13, 1958) : 1306. Mr. Rifkin of Mapam.
26. *Jerusalem Post,* July 2, 1958.
27. *Ibid.,* June 30, 1958.
28. *'Al ha-Mishmar,* July 10, 1958.

Ben-Gurion raised the question in his letter to Rabbi Maimon: "I do not know why this tumult has arisen just at this time, and I do not wish to suspect the innocent or speculate on motives."[29] The religious leadership itself admitted that, "the decision of the Government concerning the identity card registration touches perhaps only very few families."[30] The outbreak of the conflict was therefore all the more puzzling.

Some believed that the decision of the N.R.P. to withdraw from the coalition "was prompted by the tabling of a non-confidence motion in the Kneset by Mr. Mintz of Po'alei Agudat Israel on the question of the entry of a person's nationality in his identity card. The motion which was scheduled for discussion in the Kneset for next Monday would have placed the NRP in an awkward position, unless it too took some action."[31] Though this allegation may have merit, the NRP may also have been looking for opportunities to stir up trouble around the Ministry of the Interior. The NRP had considered this Ministry its legacy and exclusive domain, since Moshe Shapiro of ha-Po'el ha-Mizrahi was the first Minister of the Interior, but Mapai had bartered it first to the General Zionists and then to Ahdut ha-'Avodah.

If these were the reasons for the crisis, what then was the real meaning behind it? A perceptive observer defined it as "the burning question of what was to be considered constitutive of Jewish nationality."[32] Is nationality inseparable from religion in Judaism or is it independent of religion, both in its historical and practical sense?[33] Undoubtedly, this problem stands out in bold relief, so much so that it overshadows and hides the true problem that produced the crisis. As stated in an editorial in the *Jerusalem Post*, "The present dispute can ultimately be reduced to the question of whether the Government of Israel has the right to establish rules to decide who is entitled to membership in the Jewish nation."[34]

---

29. *Jerusalem Post,* July 3, 1958.

30. *Ha-Zofeh,* June 24, 1958, editorial.

31. *Jerusalem Post,* June 27, 1958.

32. Eliezer Goldman, *Religious Issues in Israel's Political Life* (Jerusalem: Religious Party Press, 1964) , p. 68.

33. *Divrei ha-Kneset,* Third Kneset, 488th session, 24 (July 8, 1958) :2230.

34. *Jerusalem Post,* July 4, 1958, editorial.

Indeed, the real meaning behind the crisis was not to be found in the question of determination of Jewish nationality and its connection with religion. The question of "Who is a Jew?" was less important than the question of *who decides* about a person's Jewishness in the State of Israel. To the religious and the antireligious elements, more than a theoretical decision concerning a definition of Jewishness was at stake. It was really a matter of who shall decide on military service for women, Sabbath travel, or pig raising, mixed children's playgrounds, swimming pools, and many other similar problems "where the precepts advocated by the Orthodox clash with the realities of twentieth-century society. Should life in Israel be conducted according to the rules of the Rabbinical Council or according to the secular laws adopted by elected representatives of the entire people?"[35] "Shall they (the Chief Rabbis) determine our way of life, or shall the Kneset determine it?"[36] Shall the Rabbinate be declared supreme and Israel be led toward theocracy, or shall the Kneset be proclaimed supreme, with democracy victorious?

The real meaning of the crisis, therefore, was nothing less than a crucial choice between systems of government.

Victory in Defeat for the Religious Parties

On June 22, 1958 the N.R.P. Ministers resigned from the government which steadfastly adhered to its decision of backing the Minister of the Interior on the question of registration. On July 15 the N.R.P. backed a motion of no-confidence in the Kneset introduced by the opposition Herut Party on the issue. At the conclusion of the Kneset debate which lasted four sessions in the course of two weeks, the Prime Minister introduced the following Government resolution:

To appoint a Committee of Three, consisting of the Prime Minister, the Minister of the Interior and the Minister of Justice, to examine and formulate rules for the registration

---

35. *Ibid.,* p. 5.
36. *Divrei ha-Kneset,* Third Kneset, 488th session, 24 (July 8, 1958): 2241. Minister of Interior Bar-Yehudah.

of children of mixed marriages whose parents wish to register them as Jews. The Committee of Three shall hear the opinion of Jewish sages in Israel and abroad on this question, and shall formulate registration rules, which will be in keeping both with the accepted tradition in all circles of Jewry, including all trends, both orthodox and non-orthodox, and with the special conditions prevailing in Israel, as a sovereign Jewish State in which freedom of conscience and religion are assured and as a center for the ingathering of the exiles.[37]

It was understood that until the Committee of Three would gather the necessary opinions and examine the rules, the regulations drafted by the Minister of the Interior would not be regarded as in force.

On December 3, 1958 Ben-Gurion announced to the Kneset the cancellation of all directives that were issued with regard to the registration of children of mixed marriages since the establishment of the state. In a statement to the Kneset on July 29, 1959, he added that until a further decision is made, no entry at all would be made on the identity card with regard to nationality and religion of the children of mixed marriages.

On August 3, 1959, a year and a half after the whole furor started, newspapers in Israel reported that according to the sages, whose advice was sought in Israel and abroad, the religious law is to be applied on the question of "Who is a Jew?" By this time, however, the whole issue had receded into insignificance in the light of new problems.

---

37. *Divrei ha-Kneset*, Third Kneset, 494th session, 24 (July 15, 1958) : 2314.

9
Reorganization of Government

On October 15, 1950, Prime Minister Ben-Gurion handed in his government's resignation to the President of Israel, Chaim Weizmann. The resignation surprised political observers who failed to see any motivation for it.

The government crisis arose from an attempt to reshuffle the Cabinet. On October 4, in connection with an announcement of total war against the black market flourishing in the country, the Prime Minister admitted that administrative flaws contributed to the continuation of shortages and illicit trade. He stated that "there is not enough coordination among the different Ministries, or between the different departments of one Ministry." He named specifically the Ministries of Supply, Treasury, Development, and Trade and Industry, indicating the need of governmental reorganization with regard to them.[1]

Eight days later, Ben-Gurion proposed to the Cabinet a plan of reorganization that was referred "to the parties concerned for final decision."[2] One of the proposals involved a change from the twelve-member to a thirteen-member Cabinet and the appointment of Mr. Ya'aqov Geri to the post of Minister of Trade and Industry.[3] Mr. Geri was the first nonparty, political neutral Cabinet member who was not simultaneously a member of the Kneset. This set an important precedent for future Cabinets.

1. *Davar,* October 4, 1950.
2. *Ha-Zofeh,* October 13, 1950.
3. *Jerusalem Post,* October 13, 1959.

It was understood that the Mapai and the Religious Bloc were in agreement over the need of governmental reorganization. Yet at the decisive moment, the Religious Bloc and particularly the Mizrahi declared themselves opposed to the changes. As the right-wing party of the coalition, the Mizrahi demanded that it should be given the portfolio of Trade and Industry. Moreover, the Religious Bloc wished to discuss particular grievances in the realm of religion before considering the proposals for reorganization. A substantial segment of the Religious Bloc refused to cooperate and even threatened withdrawal from the coalition if their grievances were not remedied.[4]

On October 15 Ben-Gurion resigned. Banner headlines in the Mapai news medium declared that the "Religious Bloc brought about the crisis,"[5] whereas the Mizrahi paper announced that "Ben-Gurion alone is responsible."[6]

After the Prime Minister's resignation President Weizmann consulted with party leaders and then entrusted Ben-Gurion with the formation of a new government. However, Ben-Gurion was obliged to announce to the Kneset that he had failed in the attempt. He proceeded to suggest the dissolution of the Kneset and the holding of new national elections.[7] For the interim period he proposed that the seven Mapai members of the outgoing Cabinet should constitute a temporary government.[8] Ben-Gurion's proposal for a transition government was rejected by a vote of 57 to 43.[9] The Herut, General Zionists, Mapam, and Communists voted against it, as well as the Religious Bloc of the coalition, while the Progressives, Sephardim, and Wizo (Women's International Zionist Organization) abstained from voting. According to law, therefore, until a new government is formed, the existing one was to continue in power.

---

4. *Davar*, October 15, 1950. However, a minority, led by the Minister for Religious Affairs, Rabbi Yehudah Leib Maimon, an old-time friend of Ben-Gurion, announced itself ready to cooperate with the Prime Minister.

5. *Ibid.*, October 16, 1950.

6. *Ha-Zofeh*, October 16, 1950.

7. *Divrei ha-Kneset*, First Kneset, 179th session, 7 (October 16, 1950) :5.

8. At first he also included Behor Shitreet of the Sephardi Party; later he reneged.

9. *Divrei ha-Kneset*, First Kneset, 180th session, 7 (October 17, 1950) :51.

Since Ben-Gurion failed to form a working coalition, President Weizmann delegated the task to Pinhas Rosen, the Minister of Justice, and the only Progressive member of the Cabinet. He immediately proceeded with negotiations, attempting to work out an understanding between the Mapai and the Religious Bloc. The Mapai, however, continued to uphold the position of Ben-Gurion, presenting the alternatives of immediate national elections or approval of his proposed thirteen-member Cabinet.[10]

Attitude of Coalition Partners and Opposition to the Government Reorganization

Mapai. The government reorganization proposed by Ben-Gurion did not disturb the party equilibrium in the Cabinet. No Religious Bloc Minister was to be supplanted or transferred. Only Mapai Ministers were to be exchanged, for the sole purpose of upgrading their quality. The only additional member was to be a nonpartisan candidate.

There was general agreement among the parties on the need for the reorganization. The sudden opposition of the Religious Bloc was, therefore, entirely unexpected. It demonstrated that the Religious Bloc would take advantage of a mere technicality, where neither its position nor any principle was at stake, to press for the attainment of its partisan objectives.

The Prime Minister was compelled to announce the resignation of the government in an attempt to create a new, integrated Cabinet which would not be fraught with dissension.[11] Mapai once again tried to reach an agreement with Mapam and the General Zionists, to no avail. These parties remained dogmatic and unbending in their attitudes. Though it would have been desirable to form a new Cabinet without the Religious Bloc, which had proven to be an unstable partner, Mapai was left with no other recourse. Through the mediation of Mr. Rosen, it accepted a rapprochement with the Religious Bloc. In order to avoid constant friction and government instability, however, Mapai demanded firm assurances from the

---

10. *Davar,* October 20, 1950.
11. *Jerusalem Post,* October 16, 1950, editorial.

Religious Bloc, as a condition for its participation in the Cabinet, that it would not press any new demands until the end of the Kneset term in 1953.[12]

The demands of the Religious Bloc had been unrealistic. It accused Mapai of applying coercion against the religious elements, while in fact, Mapai had supported religious aspirations to the extent that it had been called a clericalist party by its opponents. Mapai supported a law restricting business on Sabbath and Jewish festivals, a budget of hundreds of thousands of pounds for religious needs, the Religious Councils, and a religious trend in education under religious party auspices and with emphasis on religious instruction. It also voted against a written constitution solely in deference to the religious parties who were the only ones opposed to it. Yet the Religious Bloc claimed that the cause of the coalition crisis was the "uprooting of faith", by Mapai.[13]

The Religious Bloc aimed at establishing a regime which would impose a religious way of life even on those who do not wish to conform to such a situation. "It should be clear to the Religious Bloc that in this sphere Mapai reached the limit and that no further concessions could be made. It is impossible to substitute for the principle against religious compulsion, a religious way of life imposed by the state."[14]

Attitude of the Religious Bloc. The Prime Minister's proposed government reorganization offered an opportunity to clarify many issues pertaining to the conduct of government, including its attitude to the religious problems. This has been customary procedure in parliamentary democracies. However, the Prime Minister decided to take the request of the Religious Bloc for the review of grievances as a personal challenge. Thus, from the very outset it became clear that he wished to oust the Religious Bloc, and it was for that purpose that he precipitated the government crisis.

Ben-Gurion announced the resignation of the Cabinet prior to the deadline he himself gave to the coalition parties for

---

12. *Ibid.*, October 24, 1950.
13. *Divrei ha-Kneset*, First Kneset, 179th session, 7 (October 16, 1950) : 16.
14. *Davar*, October 26, 1950.

the consideration of his proposals and prior to receiving the conditions of the Religious Bloc.[15] The Religious Bloc would have desired the continuation of the existing Cabinet.[16] Even after the announcement of the resignation, it advocated negotiations that would lead to the reinstatement of the outgoing government.

The demands of the Religious Bloc were basically confined to religious issues, though they branched out into the educational, economic, military, juridical, and organizational spheres. It requested supervision over religious education; a law banning Sabbath work and prevention of import of nonkosher meats; the creation of separate religious military units and stoppage of army maneuvers on Sabbath; sole rabbinic jurisdiction in matters of personal status; the revitalization of the Ministerial Committee that was established for the purpose of investigating religious grievances; the Under-Secretaryship for Education and the portfolio for Trade and Industry.

The Religious Bloc claimed that these demands would not be an imposition on the law-abiding citizens of the state. In the words of one of its representatives, it would not wish to interfere with anybody's private life, but it should be recognized that "the public sector belongs to all. . . . Permit us to breathe its air, since we have no other air to breathe. . . . If I observe the Sabbath in the street, it does not disturb you at all; but if you transgress the Sabbath that belongs to both of us, you pierce my soul."[17]

On October 16th the Prime Minister gave an ultimatum to the Religious Ministers: "Do you or do you not agree to participate in the Government, on the basis of the organization and program that was proposed last week, without any conditions whatsoever? I will wait for your answer till twelve noon. Yes or No."[18] The Religious Ministers replied at half past twelve that a "yes or no" answer could not be forthcoming, that they needed time for further consideration, discussion and

---

15. *Ha-Zofeh,* October 16, 1950, editorial.
16. *Divrei ha-Kneset,* First Kneset, 179th session, 7 (October 16, 1950) :12.
17. *Ibid.,* 180th session (October 17, 1950) , p. 31 Avraham Shaag of the Religious Bloc.
18. *Ha-Zofeh,* October 17, 1950.

clarification of the program and work of the government, particularly on the questions of education and religion. Mapai rejected the response of the Religious Bloc.

Thereupon the Religious Bloc pointed out that "There can be no partnership when one side forces its rule upon the other by means of economic and social coercion. There can be no partnership where one side exploits the trust of the other side in order to increase its ruling power. . . . The crisis of today is the result of a great moral crisis that was caused by the majority party."[19]

As a result of the crisis the Religious Bloc became divided within its ranks. A faction led by Mr. Pinkes wished to entirely dissociate itself from the coalition. It felt so strongly on the issue, that "it made vague threats to leave the Orthodox Bloc should the majority decide to come to terms with the Mapai."[20] However, the majority continued to work for a rapproachement.

Progressives and Sephardim. The standpoint of the Progressives and the Sephardim on the Cabinet crisis is of particular interest since they, together with the Mapai and the Religious Bloc, were the component parts of the government.

The Progressives consistently supported the program of the outgoing government, while simultaneously advocating changes within its framework. They never attempted to exploit differences of opinion or a crisis in the government in order to strengthen their tactical position. They viewed "with loathsomeness the attitude of the Religious Bloc, which always stood with one foot in and the other out of the government, alternately throwing all its weight on the foot within, then on the foot without."[21] The Religious Bloc tried to exploit the situation in behalf of party interests and it should, consequently, carry the burden of blame for the crisis.

Simultaneously, however, the Progressives expressed their dissatisfaction with Ben-Gurion for his impatience in attempting to establish a government in one day. This could not succeed. It alienated not only the parties that had been by their very nature suspicious of his motives, but also those whose

---

19. *Ibid.,* October 18, 1950, editorial.
20. *Jerusalem Post,* October 24, 1950.
21. *Divrei ha-Kneset,* First Kneset, 179th session, 7 (October 16, 1950) :18.

attitude to him was friendly. As a result, the Progressives themselves became disaffiliated from the coalition.

The Sephardim would have been willing to support the government, as they did in the past, but they too objected to Ben-Gurion's precipitate approach in trying to solve the crisis within twenty-four hours. Furthermore, they would not vote for a minority government in order to prevent setting a dangerous precedent for the future.[22]

Mapam and the General Zionists. Immediately after the resignation of the government, Ben-Gurion invited Mapam and the General Zionists to participate in a new Cabinet. The former responded that "Mapam is ready, as before, to enter into negotiations for the establishment of a Government in whose center would stand the two workers parties, on the basis of a jointly agreed program."[23] It was Mapam's claim that Mapai has continually failed the people in fulfilling its pledge for the realization of socialism. Having promised peace, it has yet involved itself in the support of the United States in the Korean conflict. The Israel Defense Forces were supposed to be under general command; instead, they have been ruled by a party whose first concern seemed to be the enforcement of dietary laws in the army.

In these circumstances, and since Mapai rejected the establishment of a "Labor Front" of the two workers parties, Mapam could not join the new coalition and came out in favor of new national elections.[24]

The General Zionists rejected all overtures to join a reorganized government. Realizing that Mapai's fortunes had reached a low point because of economic mismanagement of the state, they advocated new elections at the earliest opportunity. This would help the tottering economy of the nation and would probably lead the General Zionists to a triumph at the polls. Since the party did not have confidence in the existing Cabinet, it could not vote in behalf of a minority Mapai government for the transitional period preceding the elections.[25]

---

22. *Ibid.*, 180th session, 7 (October 17, 1950) :26.
23. *Ibid.*, 179th session, 7 (October 16, 1950) :9.
24. *Ibid.*
25. *Ibid.*, p. 18.

Bargaining for Power

Under the guidance of Pinhas Rosen, the negotiations for the creation of a new government proceeded mainly between two parties: the Religious Bloc and Mapai. At the early stages of negotiation the Religious Bloc began to modify its demands by narrowing them to two religious issues: it requested a government assurance that meat imports, for which the state appropriated foreign exchange, would conform to religious dietary laws, and it demanded a Sabbath observance law banning interurban transport services on Sabbath and religious holidays.

Other issues became less critical or found their appropriate solution. The education issue was resolved when it was agreed to establish separate divisions in the Ministry of Education for each of the school trends, allowing the Religious Bloc greater control of the religious schools. In return the Religious Bloc gave up its demand for a Deputy to the Ministry.

The portfolio of Trade and Industry, demanded by the Mizrahi, stopped being a stumbling-block when Ya'aqov Geri (the incumbent nonparty Minister) was understood to have agreed to the appointment of Herman Hollander of the Religious Bloc either as Under-Secretary or Director General of the Ministry.[26]

Eventually the Religious Bloc further modified its demands on the issue of Sabbath observance. It expressed satisfaction with an undertaking in principle to pass a Sabbath law during the Kneset term. In turn, Mapai agreed to uphold the ruling adopted by the Provisional Government which provided that the import of meat should be handled by the Minister concerned with food supplies in conjunction with the Minister for Religious Affairs.[27]

The one controversial issue that was still pending dealt with the demand of the Religious Bloc for the establishment of a Committee of Ministers to examine problematic religious issues. Mapai was opposed to this, claiming that such matters should be brought up in the Cabinet as routine business. Mapai further demanded a virtual moratorium on religious issues in

26. *Jerusalem Post*, October 24, 1950.
27. *Ibid.*, October 25, 1950.

the Kneset for the balance of the current tenure, a standpoint unacceptable to the Religious Bloc.[28]

A compromise formula was finally reached between the two parties according to which a Committee of Ministers would be formed, without setting a time limit for their investigations. Meanwhile, status quo was to prevail on religious practices. Thus, the Religious Bloc would stop agitating for a law of Sabbath observance, and Mapai would abstain from impairing rabbinical control over marriage, divorce, wills and alimony, though it was pledged to introduce legislation providing equal rights for women. Mapai also moderated its demand for a guarantee from the Religious Bloc that it would not precipitate a crisis until the termination of the Kneset term in 1953. It became satisfied with an affirmation of a desire for stable government—a rather vague promise.[29]

The negotiations concluded with a seven-point agreement between Mapai and the Religious Bloc that was presented to the Kneset, together with the newly formed government.[30] The agreement confirmed the ten-point coalition program of March 1949; laid renewed stress on collective responsibility of members of government; provided for a four-year Kneset term; declared that the coalition partners would make their determination known to the Kneset to participate in the coalition until the expiration of its term in 1953; assured equality of rights and freedom of conscience in economic, educational, religious and cultural matters to all citizens; promised the setting up of a Ministerial Committee that would clarify religious questions, with the understanding that until these questions are resolved, there would be no change in status quo; granted the ministers power to appoint deputy ministers. Ben-Gurion neglected to mention the agreement which would reaffirm the ruling of the Provisional Government with regard to import of meat, assuring religious supervision in that sphere.

Mizrahi vacillated over joining the government. At first it decided not to join the new Cabinet, though it gave assurances that it would not vote against it.[31] Within twenty-four hours,

---

28. *Ibid.*, October 26, 1950.
29. *Ibid.*, October 29, 1950.
30. *Divrei ha-Kneset*, First Kneset, 184th session, 7 (October 30, 1950): 102.
31. *Ha-Zofeh*, October 30, 1950.

the party reversed its position and decided to participate in the coalition.[32]

Analysis of the New Government

The only substantial difference between the outgoing and the incoming government was the addition of the nonpartisan Ya'aqov Geri as the Minister of Trade and Industry. Otherwise the same four parties continued in the coalition with identical representation. Mapai retained seven key Cabinet posts, thereby continuing to control and dominate the Government. Despite repeated attempts to bring the Mapam and the General Zionists into the coalition, they persistently refused to join.[33] Their refusal was undoubtedly based on the assumption that new elections may be in the offing, wherein the opposition parties could expect to improve their position.

Thus, despite a government crisis that shook the nation and the Kneset, little changed. The "family quarrel" between the Religious Bloc and Mapai had once again come out into the open, their struggle for mutual concessions upsetting the legislative process.

When on October 30, 1950, Ben-Gurion presented his new government to the Kneset, the Religious Bloc congratulated itself on its success. In the Ministry of Education a special branch for religious education was established, headed by a member of the Po'alei Agudat Israel, to secure its autonomy and undiluted influence. Concerning the import of meat, status quo was to prevail in consonance with the agreement reached under the Provisional Government (whereby the Ministry for Religious Affairs would share control over all meat imports with the Ministry responsible for food supplies). All other religious demands, among them a law describing Sabbath observance, reforms in behalf of observant men in the army, or rabbinical jurisdiction, would be taken up by a Committee of Ministers.[34]

---

32. *Ibid.*, November 1, 1959.
33. On October 23, Mr. Rosen offered the General Zionists two Cabinet seats including the Trade and Industry and Interior portfolios. The General Zionists refused.
34. *Divrei ha-Kneset*, First Kneset, 185th session, 7 (October 31, 1950): 111.

Mapai also had reasons to be satisfied. It succeeded in a much needed government reorganization. Basically, the Cabinet reshuffle was necessitated by a mixture of economic and political factors. Economically, the situation in the country had drastically deteriorated. Essential supplies of food and clothing were inadequate and the blame was placed squarely upon the Mapai Minister of Supplies and Rationing, Dov Joseph. In view of the fast approaching municipal elections Mapai had reasons to worry that the economic adversity would mar its political future. Hence it had to rid itself of the politically explosive Ministry without, however, tipping the balance in the Cabinet. Despite the maneuvers of the Religious Bloc, Mapai accomplished its goal and emerged unimpaired from the crisis.

As for the majority's concessions to the Religious Bloc, Mapai could claim that they did not entail any change in policy. The establishment of the Ministerial Committee, which was to handle religious problems, helped in postponing decisions on the issue and in preserving the status quo. This is exactly what Mapai hoped to accomplish with the Religious Bloc. In the course of the Kneset debate on the government crisis, Ben-Gurion admitted his readiness to reach an accommodation with the Religious Bloc, if necessary at the price of compromise, in an effort to achieve coexistence between religious and irreligious Jews.[35] In a sense, therefore, Mapai could feel that it had resisted the pressures of the religionists and had secured a stable government for the balance of its constitutional tenure.

The Cabinet crisis, lasting two weeks, hurt the image of the government in the eyes of the voters. The wrangling of coalition partners over a portfolio and the squeeze tactic employed by a minority group demonstrated that party interests were dominant within the structure of government. It became obvious that organizational requirements, personal qualifications and the will of the majority were subordinated to the attainment of best results in interparty bargaining.

---

35. *Ibid.*, 180th session, 7 (October 17, 1950) :36. Ben-Gurion said, "I yet have to admit one sin: the sin of compromise."

10

Display of the Red Flag

On May 1, 1953, a workers' holiday in Israel, the red flag
of the workers was displayed and their anthem sung in some
public schools that belonged to the workers' trend in education.
As was already noted, Israel's system of education incorporated
four trends, one of which was Labor.[1] In anticipation of the
imminent passage of the State Education Law that would dissolve the trends and combine them into a united national
system of education, a step agreed upon by the members of
the coalition, the General Zionists promptly objected to the
use of schools for party purposes.[2] They requested that the
display of the red flag and the singing of the workers' anthem
be placed on the agenda of the Cabinet.[3] They demanded a ban
on similar action in all schools that were about to become
national institutions when the State Education Law was passed.
Their claim was that the schools must serve the nation and not
a class or party.

Mapai's Kneset membership was in agreement with the
General Zionist stand.[4] Before the month drew to an end,
however, the Central Committee of Mapai endorsed the action
of the labor demonstrators. It decided that the new Education
Law should permit the display of the red flag and the singing
of the "International" in some schools, at the request of parents,

---

1. See Chapter 6, "Crisis Over Religious Education: Act One."
2. *Ha-Boqer*, May 3, 1953.
3. *Ibid.*, May 13, 1953.
4. *Ibid.*

on May Day and on the Histadrut holiday.[5] Thereupon the four General Zionist Ministers handed in their resignations to Prime Minister Ben-Gurion. They announced that the decision of the Central Committtee of Mapai amounted to a breach of the agreement designed to create a national school system. It was indicative of Mapai's attitude that considerations of party interests were still paramount to the interest of the nation.[6]

In accordance with the law, the Prime Minister assumed the responsibility for the four vacated portfolios. He announced to the Kneset the resignation of the General Zionist Ministers, but avoided a vote of confidence in the hope that the crisis could be settled through party negotiation. Technically speaking, the government was not in immediate jeopardy, since it still commanded the sixty-four votes of Mapai, ha-Po'el ha-Mizrahi, Mizrahi, the Progressives, and the Minorities in the Kneset, thus assuring it a narrow majority.

Efforts to Bridge the Crisis

"I am firmly convinced,"declared Ben-Gurion to the Kneset, "that there is no tangible basis for the present crisis. There is only a temporary misunderstanding that, with mutual good-will, could be overcome."[7] Ben-Gurion agreed with the General Zionist stand against the display of the red flags, though officially he had to represent the Central Committee of his party which outvoted him on the issue. The compromise proposals made by Mapai in the hope of mending the breach were refused by the General Zionists, who claimed that in the matter of national education there could be no place for compromise.[8]

In order to secure the continuation of government, Mapai made a tentative effort toward coalition negotiations with other parties. However, discussions with Mapam broke off at their first stage, when Mapam demanded the preservation of the Labor trend in education and the assertion of neutrality in

5. *Jerusalem Post*, May 28, 1953.
6. *Ha-Boqer*, May 26, 1953.
7. *Divrei ha-Kneset*, Second Kneset, 236th session, 14 (May 27, 1953): 1418.
8. *Ha-Boqer*, May 27, 1953.

foreign affairs. Mapai rejected both of these demands.[9] The Agudah parties also expressed willingness to join the government if the status quo in education would be preserved and the trends left unchanged. Instead, Mapai was ready to promise the religious party that the Compulsory Service Law for women would not be enforced, that it would enlarge state support for the separate Agudah education system, and would support the prohibition of pig raising. But Agudah remained insistent on its condition regarding education.[10]

After a lapse of ten days, it became clear that if he wished to broaden the coalition Ben-Gurion had only two alternatives: either to patch up the Mapai–General Zionist coalition or to call for new Kneset elections. Since Mapai was eager to avoid new elections at this time, and since the General Zionists refused to compromise, the Mapai Central Committee decided to capitulate. As a face-saving device, so that its surrender to the General Zionists on the disputed point should not be utilized by rival and foe alike to their political advantage, the Central Committee left the final decision on the use of the labor flag to the supreme Party Council and a possible party referendum.[11] This was equivalent to a declaration that the Central Committee's decision was not final and that a reconsideration of the issue was in order.

The Cabinet crisis was thus believed to be virtually over. However, the session where the General Zionist Ministers were presented to the Kneset for reinstatement held a few surprises in store. Prior to the final vote on the new Cabinet, the General Zionists requested a recess with the implicit threat of a last minute change of heart. For two and a half hours the Kneset was held in suspense, to the chagrin of the government supporters and the undisguised delight of the Opposition, while negotiations were conducted behind the scenes by leaders of Mapai and the General Zionists.

Evidently, remarks made by Meir Argov of Mapai on the floor of the Kneset, had a disturbing effect on the General Zionists. He stated that in the unified national school system

9. *Davar*, May 29, 1953, also May 31, 1953, editorial.
10. *Ha-Zofeh*, May 29, 1953.
11. *Jerusalem Post*, June 1, 1953.

there shall be a minimum required curriculum, which shall be complemented at the parents' desire by instruction on the values of labor and labor unions. He further declared that, by decision of the Mapai Central Committee, the Labor flag could be used in schools under certain conditions if parents should request it. However, due to the importance of the matter, the party's National Convention would discuss it within the next few months.[12] Undoubtedly, Argov's remarks were meant for publicity purposes, but the General Zionists chose to take them literally.

At the conclusion of their caucus meeting, the General Zionists made a statement before the Kneset. They refused Argov's interpretation of the meaning of complementary instruction on the values of labor and announced the following agreement with Prime Minister Ben-Gurion:

1. The Law of National Education shall, after its final approval by the Government, be placed before the Kneset at the earliest opportunity and shall be approved by it.
2. With the passing of the Law of National Education the Minister of Education shall issue instructions to all national schools that, until the passage of a Unified Flag and Anthem Law for all the institutions of state, only the state's flag and anthem be used in the national schools.
3. A declaration will be made that within a few months the Government will present to the Kneset for its confirmation a law of the flag and the anthem for all institutions of State and the national schools.[13]

Following the statement, Meir Argov apologized for a snide remark on private economy.[14] General Zionist victory was complete. The minor coalition partner emerged triumphant, splitting the ranks of Mapai in the process.

The proposed coalition, a replica of its predecessor, consisting of Mapai, the General Zionists, Mizrahi, ha-Po'el ha-Mizrahi and the Progressives, was approved by a vote of 72 to 24 with two abstentions.[15]

---

12. *Divrei ha-Kneset,* Second Kneset, 241st session, 14 (June 3, 1953): 1499.
13. *Ibid.,* p. 1500. Elimeleh Rimlat, General Zionist.
14. *Ibid.,* p. 1501.
15. *Ibid.,* p. 1502.

Analysis of the Red Flag Crisis

In political quarters it was generally accepted that "the precipitate resignation of the General Zionists from the government was influenced by other considerations than the decision of the Central Committee of Mapai on the 'flag issue.' "[16] Opinions varied as to the real reason for "the whole sorry episode," which was designated by a member of the opposition in the Kneset as "a mystery."[17]

Some claimed that the General Zionists needed a crisis to cover up their failure in fulfilling their promises to their voters in the economic field. The party vowed to fight for relaxation of all economic controls. However, once the party assumed a position of responsibility, it realized the detrimental effect such a step would have on the country. To save face it sought a way out of the coalition.[18]

Others stated that the true reason for the crisis could be found inside the General Zionist party. Reportedly, already two weeks earlier, possibly in conjunction with the ongoing budget debate in the Kneset, the party's leaders decided to withdraw from the government under the pressure of vested middle class interests who saw their economic and social aims frustrated and who were disappointed by their Ministers.[19] Thus, the resignation of the General Zionists may have been motivated by an endeavor to avoid a split in the party.[20]

Indeed, during the Kneset debate on the budget which was then proceeding, a rift appeared to develop between the General Zionists and the Mapai. Differences of opinion were expressed on the problems of education, economy and ways to relieve the burden of unemployment.[21] A General Zionist member strongly criticized the approach of the Treasury (under a Mapai Minister) for its lack of understanding of the financial prob-

16. *Jerusalem Post*, May 26, 1953.
17. *Divrei ha-Kneset*, Second Kneset, 241st session, 14 (June 3, 1953) : 1489. Y. Bader of Herut.
18. *Jerusalem Post*, May 26, 1953.
19. *Davar*, May 27, 1953, editorial.
20. Three weeks prior to the crisis newspapers reported that "tension within the coalition is growing . . . although reports of a possible dissolution may be considered tendentious." Jerusalem Post, May 5, 1953.
21. *Ha-Boqer*, May 6, 1953.

lems at hand. The specific demands of the General Zionists dealt with ending the rationing of goods. The party was also opposed to the imposition of an unemployment tax on the employers in behalf of the jobless..[22]

During the same budget debate, the General Zionists voiced additional grievances. They introduced a strong complaint that the Minister of Commerce and Industry (under a General Zionist Minister) was not given the opportunity to perform the functions for which it was created. Many of the tasks that would, by their very nature, fall into its province, were transferred to other Ministries, presumably to keep them under Mapai control. The budget, the General Zionists protested, did not demonstrate a will to economize. To the contrary. It spoke of establishing new offices and branches within the Ministry of the Treasury and planned to pay for them by increasing the burden of taxation. The implication was clear: Mapai wished to offer new positions as rewards to its faithful while centralizing the conduct of government in Mapai Ministries. The General Zionists would be left with the illusion of responsibilities, presiding over impotent Ministries stripped of all power, yet the middle classes supporting them would carry the brunt of the tax burden.

In describing and analyzing the crisis one cannot omit the possibility that the General Zionists utilized it as a technique to preserve their oppositional stance in the eyes of the voters. It was the party's opposition to the government that seemed to have contributed most to its phenomenal rise in the 1951 Kneset elections. The party was concerned that it may have lost this advantage, since it became associated and identified with the coalition.

The flag issue offered the General Zionists an ingenious excuse to disassociate from the government on ideological grounds, while simultaneously voicing their grievances and protesting against a noncooperative Cabinet majority. With their action they also hoped to satisfy the militant vested interests within the party and to prove their oppositional skill to the voters.

Despite these explanations, the crisis still remained somewhat

22. *Ibid.*

of a puzzle. Curiously enough, on economic issues most vital to the General Zionist platform, an acceptable compromise seemed to have been reached between the two parties just before the withdrawal of the General Zionist Ministers. General Zionist leaders had succeeded in reducing the Work Relief Tax to 15 million pounds from 17 million pounds demanded by Mapai. Likewise they served their voters well by gaining for them a reduction in property tax.[23] At their national convention they expressed satisfaction at the recent liberalization of the economy.[24] Yet, despite their favorable balance sheet in the Cabinet, the General Zionists precipitated a crisis on an issue that was as insignificant as it was dramatic.

To Mapai the crisis demonstrated the inability of the General Zionists to be constructive and responsible government partners.[25] They brought severe embarrassment to the government in the international arena, since the disputed red flag has been widely associated with communism.[26] The crisis was also poorly timed from a domestic point of view. The insecure borders and the problem of unemployment required that drastic measures be taken by a strong and unified Cabinet. But above all, Mapai had a right to be unhappy with the General Zionist choice of the labor flag issue to bring the crisis about. The whole matter was not close to middle-class hearts. It was only remotely linked to the question of a unified national system of education. It could easily have been handled in a separate bill originating in the Cabinet, in a quiet and legal way, instead of precipitately in public.

By their resignation from the government, the General Zionist Ministers catapulted a minor ideological issue into the forefront of national and international attention. In doing so, they elicited an outcry of betrayal from the left against Mapai, and succeeded in introducing confusion and disarray in Mapai ranks. The red flag issue was emotion-charged and it required time for the minority within Mapai, led by Ben-Gurion, to convince the rank and file that the prohibition of

23. *Jerusalem Post*, May 27, 1953.
24. *Ha-Boqer*, May 15, 1953.
25. *Davar*, May 26, 1953, editorial.
26. *Jerusalem Post*, May 27, 1953.

red flags in public would not signal the demise of socialism.

Thus, Mapai saw the crisis not as a question of principle to the General Zionists, but as an act of malicious mischief. The General Zionists did not take a stand to safeguard their own free enterprise party platform. Instead they penetrated into the socialist camp to cause disruption over its flag and to place Mapai in a compromising position.

The Crisis and the Religious Parties

Two questions must be considered: the attitude of the religious parties to the crisis and the position of the religious parties as a result of the crisis.

This was the first government since the establishment of the state in which the religious parties were not the major partner. It was therefore of crucial significance to them to what degree Mapai and the General Zionists would be capable of working out a comfortable basis of cooperation in practice. If the two major coalition partners had developed sufficient mutual trust and a strong enough appreciation of their common loyalties to the state, Mapai's need for the religious parties would have correspondingly dwindled and the religious establishment may have been placed in jeopardy. Consequently, the religious elements were greatly relieved, if not jubilant, at the breakdown of the coalition. An observer reported that "the religious parties of the coalition (Mizrahi and ha-Po'el ha-Mizrahi) as well as of the opposition (Agudah and Po'alei Agudat Israel) could not hide their satisfaction at the prevailing situation."[27]

The religious parties blasted away at the irresponsibility and blackmail tactics of the General Zionists for utilizing the flag as an excuse to break the artificial coalition.[28] Religious spokesmen pointed out that the General Zionists lack "the traits of patience and responsibility that are always required as basic conditions for participation in the yoke of govern-

---

27. *Ha-Boqer,* May 26, 1953.
28. *Ha-Zofeh,* May 26, editorial.

ment."[29] Rabbi Meir Levin of Agudat Israel said that they continually "promised help and salvation in the economic field but did not improve the situation at all. Instead, they worsened it.[30] "To our sorrow," continued the Agudah leader, "religious Jewry must remember that the General Zionists forced the implementation of unified education in order to cancel out religious education. They did not want to postpone the implementation even for one year. Of all the salvation and comfort that they promised in the economic field, all that remained is the liquidation of religious education."[31]

The vehemence of the religious attack against the General Zionists was matched only by the Progressives who accused their former colleagues of attempting to undermine the government with recklessness and thoughtlessness on an issue of no consequence.[32]

On the merits of the flag issue itself the religious parties did not agree. The ha-Po'el ha-Mizrahi and the Agudah defended the decision of Mapai's Central Committee that the labor flag should be permitted for use on labor holidays. They claimed that parents should have a right to cherish symbols, and they should be respected even by those who are opposed to them.[33] Besides, did not the tribes of Israel encamp around their tribal flags in the Wilderness![34] However, the Mizrahi came out unequivocally for a state that would tolerate only one flag and one anthem.[35]

The flag crisis precipitated by the General Zionists undoubtedly strengthened the position of the religious parties. The General Zionists, who had given Mapai a difficult stretch of five months as coalition partners with their economic demands, had proven their unreliability and fickleness by strik-

---

29. *Divrei ha-Kneset*, Second Kneset, 241st session, 14 (June 3, 1953) : 1490. M. Hazani of ha-Po'el ha-Mizrahi.
30. *Ibid.*, p. 1492.
31. *Ibid.*, p. 1493.
32. *Ibid.*, 1498. Izhar Harari of the Progressives.
33. *Ha-Zofeh*, May 26, 1953.
34. *Divrei ha-Kneset*, Second Kneset, 241st session, 14 (June 3, 1953) : 1492. Rabbi Y. M. Levin of Agudat Israel.
35. *Ibid.*, p. 1496. Mordehai Nuruk of Mizrahi.

ing at Mapai by subterfuge in a sensitive ideological area. The religious parties could rightly deduce that the Mapai–General Zionist partnership would not be based on mutual trust, but rather on mutual need, coupled with deepseated mutual suspicion and anxiety.

Though the Mizrahi and ha-Po'el ha-Mizrahi continued as minor partners in the new coalition, the religious parties emerged unscathed from the crisis with their bargaining power strengthened and their demands respected. The very same year the religious parties scored a major victory with the passage of the Law of Rabbinical Jurisdiction, that confirmed the undisputed right of Rabbinical Courts to sole authority in matters of marriage and divorce.[36] It was noteworthy that, despite the backing of a strong secular majority in the Kneset as well as in the Cabinet, Ben-Gurion and Mapai supported the Law of Rabbinic Jurisdiction. This support was not rooted in the personal convictions of members of Mapai, but rather in a pragmatic approach to politics. To Mapai it was a dictate of realism to preserve for itself a coalition partner who would not block its main economic and foreign policy objectives and whose interests were largely confined to relatively limited objectives.

36. *Laws of the State of Israel* 7:139.

11

Breach of Collective Responsibility: The Case of Abstention

On June 28, 1955, the Herut and the Communist parties introduced in the Kneset two separate motions of no-confidence in the government. The General Zionists were expected to vote with the government since, as members of the coalition, they were subject to the rule of collective responsibility. Instead, however, they abstained. This led to a Cabinet crisis and the resignation of the government.

Motions of censure were introduced by the two opposition parties regarding the notorious Kastner Case. Dr. Israel Kastner was head of the Jewish Rescue Committee in Budapest during the Nazi occupation of Hungary in 1944. He was accused by a man named Greenwald of having collaborated with the Nazis in the mass murder of Hungarian Jewry. Thereupon the Attorney General's office brought a libel suit against Greenwald. In his verdict, however, Judge Benjamin Halevy declared that he found Greenwald's accusation substantiated. Though officially Kastner was not on trial, this was nevertheless tantamount to a judgment of guilty against him. The verdict insinuating Kastner's guilt was promptly appealed by the Attorney General with the concurrence of high government officials.

Because of the important position Kastner had held during and after the war in the hierarchy of the Jewish Agency and Zionist Mapai leadership, the two extreme opposition parties were eager to exploit the theme of "guilt by association," to the great embarrassment of the government. Indeed, the day after judgment was rendered in the Greenwald-Kastner Case, the *Jerusalem Post* had occasion to bemoan in an editorial that "its exploitation for purposes of party politics has already begun."[1]

The Herut motion of censure accused the Attorney General of illegal and inconsiderate action when he chose to bring the libel suit against Greenwald, instead of permitting Kastner to handle the case for himself. Since the Attorney General's office was committed to one side, it could not view the case impartially any longer. Herut further accused the government of acting precipitately in favor of Kastner in its prompt appeal of Judge Halevy's verdict. The international implications of the case were also highlighted. It was not feasible to demand the condemnation of Nazis in other lands while the government of Israel sheltered a collaborator in its midst. Herut contended that such protection was extended to Dr. Kastner solely because he was a high-ranking member of Mapai.[2]

The Communist motion attacked the government for attempting to cover up Kastner's guilt which it did by throwing its weight into the libel suit against Greenwald and by standing up in Kastner's defense after the Court passed judgment over him.[3]

Government spokesmen explained that the Office of the Attorney General is independent of the Ministry of Justice and the government, and that they do not interfere in its conduct. The Attorney General decided to act for Kastner since he had been accused by Greenwald in his capacity as a public servant. The appeal was a logical consequence of the verdict. The Attorney General himself stated that "if what had been said about Kastner was true, his penalty was death."[4] The appeal in-

---

1. *Jerusalem Post*, June 23, 1955.
2. *Divrei ha-Kneset*, Second Kneset, 620th session, 18 (June 28, 1955): 2107. Yohanan Bader of Herut.
3. *Ibid.*, p. 2109. Esther Vilenska, Communist.
4. *Ibid.*, p. 2116. Pinhas Rosen, Minister of Justice.

volved no affront to the integrity of the judge. It was an elementary obligation to a citizen of the state, as well as to history, which is entitled to an exhaustive scrutiny of the tragic events of the holocaust by a higher court instead of only by a one-man bench. The action of the government did by no means wish to prejudge the case.[5]

The General Zionists, though members of the coalition, were critical of the Attorney General for undertaking judicial action in the Kastner case without thorough prior investigation of the situation. They regretted the impression left behind by the action of the government that, instead of considering the true facts, it had hastened to whitewash itself and particularly Mapai. The General Zionists speaker declared, that under the circumstances, the government compounded the error of the Attorney General when it appealed the case, thus taking a stand in defense of Kastner after he was condemned by a respected judicial authority. The hasty appeal supported the point of view that powerful interests who had reason to be concerned with their own rehabilitation applied pressure on the Attorney General and the Minister of Justice to initiate the appeal. The General Zionist stand was an implied accusation of Mapai involvement in the distortion of justice. It came as no surprise when the General Zionists declared their abstention in the voting.[6]

Collective Cabinet Responsibility

The government did not have to resign as a result of the no-confidence motions which barely mustered a few votes.[7] The abstention of the General Zionists in the crucial vote indicated, however, that the coalition shifted to an uncertain course. Instead of exposing himself and the government to further General Zionist coalition maneuvers, Prime Minister Moshe Sharett handed in his resignation to the President. According to the Transition Law, this move brought down the govern-

5. *Ibid.*, p. 2109. Prime Minister Moshe Sharett.
6. *Ibid.*, p. 2114. Hayim Ariav, General Zionist.
7. The Herut motion of no-confidence was defeated by a vote of 9 to 50, with 29 abstentions. On the Communist motion only the five Communists voted for censure. *Davar*, June 29, 1955.

ment.[8] The Prime Minister made the following explanatory statement to the press:

> To my regret, I must announce that after what happened in the Kneset yesterday, I saw no alternative but to present my resignation as Prime Minister. . . .
>
> When I said "what happened yesterday" I meant one thing and one thing only: the failure of the members of the General Zionist Kneset faction, and of the General Zionist Ministers in particular, to vote against the non-confidence motion presented by the Herut party.
>
> The General Zionist Ministers apparently assumed that even after the abstention on the vote of non-confidence in the Government of which they are members they could remain in it. This assumption did not seem reasonable to me.
>
> I hereby assert that by their abstention, the General Zionist Ministers broke the most basic rule of any coalition Government which is in the nature of an axiom of collective responsibility. By abstaining, it was as if they said that they were doubtful whether this government of which they themselves are members, is worthy of the confidence of the Kneset, and that it did not matter to them if it would fall as a result of this vote. Such a practice is bound to destroy the stability and undermine the foundations of any future coalition government. It is a complete negation of every elementary concept of collective responsibility, without which no regular parliamentary government in a democratic country can survive. The Government, with all the groups and individuals which make it up, must appear as one solid body, otherwise it is not a government at all. There is a supreme and decisive national reason for observing most jealously this central principle, for not deviating from it, and not compromising with its violation. A party which does not understand this simple truth demonstrates its lack of political maturity and its fitness for partnership in a democratic coalition. . . .
>
> I felt it my duty and an imperative necessity for the Government as a whole not to acquiesce in this pernicious precedent, which dooms Israel statecraft in its formative period—and that is why I resigned.[9]

---

8. *Divrei ha-Kneset,* Second Kneset, 623rd session, 18 (June 29, 1955): 2146.

9. *Jerusalem Post,* June 30, 1955.

Moshe Sharett wanted to make it clear that the resignation of the government was the result solely of the breakdown of the principle of collective responsibility and had nothing to do with the Kastner case. In answering questions of newspapermen he made a distinction between abstention during the regular course of Kneset business and a motion of no-confidence, on which the very survival of the government depends. In the second case abstention of coalition parties, and especially Ministers, is intolerable.[10] He pointed out that the day prior to the Kneset debate he warned the General Zionists that their abstention in voting would force him to demand their resignation from the government. They replied that Ministers could not be compelled to resign, unless the Prime Minister brings down the government by his own resignation.[11]

The General Zionists countered that to them the issue was purely a matter of conscience. The Kastner case was not written into the coalition agreement, and they had a right to vote on it as they pleased without considering their vote a breach of joint responsibility.[12] General Zionist party leaders demanded the privilege of following their conscience at an extraordinary Cabinet session. This was denied to them, though it was sometimes extended to the ha-Po'el ha-Mizrahi on religious matters. According to the General Zionists, the majority in the Cabinet could blame only itself for the crisis.

The True Causes of the Crisis

Due to the proximity of the national elections to be held in less than a month, the conclusion was inescapable that the General Zionists utilized the Kastner case for the purpose of freeing themselves from the shackles of government and its collective responsibility. They felt that identification with the government would weaken their chances in the elections. Mapai charged that, "the election high-command of the General Zionists considered it imperative to demand that the party abstain

10. *Davar*, June 30, 1955.
11. *Divrei ha-Kneset*, Second Kneset, 623rd session, 18 (June 29, 1955): 2146.
12. *Ibid.*, p. 2148.

from voting in the Government and in the Kneset, in the hope that this abstention will protect them from the attacks of Herut in the election campaign."[13]

Government and opposition spokesmen were unanimous in accusing the General Zionists of irresponsible action. Menahem Begin, the leader of Herut, reproached them for their opportunism. If the Kastner case presented a question of conscience, why did they not vote against the government? If it was a corrupt government, how could the General Zionists tolerate it and associate with it? The situation only points out the corruption of the General Zionists themselves.[14] Elazar Peri of Mapam stated that the General Zionists exploited Mapai "in a tactical manner solely for election purposes.[15] Ben-Yehuda of Ahdut ha-'Avodah pointed out the unfairness of identifying any individual act in the tragic period of the Jewish people with a specific party or parties. "The technical game of a non-confidence motion two days before the expiration of the Kneset term . . . will be judged by the whole population of citizens in the country."[16] Yizhar Harari of the Progressives called the conscience cited by the General Zionists "a conscience brought forth by the fear of elections."[17] His colleague, Pinhas Rosen, added that the situation should not have been exploited by the General Zionists as if all that was involved concerned the acquisition of another half a portfolio, or even a whole portfolio.[18] Speakers of the religious parties considered it an unfortunate phenomenon that such a sensitive and tragic issue should be utilized as a political weapon and an election price.[19] In the circumstances, the act of the General Zionists can be seen only in the light of the election campaign going on in the country.[20] Yizhaq Meir Levin of Agudat Israel pleaded, "Do not make use of our martyrs' blood for election purposes."[21]

---

13. *Davar,* June 29, 1955.
14. *Divrei ha-Kneset,* Second Kneset, 623rd session, 18 (June 29, 1955) : 2150.
15. *Ibid.,* p. 2154.
16. *Ibid.,* 620th session, 18 (June 28, 1955) :2110.
17. *Ibid.,* 623rd session, 18 (June 29, 1955) :2156.
18. *Ibid.,* 620th session, 18 (June 28, 1955) :2116.
19. *Ibid.,* p. 2114. Michael Hazani of ha-Po'el ha-Mizrahi.
20. *Ibid.,* 623rd session, 18 (June 29, 1955) :2157.
21. *Ibid.,* p. 2159.

A General Zionist speaker expressed his satisfaction in draw-ing fire from both sides of the Kneset and assured the Assem-bly that this would certainly assist his party in the election.[22] However, the General Zionists countercharged that actually the Mapai party wanted to break off with them and utilized the flimsy excuse of an alleged breach of cabinet discipline to ac-complish their objective. "As for the causes that led Mapai to bring about the Government crisis, it is difficult to hide from the possibility that the thing was planned in advance," said Mr. Sapir.[23]

It was supposedly an open secret that Mapai was tired of the partnership and was anxious to find a way to break it up.[24] A left-wing source offered some comfort to the General Zionists in stating that the election tacticians of Mapai decided, sev-eral days prior to the confidence vote on Kastner, to assume an attitude toward the General Zionists as if they were outside the coalition.[25] Indeed, the General Zionists did not want the crisis, declared Mr. Ariav. If they had wanted it, they could have voted against the government instead of abstaining. "We thought that the government will conclude its term till the elections."[26] Thus, the General Zionists attempted to shift the guilt for breaking up the coalition to Mapai and attributed Mapai's actions mainly to two motives: To get ride of the General Zionists, their most challenging partner with the greatest potential of forming the alternative government; and to "cover up for Kastner and his collaborating colleagues, the men of Mapai, who were working on the salvation of Hun-garian Jewry and were found guilty of delivering them to the Nazis."[27]

Who Is the Government?

With the rapid approach of the new elections, apparently the General Zionists felt that they had no choice but to break

---

22. *Ibid.*, p. 2160.
23. *Ha-Boqer,* June 30, 1955.
24. *Ha-Arez,* June 30, 1955.
25. *La-Merhav,* June 29, 1955.
26. *Ha-Boqer,* June 30, 1955.
27. *Ibid.,* June 29, 1955.

with the coalition. Their chance of being considered Mapai's alternative was greatly diminished while serving with the rival party in one government. The party most closely aligned to the General Zionists on the right, the Herut, exploited their cooperation with the government to the hilt and courted the General Zionist electorate. They were, therefore, looking for a way out of the coalition in order to assume once again the role of a vigorous opposition. This was the role that had gained the party twenty votes in the former Kneset.

It would, however, be wrong to assume that the sole consideration in the decision of the General Zionists was to defy the government of which they were a member. They had long been irked by Mapai's attitude in identifying itself, and itself alone, with the government. While the General Zionists could not deny that Mapai formed the coalition, they protested that Mapai was not the government by itself. Lacking a majority, it could not establish a Cabinet by itself and was, therefore, as much dependent on the other parties as these were on Mapai. The General Zionists wanted to be considered equal partners, and they resented Mapai's somewhat superior and condescending approach to the other parties. It seemed as if Mapai would be the very embodiment of government, mediating among the interested parties to pacify them until they could be brought together in one coalition. A General Zionist leader, Josef Sapir, shed some light on this subject while addressing the Kneset:

> We were asked why we did not resign yesterday or this morning? We did not resign because we do not recognize that the government of Israel is the government of Mapai together with those whom she chooses to attach, or disattach, from the government. The Government we participated in was a collective government, and if there is no partnership in it any more—it stands dissolved. But it is not a government of Mapai who determines by her good will or ill will whom to join to it or release from it, as she pleases. Let her try to do that to other parties! To us such a thing will not be done!

(Interjection from Ben-Gurion: "It was done today!")

Today a government was dissolved through the resignation of the Prime Minister before the President of the State. The outgoing government is no more in existence and the Prime Minister designate, appointed by the President, appears before the Kneset requesting its confidence in a new government. Ministers did not leave the government and were not released from it.[28]

Another leader of the General Zionists underscored his party's position in the government under Mapai tutelage, clearly accenting General Zionist resentment for being considered a subordinate party.

There is one basic fact in this country: Two outlooks are fighting over the character of the state and the Government —Mapai on one side, and the General Zionists on the opposite side, with all due respect to the other parties. . . . A coalition Government can proceed only in one way, and this way can be neither the way of Mapai nor the way of the General Zionists, but only the way of compromise—on occasion a better, on occasion a worse compromise. All our strength in the Government consisted of proposing and amending, for you (of Mapai) were nine, supported by three satellites, and we were only four. Our whole duty in the Government consisted of making suggestions and improvements to Mapai's outlook on the state.[29]

The General Zionists did not stand on solid ground in their argument. A Progressive spokesman projected the situation in a different perspective.

Member of Kneset Sapir would have had the right to argue and to boast if it were possible to think that his party could be a member of the Government anytime she wants and could cease to be a member anytime she wants.

It seems, however, that 'by sheer chance' you ceased to be in the Government exactly when Mapai so desired. You also became attached to the Government when Mapai wanted you to become attached. You would not have been members of

28. *Divrei ha-Kneset*, Second Kneset, 623rd session, 18 (June 29, 1955) : 2148.

29. *Ibid.*, p. 2162. Josef Serlin of the General Zionists.

the Government without Mapai's consent. In other words, you never remained outside because you chose to stay out.[30]

Mr. Serlin's remarks made it clear that the struggle, as the General Zionists saw it, was strictly between Mapai and the General Zionists. The other parties were considered subordinate. The impression made by his remarks was that if the General Zionists had been in Mapai's place with the substantial plurality to their disposal, they would have been ready to be more compromising on their program than Mapai. The General Zionists did not have the opportunity to substantiate this statement in practice. Should they gain such an opportunity, it is highly doubtful that they would not take advantage of their power to attain objectives commensurate with their influence. Their complaints were therefore unrealistic and were rooted in the frustrations of a party that failed to attain the power of which it considered itself worthy, first in the elections and then in the technique of coalition bargaining.

The conclusion was inescapable. Despite opposition objections, the question of "Who is the government?" could be answered only in one way: Mapai is the government.

The Crisis and the Religious Parties

Once again the religious parties emerged from a government crisis with a definite improvement in their strategic position. The religious parties of the coalition backed Mapai completely on the confidence motion. They proved their trustworthiness to Mapai. Working to their advantage was the disappointing behavior of the General Zionists. To the extent that the General Zionists were becoming less desirable as a possible future coalition partner, the religious parties were becoming more desirable.

The religious parties fully exploited the situation. They hastened to point out the hypocritical attitude of the General Zionists regarding the no-confidence motion, as well as throughout their stay in the government. The General Zionists at-

---

30. *Ibid.,* p. 2156. Yizhar Harari of Progressives.

tempted to be in the government and in the opposition simultaneously, bringing about crises of government and making the work of the coalition unrewarding and frustrating. However, "this time their tactics recognized no boundaries, when they desired to attack the Government by employing the Kastner case in the election campaign and at the same time wished to continue sitting in the Government that they did not consider worthy of their confidence. . . . Experience proves that the General Zionists did not yet mature sufficiently to undertake governmental responsibility."[31]

Besides condemning the General Zionists on technical grounds for the purpose of improving their tactical position, the religious parties also attacked them on religious grounds. Yizhaq Rafael of the ha-Po'el ha-Mizrahi declared that the religious people became disillusioned with the General Zionists. They expected from a conservative party a conservative stand and a defense of tradition. Instead, the General Zionists fought religion on the issues of religious education, Sabbath observance in Jerusalem, the law of marriage and divorce, the law of religious judges, and other Toraitic laws. The religious adherents were also mindful of the "organized sabotage by the Ministry of Commerce and Industry of the effort to extirpate the shame of pig raising from the land. We received an offer of compromise [from the government] and were hopeful to restrain this shameful activity by administrative means and regulations, but the Ministry of Commerce and Industry, headed by Mr. Bernstein [General Zionist] in an organized fashion undermined these means, and so we reached the same abject state wherein we were before."[32]

Similarly, Yizhaq Meir Levin of the Agudat Israel expressed his satisfaction that the General Zionists would no longer be in the government, since they wanted national service for religious women and the abolition of trends, yet no support for religious education. They were also to be blamed for the spread of pig raising in the country, for an autopsy law unfavorable to religious elements and for pressures in behalf of civil mar-

31. *Ha-Zofeh,* June 30, 1955, editorial.
32. *Divrei ha-Kneset,* Second Kneset, 623rd session, 18 (June 29, 1955) : 2157.

riage.[33] The Po'alei Agudat Israel substantially concurred with these complaints.[34]

The General Zionists were reciprocally hostile in their attitude to the religious parties. Josef Serlin, addressing himself to them, said: "Who will believe that you are talking in the name of religion and that you are really aspiring for religion? And who will believe that you are talking in the name of tradition and that this is really the tradition?"[35]

A surprising move was made by the Yemenite member affiliated with the General Zionists. He announced that, since he represents a party of religious people and workers, he is obliged to dissociate himself from the General Zionist Party and will vote for the government.[36] The Po'alei Agudat Israel, that was formerly in opposition, also declared that its vote will support the Cabinet. Of the religious parties only the Agudat Israel abstained in the no-confidence motion.

There was another element in the crisis that helped the position of the religious parties. The General Zionists had an affinity to evoke a crisis on issues that had nothing to do with their basic platform and principles. The crisis of the Kastner case as well as the former crisis of the display of the red flag involved principles that were remote from economics, the acknowledged main concern of the General Zionists. When the General Zionists utilized these issues against the government, they took Mapai by surprise. Their attitude was interpreted as an act of hostility, utilizing the first convenient pretext to break the ranks of the Cabinet.

The religious parties contributed their share to the growing number of government crises. But in every instance the problem was built up progressively to its crescendo instead of making a sudden appearance. More significantly, it was a problem connected with some aspect of religious life, the main concern of the religious parties. This made the crises brought about by the religious militants, if not less irritating, at least more acceptable.

---

33. *Ibid.*
34. *Ibid.*, Kalman Kahana.
35. *Ibid.*, p. 2161.
36. *Ibid.*, p. 2160, Shimon Greidi.

The New Government

The new government was created on the very same day that Moshe Sharett handed in his resignation, thereby bringing down the former government. The only difference between the two governments was that the General Zionists, who were present in the former, were absent in the latter .

The creation of the new government by Moshe Sharett was recognized as a masterstroke of politics. It effectively eliminated the General Zionists from the coalition, and particularly from the Ministry of the Interior, which oversees the conduct of elections, on the eve of the dissolution of the Kneset and the forthcoming national and municipal elections. The new coalition could act only in a caretaker government capacity. However, if it had not been legally installed, the Ministers of the outgoing government could have held on to their respective Ministries until a new government had been formed following the elections. This could have opened the way to General Zionist obstruction within the government.

Postscript on the Kastner Case

The Kastner case did not close until January 1958 (between January 16 and 22) when the Supreme Court of Israel, sitting as a Court of Criminal Appeals, cleared him of the charges of collaboration with the Nazis and of contributing to the destruction of Hungarian Jewry. Five members of the Court sat on the bench. It was the first time that the Court was composed of more than three members in hearing a case. The verdict took three days to deliver. Dr. Kastner himself did not live to see his own vindication. In March 1957 he was assassinated by a group of terrorists who claimed to act in behalf of the victims of Nazi terror. They were sentenced to life imprisonment only three weeks before Kastner was legally vindicated.[37]

---

37. *Israel Weekly Digest,* no. 17 (January 23, 1958) .

12

Breach of Collective Responsibility: The Case of Indiscretion

On December 31, 1957, Prime Minister Ben-Gurion resigned in protest of a security leakage stemming from a breach of joint Cabinet responsibility by one of the coalition partners. Events leading up to the resignation started at the Cabinet meeting two weeks earlier. There Ben-Gurion had sought approval for a visit by a high-ranking Israeli official to Germany, in order to negotiate the acquisition of strategic material and armaments. The Cabinet vote on the issue was close, with seven Mapai Ministers supporting the visit and two abstaining. The six Ahdut ha-'Avodah, Mapam, Progressive, and ha-Po'el ha-Mizrahi Ministers voted against it. By a majority of one, the visit was approved over strenuous Ahdut ha-'Avodah and Mapam objections.[1] The leftist parties were suspicious that the contact with Germany was intended for the purpose of establishing a link with NATO, an allegation denied by Mapai.[2]

However, Ahdut ha-'Avodah was not content with voicing its objections within the Cabinet. Contrary to the pledge of Cabinet secrecy, it published in the party organ *La-Merhav* in-

1. *Jerusalem Post*, December 18, 1957.
2. *Davar*, December 20, 1957.

formation pertaining to the decision of the Cabinet and warned that "the refusal of Mapai to cancel the decision would jeopardize the very existence of the coalition."[3] As a result of the *La-Merhav* disclosure of what was supposed to have been a highly confidential mission, Ben-Gurion canceled all plans for the visit of a distinguished Israeli representative to Germany. The aim which Ahdut ha-'Avodah sought to achieve had been attained.[4]

The highly irregular action by Ahdut ha-'Avodah had its immediate repercussions. Following an emergency meeting of Mapai Ministers under the chairmanship of Ben-Gurion, the Secretary of Mapai, Giora Josephthal, issued the following communiqué:

> Ahdut ha-'Avodah, following narrow party interests, had frustrated a security matter of supreme importance to the state. No such act has ever been committed in the history of the state, not even by an opposition party whose representatives participate in sessions of the Kneset Foreign Affairs and Security Committee. The meeting was united in its determination not to pass over in silence such sabotage of security. All the members who took part in the meeting, without exception supported the stand of the Prime Minister, that such an act was completely incompatible with membership in the Cabinet and that the party and its Cabinet members must draw the proper conclusions.[5]

This amounted to an indirect request that Ahdut ha-'Avodah resign from the coalition. However, the party made it clear that it had no intention of resigning. It was supported in this resolve by Mapam.

If both left-wing parties had withdrawn from the coalition, the government would still have been left with a bare majority of sixty-one in the Kneset (Mapai—40; NRP—11; Progressives—5; Arab parties—5). However, in order to avoid the reduction of the government to such a bare minimum, strenuous efforts were made by some Mapai members and the Progressives to

3. *La-Merhav*, December 17, 1957.
4. *La-Merhav*, December 19, 1957.
5. *Israel Digest*, December 27, 1957.

persuade the Ahdut ha-'Avodah to overcome considerations of prestige and to admit its error.

As a corollary or an alternative to a forthright admission of guilt, the Minister of Justice, Pinhas Rosen, proposed that a law be adopted enabling the Prime Minister to dismiss an indiscreet Minister with the consent of 60 percent of the Cabinet. However, Mapam and the NRP were firmly opposed to Rosen's suggestion. Mapam indicated that a simple censure of Ahdut ha-'Avodah by the Cabinet, as well as a determination that in the future the Prime Minister would consult the Cabinet on all matters of security and foreign affairs, should suffice.[6]

Of the coalition partners only the NRP would have been pleased to see a government without the Ahdut ha-'Avodah because of its continual antireligious stand.[7] In its turn, the Ahdut ha-'Avodah, having accomplished its goal, would have liked to see the incident closed and forgotten, but without loss of face.[8]

On December 30 a decision of the Cabinet was made public, declaring that "The Government considers the publicity given last week by Ahdut ha-'Avodah to the Government's confidential decision to be harmful to the state and a grave violation of the principle of the collective responsibility of the Government for its decisions."[9] Simultaneously, the Prime Minister announced his resignation in view of the fact that no solution could be found to the prevailing crisis.

Formation of New Government

On December 31, 1957, Ben-Gurion submitted his resignation to the President. On the same day the President began consultations with the leaders of all parties represented in the Kneset. At the termination of these meetings, he invited Ben-Gurion to form a new Cabinet. Ben-Gurion accepted the mandate with two stipulations that became the basis of the nego-

6. *Jerusalem Post,* December 25, 1957.
7. *Ibid.,* December 22, 1957.
8. *La-Merhav,* December 18, 1957.
9. *Israel Weekly Digest* 1, no. 14 (January 2, 1958).

tiations conducted by Mapai: collective responsibility of the Cabinet and the parties comprising it must be strengthened and absolute secrecy of all Cabinet discussions on security and foreign affairs must be maintained.[10]

Mapai's main concern was to avoid the repetition of a government crisis due to procedural failures. To that end, Levi Eshkol, the Mapai Minister of Finance, proposed a "Six Point" program. Its most controversial articles stated that the Cabinet should have the right by a two-thirds vote to dismiss a Minister for divulging its secrets either directly or through his party newspaper and that Kneset members of a coalition party should be forbidden to abstain in a Kneset vote on Cabinet bills without prior agreement with the Cabinet.[11] These two points were specifically reiterated by Ben-Gurion in a letter "to all former partners in the coalition," with one significant addition: "If Ministers or Kneset factions find it necessary to abstain without Cabinet consent, or to vote against these decisions, then their representatives must undertake to resign from the Cabinet prior to the vote."[12]

Ahdut ha-'Avodah and Mapam countered with proposals calling for a "bona fide" understanding among all partners of the coalition on matters of collective responsibility. They requested that coalition members should have a right to abstain from a vote in the Kneset rather than go contrary to their conscience. In particular, the two leftist parties wished to dissociate themselves from any decision that may draw Israel into a military alliance. In addition, they also sought ways and means to secure greater participation of all Ministers in major policy plans, especially on matters of security and foreign policy.[13] The Ahdut ha-'Avodah warned that should Ben-Gurion form a coalition without it, the party would not join at a later stage. It would either be in from the beginning or not at all.[14]

The Progressives had one major objection to Mapai's pro-

---

10. *Divrei ha-Kneset*, Third Kneset, 387th session, 23 (January 7, 1958) : 563.

11. *Jerusalem Post*, December 29, 1957.

12. *Ibid.*, January 5, 1958.

13. *Ibid.*, January 6, 1958.

14. *Ha-Zofeh*, January 2, 1958.

posals, namely, that the press should be held responsible
for printing unauthorized news of Cabinet meetings.[15] The
Progressives were eager to see a functioning coalition re-estab-
lished in order not to leave the country without properly constituted leadership. Although they were not especially happy
with the former leftist-oriented coalition that included the
Ahdut ha-'Avodah and the Mapam, they preferred it above a
narrow coalition with only the Mapai and the religious parties.
The Progressives made it clear that, should a narrow coalition
have to be established, they would demand firm assurances from
Mapai that the NRP would not be allowed to use its strengthened position to force its program on the coalition.[16]

In line with the fears expressed by the Progressives, a *Jerusalem Post* editorial stated that "it does not seem to be the right
moment for a practical minded Prime Minister to rid himself
of pressure exercised from the Left in such a manner as to ex-
pose his Government more than ever to pressure exercised by
the religious group. It is becoming clearer at every step that
coalition Government is Government by threat and extortion
and a daily invitation to political irresponsibility."[17]

Position of the Religious Parties

The NRP was perfectly content with the Cabinet crisis
brought about by the Ahdut ha-'Avodah and eagerly exploited
it in the following directions: It requested that the new government should consist "of all the elements that approve of high
ideals for this country."[18] This was elaborated on to mean that
the Agudah parties should be included in the new coalition. On
the other hand, it accused the Ahdut ha-'Avodah of political
immaturity and incompetence to assume the burden of collective Cabinet responsibility, and so it was not ready to become
a component element of a new coalition.

The NRP, cognizant of the fact that Ben-Gurion indicated
his unwillingness to sit in a Cabinet with the two Ahdut ha-

---

15. *Jerusalem Post*, January 6, 1958.
16. *Ibid.*, January 2, 1958.
17. *Ibid.*, December 19, 1957.
18. *Ha-Zofeh*, January 1, 1958.

'Avodah Ministers[19] and that he had no intention of including the General Zionists in his new government,[20] expected the formation of a narrow coalition. Indeed, they demanded that additional Ministers be allowed from their ranks, and should Ben-Gurion decide to continue the Cabinet with the present number of Ministers (twelve), it requested that additional portfolios be allocated to the religious Ministers in the Cabinet.[21]

In addition to these procedural considerations, the NRP made it clear that it accepted Ben-Gurion's invitation to participate in the new coalition on certain conditions. It demanded a Sabbath Observance Law, as well as an amendment to the Religious Schools Law, permitting the transfer of state schools from secular to religious supervision and vice versa at the request of the parents. The demand was all the more forceful in that it stipulated that this agreement be implemented within the next three months (!).[22]

In their response to Ben-Gurion's proposals regarding joint Cabinet responsibility, the NRP tacked on an amendment which would have imposed a limitation on the other coalition partners in spreading what the religious parties call "anti-religious propaganda."[23] The amendment was not accepted.

Toward Enforcement of Joint Cabinet Responsibility

On January 6, 1958, Ben-Gurion presented his reconstituted Cabinet to the Kneset for approval. It was approved the following day by a vote of seventy-six to thirty-three.[24] The Cabinet was identical in composition to its predecessor. The agreement, serving as the functioning basis of the coalition, was also inherited from its predecessor practically unchanged. The only change consisted in an addition to the article stating the procedural rule of joint Cabinet responsibility. It was presented by the Prime Minister to the Kneset as follows:

19. *Jerusalem Post,* December 19, 1957, editorial.
20. *Ibid.,* January 2, 1958.
21. *La-Merhav,* January 2, 1958.
22. *Ha-Zofeh,* January 6, 1958.
23. *La-Merhav,* January 5, 1958.
24. *Divrei ha-Kneset,* Third Kneset, 388th session, 23 (January 7, 1958): 590.

Collective responsibility will bind all the members of the Cabinet and the coalition parties to vote in the Kneset for all the decisions of the Government and laws proposed by it to the Kneset.

The Government may permit a party to abstain from voting in certain circumstances. A party may also permit one or several of its members to abstain from voting.

The details of such abstention and the circumstances under which it may be permitted will be determined by the Government.

If one or more Ministers feel themselves compelled to abstain from voting without the agreement of the Government, the Minister or Ministers concerned must resign from the Government.

A vote by a party against a Government decision shall be treated as equivalent to the abstention of a Minister without the agreement of the Government.

The Ministers bind themselves in accordance with the coalition agreement to preserve complete secrecy in regard to all deliberations in the Government and its committees in matters of security and foreign policy, without any exception.

If the Government decides that secrecy shall also apply to its deliberations on any other matter, the Ministers are also bound to secrecy in that case.

In order to guarantee the secrecy required, a State Secrets Law, applying both to the person revealing the secret and to the newspaper publishing it, will be submitted to the Kneset at the earliest possible moment on behalf of the coalition parties.

The Law will define those matters included in the category of state secrets the publication of which is forbidden. It will in any case include the deliberations of the Cabinet on matters of security and foreign affairs, as well as such other deliberations as the Government itself does not release for publication.[25]

Despite the best efforts of Ben-Gurion to reinforce collective responsibility, these articles were of dubious value. Ya'aqov Hazan of Mapam pointed out that, "In reality they will not strengthen the Government and he who builds its future on

---

25. *Israel Digest,* January 16, 1958, from *Divrei ha-Kneset,* Third Kneset, 387th session, 23 (January 7, 1958) :564.

them, builds castles on shifting sands."[26] The only remedy they proposed in case a Minister or a coalition party member wished to vote against the government or abstain on a no-confidence motion, was the pious wish that the member resign from the Cabinet. There was nothing new in this declaration. As early as February 21, 1950, in connection with a Cabinet crisis precipitated by the Religious Bloc, the Prime Minister presented to the Kneset in the name of the Cabinet a statement to the effect that any Minister "declining to implement decisions of the Cabinet shall be considered as having resigned."[27] It did not remedy the situation, as the crisis brought about by Ahdut ha-'Avodah in December 1957 amply demonstrated.

Results of the Crisis

If better coalition discipline could not be worked out, what, then, were the results of the crisis?

Mapai once again demonstrated the inability of the political system to maintain its equilibrium, despite the best efforts of the responsible parties involved. It could, therefore, proceed to agitate for a change in the electoral system in order to bring about a strong majority party that could create a government without bickering and compromise.

Ahdut ha-'Avodah proved to Mapai that it would not accept the position of a second-rate party in a government that can be overruled at Mapai's will. The government is not Mapai alone, but Mapai plus Ahdut ha-'Avodah and the other coalition partners who reached an agreement on a joint effort. By bringing the crisis about, Ahdut ha-'Avodah proved that its agreement must be obtained by the Prime Minister in all important matters of crucial importance to the security of the state.

The NRP succeeded in pressing forward with their demands regarding a Sabbath Observance Law and the religious school system. Though their requests were not put in a formal agreement, it is quite likely that they extracted oral promises from the Prime Minister that the passage of bills in these areas would

---

26. *Divrei ha-Kneset*, Third Kneset, 387th session, 23 (January 7, 1958) : 575.

27. *Ibid.*, First Kneset, 118th session (February 23, 1950) , p. 830.

be expedited.[28] Yizhaq Rafael of the NRP declared that "this Government will present to the Kneset a Sabbath Law whose need has become urgent because of the breaches in the wall of Sabbath observance . . . by the partial employ of trains, also in the work on the airfield, flights of El-Al planes and similar. The articles in the agreement concerning education that will be materialized shall offer legal right to transfer a school from one outlook to another at the request of the parents. . . . This Government will fulfill these (aspirations) without delay."[29]

The NRP had made it clear that it will consider itself freed of the principle of collective responsibility should any bill which conflicted with the Torah be presented by the government to the Kneset.[30] Within six months it faced a dilemma brought about by the instructions issued by the Ahdut ha-'Avodah Minister of Interior concerning registration of nationality, when the NRP declined to support the government in the Kneset.[31] However, prior to voting against the government, it voluntarily resigned from the coalition.[32]

28. *Ha-Zofeh,* January 7, 1958. *La-Merhav,* January 1, 1958, reported that the NRP received assurances from Mapai that their demands regarding Sabbath and the school system would be fulfilled.

29. *Divrei ha-Kneset,* Third Kneset, 387th session, 23 (January 7, 1958): 570.

30. *Ha-Zofeh,* January 7, 1958.

31. See Chapter 8, "Who Is a Jew?"

32. Yizhaq Rafael spoke up strongly in the Kneset against the Ahdut ha-'Avodah, declaring that it had shaken the foundation of the coalition more than once by its incitement against religion from sheer elementary ignorance of Judaism and its sources. *Divrei ha-Kneset,* Third Kneset, 387th session, 23 (January 7, 1958) :569. Answering, Yigal Alon of the Ahdut ha-'Avodah stated, "we have never denied, to the contrary, we confirm the privilege of every religious Jew and of every citizen of another faith to live according to his religion and conscience. We will not attempt to impose by law, on religious Jews, a way of life that is not welcome to them. . . . The thing we are fighting for is that the secular part of the population, Jew as well as non-Jew, should be granted the freedom to live according to its conscience and belief." *Ibid.,* p. 577.

13
Breach of Collective Responsibility: The Case of Outright Opposition

On July 5, 1959, Ben-Gurion submitted his resignation to the President following the refusal of four dissident Ministers to withdraw from the Coalition.[1] The Prime Minister's resignation, in accordance with the Transition Law 1949 (par. 11g), was tantamount to the resignation of the government.

The crisis resulted from a Kneset debate on a motion submitted by Ben-Gurion in behalf of the government. The motion read: "The Kneset opposes the cancellation of the sale of arms to the Federal German Republic."[2]

The emotional impact of the sale of arms to Germany, the country held responsible for the death of six million Jews during the Second World War, could not be underestimated. However, the transaction was considered so vital to Israel's security that the majority of the Cabinet, as well as the Foreign Affairs and Security Committee of the Kneset, decided in favor of it. After repeated discussions, the Cabinet resolved by majority on the eve of the Kneset debate unanimously to support the arms deal. Ministers who wished to take independent action,

---

1. *Davar,* July 6, 1959.
2. *Divrei ha-Kneset,* Third Kneset, 662nd session, 27 (June 30, 1959): 2393.

or whose parties would not concur with the Cabinet majority, were expected to resign before the decisive vote in the Kneset was taken. Despite all these preliminary arrangements, the Mapam and the Ahdut ha-'Avodah voted with the opposition and against the government of which they were members. Although the government policy was supported by a vote of 57 against 45 with six abstentions,[3] the breach of joint Cabinet responsibility by the four left-wing Ministers gave rise to a serious political crisis. An official Cabinet communiqué stated: "At the weekly Cabinet meeting held on July 5 under the chairmanship of the Minister of Finance, Levi Eshkol, it was decided that, in accordance with the terms of 'the coalition agreement and the principle of collective responsibility by which the Government operates under force of law, Ministers Bentov, Barzilai, Bar-Yehuda and Carmel are obliged to resign from the Government, and they are called upon to do so without delay.' "[4] The same communiqué repeated Ben-Gurion's warning that if the four Ministers did not resign, he would be forced to do so, thus bringing down the government.[5] A *Davar* editorial pointed out: "Is it possible to preserve a secure national existence under such a governmental system where anybody does as he pleases? Should not an end be put to that?"[6]

Because the Mapam and the Ahdut ha-'Avodah Ministers refused to abide by the Cabinet decision, Ben-Gurion submitted his letter of resignation to President Ben-Zvi the same evening.

Since the Cabinet Ministers and members of the Foreign Affairs Committee of the Kneset had full knowledge of the arms deal for six months[7] and new elections to the Kneset were expected to be held shortly, the outbreak of the Cabinet crisis was viewed as the beginning of the election campaign. In that light, Mapai charged its left-wing coalition partners with "ir-

3. *Ibid.*, 663rd session, 27 (July 1, 1959) :2416.

4. *Jerusalem Post,* July 6, 1959.

5. It should be noted that Article Four of the "Six Articles" agreement adopted in January 1958 by all coalition partners stated: "If any of the Ministers feel compelled to abstain from voting without the agreement of the Government, the Minister or Ministers concerned must resign from the Government." For details, see preceding chapter.

6. *Davar,* June 28, 1959.

7. *Ibid.*

responsibility of the highest level and with using security matters of supreme national importance for electioneering purposes."[8]

Toward New Elections: Courting the NRP

With the resignation of the Cabinet, interparty talks intensified in an attempt to establish a caretaker government for the period of national elections. Two alternatives were explored: The first would have centered around Mapai, with the General Zionists, the Progressives and the NRP as partners; the second would have included Mapam, Ahdut ha-'Avodah, Herut, and the NRP.[9]

Not one of the alternatives materialized, since the gap between the parties was too wide, and they preferred to keep their hands free for the election campaign. Nevertheless, there was one remarkable thing in the exploratory discussions for a caretaker government: both sides, Mapai as well as the opposition, counted on the NRP. It was the only party whose name was associated with both camps. Obviously, the NRP was a desirable coalition partner and available for a price that even the antireligious parties were willing to pay in order to secure control of the government.

On July 15, after consultation with leaders of all Kneset parties, the President requested Ben-Gurion to form a new government. Within a week Ben-Gurion informed the President of his inability to do so and was therefore returning the mandate with which he was entrusted. He was then instructed by the President to continue in office as the head of the caretaker government in its present constitution until a new government could be established after the elections to the Fourth Kneset.[10]

The election campaign was the longest and quietest on record. It held few surprises. One of them was the proliferation of parties in the campaign. Twenty-six lists of candidates were submitted to the Central Election Committee for approval.[11]

---

8. *Jerusalem Post,* June 28, 1959.
9. *Ibid.,* July 9, 1959.
10. *Davar,* July 22, 1959.
11. *Jerusalem Post,* September 9, 1959.

By contrast, only twenty were submitted for the 1951 election, and twenty-three for the elections in 1955. Of the twenty-six lists only twelve were represented in the Third Kneset. Seven were in existence since the inception of the Kneset in January 1949. This was sufficient indication that the nation was moving away from national consolidation. The Mapai organ *Davar* termed the phenomenon a pathological fissure in the country's edifice which could be cured only by a change in the electoral system.[12]

Indeed, the electoral system was one of the main issues in the election campaign. Mapai advocated the introduction of constituency elections in place of the present system wherein the whole country served as one constituency.[13] It was supported by the General Zionists in this endeavor.[14] On the other hand, the leftist parties were decisively opposed to such a change. The Mapam platform, as well as the party's foremost leaders, declared their uncompromising opposition to the method of constituency elections that "would not improve Israeli democracy and would not give it stronger foundations, but, instead, would destroy it."[15] Y. Tabenkin, the chief ideologist of the Ahdut ha-'Avodah, accused Mapai of advocating electoral reform in "an attempt to introduce the cult of the personality" and to concentrate absolute power in a Mapai government.[16] In its platform the Ahdut ha-'Avodah declared that "it will fight with all its strength against the goal of eradicating democracy by means of changing the electoral system of proportional representation to a system of constituency and majority elections."[17]

The Progressives shared the antipathy of the leftists toward electoral reform but for reasons of their own. The changes advocated by Mapai and the General Zionists, if translated into

---

12. *Davar*, September 9, 1959, editorial.
13. David Ben-Gurion, "Democracy in Danger," *Jerusalem Post*, September 11, 1959, p. 4.
14. *Jerusalem Post*, October 14, 1959.
15. *'Al ha-Mishmar*, October 9, 1959, "Platform of Mapam for the Fourth Kneset. "Also Ya'aqov Hazan in *Divrei ha-Kneset*, Fourth Kneset, 9th session, 28 (December 16, 1959) :98.
16. *Jerusalem Post*, October 7, 1959.
17. *La-Merhav*, October 16, 1959, "Platform of the Ahdut ha-'Avodah for the Fourth Kneset."

law, would have sounded the death knell of the small parties, including the Progressives.

Another main issue, besides the change in the electoral system, was the aspiration to change the complexion of government. In essence, the two were but corollaries of each other. The parties in favor of changing the system of elections were hoping to strengthen the government by eliminating small parties which barter their votes for concessions that seem crucial to them, at the expense of the majority and true democracy. The parties that were determined to preserve the functioning electoral system reasoned that the government would be strengthened and democracy would be saved if Mapai's power and dictatorial tendencies could be restrained.

A surprising factor in the election campaign was the extent to which the three major parties who aspired to form the next government courted the religious voters and their parties. Ben-Gurion announced in the Kneset that the question of "Who is a Jew," which motivated the NRP to withdraw from the coalition in June 1958, can be removed once and for all from the agenda. He intimated that arrangements in registering nationals would be made in conformity with religious law.[18] This announcement removed a major obstacle to the NRP's joining a Mapai-created coalition after the elections.

The General Zionists, who had repeatedly been criticized by religious spokesmen for their advocacy of civil marriage and for their opposition to religious aspirations, placed the son of Chief Rabbi Nissim on their list of candidates. This in itself would have caused a sensation, but in addition, the twenty-three-year-old Moshe Nissim was put high on the list, in the almost safe seventh place![19] The General Zionists hoped that their tactic would accomplish two things: it would attract the religious vote and, simultaneously, the vote of the Sephardi community of which Moshe Nissim was a member.

The Herut declared in its platform that "the instructions issued by the outgoing Government for the registration of the population should be declared null and void; (in heavy print:)

18. *Divrei ha-Kneset,* Third Kneset, 685th session, 27 (July 29, 1959) : 2782.
19. *Jerusalem Post,* September 11, 1959.

As far as a Jew is concerned there is no distinction between nationality and religion."[20] This was a provocative attempt to exploit the passions of the religious elements against Mapai, that were awakened in conjunction with the government instruction for registration and that conflicted with the religious definition of who is a Jew.

The courting of the religious adherents by the three largest parties contrasted with the sentiments of the population. The *Jerusalem Post* declared that "the majority of Israelis have come to be irritated beyond measure at all the pious filibustering that goes on—round the question of national service, the playground, the swimming-pool in the German Colony, the Haifa subway, and what not. The growing popular resentment against religion is alarming."[21]

The quote made reference to several irritants in religious-secular relations. The Jerusalem municipality intended to build a playground near the religious quarter of Meah Shearim. Religious militants objected, since it would injure their sensibilities to have a coeducational playground so close to their homes, and since it could also be considered a desecration of the Holy City. When it was made public that a swimming pool would be built in Jerusalem, the religious militants objected once again since it would be open to mixed bathing, which is forbidden by religious law and would undermine the morality of the population.[22] And when the long-awaited Haifa subway (the Carmelit) was ready for use, its opening had to be delayed because of the controversy over whether the Carmelit will operate on the Sabbath. In order to avoid stirring up a hornet's nest, a decision on the issue was postponed until after the elections. Till then the Carmelit was to rest from Friday afternoon till Saturday night. Each of these and similar issues awakened a storm of protest, with public demonstrations and boycotts on both sides. For example, the decision with regard to the Haifa subway brought a protest resignation from the

---

20. *Working Platform for a National-Liberal Government Headed by the Herut Movement.* Herut, 1959.

21. *Jerusalem Post,* October 2, 1959.

22. *Ha-Zofeh,* March 16, 1958. *Divrei ha-Kneset,* Third Kneset, 433rd session, 23 (March 12, 1958) :1274, discussion on Jerusalem swimming pool.

Deputy Mayor of Haifa, Y. Nussbaum, who represented Mapam in the City Council.[23]

The attitude of the former small coalition partners to the religious elements was more in line with popular sentiment. Mapam called for "the abolition of all coercion on one's conscience, full freedom for the secular and religious way of life, and a demand for a legal pledge to prevent religious coercion in the life of the citizen and the public."[24] Ahdut ha-'Avodah went somewhat further in its platform in demanding separation of state and religion and a secular imprint on the character of the state.[25] It also demanded civil marriage and divorce, and military or national service for Yeshiva (rabbinical) students.[26] The Progressives were more cautious. Their leader, P. Rosen, stated that he did not at present advocate separation between religion and state for fear of a possible aggravation of the prevailing tension around this problem. Then he added, "We will, however, demand freedom of action in the Cabinet and in the Kneset on all matters of principle connected with religion."[27] The implication was clear: even if the Cabinet should be forced to introduce legislation on religious issues, the Progressives declared that they would not support it.

The conclusion was inescapable that, though religion had become extremely controversial and was viewed in a negative light by the majority of the population, only the smaller parties dared to speak their mind concerning it. The larger parties, who had hopes of possibly forming the next government, had to court the religious parties because of their indispensability to a functioning coalition.

Post-Election Bargaining

Elections to the Fourth Kneset took place on November 3, 1959. Their results were most favorable to Mapai, which acquired 47 seats in the Kneset, an increase of seven over the

23. *Jerusalem Post,* October 9, 1959.
24. *'Al ha-Mishmar,* October 9, 1959, "Platform of Mapam for 4th Kneset."
25. *La-Merhav,* October 16, 1959.
26. *Jerusalem Post,* October 7, 1959.
27. *Davar,* October 23, 1959.

Third Kneset. When the five supporting Arab votes were added on, Mapai was only nine votes short of an absolute majority. Of the other parties, Herut gained two additional seats, increasing its total to 17, the NRP acquired 12, an increase of one, and the Progressives increased by one to six. Mapam remained unchanged with nine seats, so did the joint list of the Agudah parties, whereas Ahdut ha'Avodah lost three, dropping its representation to seven, the General Zionists dropped to eight from 13, and the Communists to three from six.

Bargaining for Power: Standpoint of Mapai

Mapai found itself in an extremely favorable bargaining position. It had no reason to expect any difficulty in picking up the necessary party or parties to give it a comfortable edge in the Kneset. The following alternatives were available: A coalition of Mapai with either Ahdut ha-'Avodah and Mapam, or with the General Zionists at the center. With its commanding lead of 52 votes Mapai was in no need of the NRP.

Two days after the elections a political observer stated: "One thing is clear: there is almost no likelihood that the outgoing Cabinet will be reconstituted. The most likely team is Mapai, Progressives, and the General Zionists."[28] The prognosticator felt on safe ground, since Ahdut ha-'Avodah had proved to be a most difficult partner. Twice it had broken the agreement on joint Cabinet responsibility and had succeeded in eliciting a statement from Ben-Gurion that he would not sit in one Cabinet with the Ahdut Ministers.

Hardly a week after the elections, Ben-Gurion unexpectedly announced that he was willing to forgive the left-wing parties and forget their slanders. But, he added, "you have to decide whether you are sitting in the coalition or in the opposition. You cannot have it both ways. The choice is in your hands."[29]

As in the past, at the time of constituting a government, Mapai declared that it hoped to establish a broad coalition to include all parties except Herut and the Communists. It then presented the parties that came into consideration with an out-

---

28. *Jerusalem Post*, November 5, 1959.
29. *Davar*, November 9, 1959.

line of its key principles on which the coalition was to be based. These principles were essentially similar to the program of the former government, with the following additions: the coalition shall introduce legislation leading to constituency elections, as well as to the enforcement of more stringent Cabinet responsibility.[30] Mapai also wanted the establishment of a state secondary school system that would offer free secular instruction.

Ben-Gurion went so far as to state that Mapai's main objective in the Fourth Kneset was to change "the accursed election system."[31] Only the General Zionists, however, saw eye to eye with Mapai on that issue. The two parties controlled altogether 60 votes, but, according to Kneset regulations, a change in the electoral system demanded an absolute majority of 61 votes.[32] All the other possible coalition partners were opposed to constituency elections.

Since the change of the electoral system was Mapai's main aim, it seemed plausible that the General Zionists should be their most desirable partner. Indeed, Ben-Gurion endeavored to come to a quick understanding with them, as well as with Agudat Israel and possibly the Progressives. In order to pacify the left wing of his own party, which preferred the leftist parties to the General Zionists in a coalition, he added the stipulation that some of the portfolios in the narrow coalition would remain unallocated and reserved for a short time, in case Mapam and Ahdut ha-'Avodah decided to join.[33]

However, Mapai's policy planning body, the "Havereinu," was opposed to a narrow coalition and asked Ben-Gurion to continue negotiations with the two leftist parties.[34]

Bargaining for Power: Standpoint of Agudat Israel

The first unconditional refusal to join the government came from Agudat Israel.[35] Mapai was willing to agree to only one

30. Ibid.
31. Jerusalem Post, November 9, 1959.
32. In the last stage of the Third Kneset, the so-called "Nir Bill" was passed with the singular aim in mind to thwart Mapai from introducing constituency elections.
33. Jerusalem Post, November 17, 1959.
34. Davar, November 18, 1959.
35. Ibid., November 20, 1959.

of the party's demands, namely, that government support for religious schools be increased to 85 percent. Concerning legislation for the strict observance of Sabbath, the imposition of severe limitations on postmortems, the prohibition of the sale of pork, the abolition of work permits for Jews on Sabbath, or the total exemption of girls from military service, Mapai would not make any promises beyond the assurance that they would be given further consideration by the next government.[36] Mapai regretted the negative decision of the Supreme Rabbinical Council, the highest authority of the Agudah party, since by reaching an agreement with the Agudah, it had hoped to outflank the demanding NRP. A week later the NRP decided to remain in opposition "for the time being," rather than serve in a government where it would be consigned to play a minor role.[37]

Bargaining for Power: Standpoint of the General Zionists

The refusal of the Agudat Israel to join the coalition did not at all diminish Mapai's hopes of attracting the General Zionists and the leftist parties into the government.

The real complications in the coalition talks began when the Ahdut ha-'Avodah and Mapam decided against joining a government that would include the General Zionists.[38] They were gravely concerned with the General Zionist demands and the compromises the socialist parties would have to make in the economic field. The General Zionists wanted the abolition of foreign currency controls, the nationalization of health services, the depolitization of the civil service, the reduction of military service for girls from two years to one year, and, above all, the reduction and the reform of income tax.[39] A Mapam leader stated, "With the exception of our mutual love for the nation, a mutual concern for the Jewish people and its security, and our encouragement of immigration, we have nothing in common regarding the ways and means of building up the nation,

---

36. *Jerusalem Post,* November 17, 1959.
37. *Ibid.,* November 27, 1959.
38. *Davar,* November 25, 1959.
39. *Jerusalem Post,* November 24, 1959.

safeguarding immigration and enhancing security. On these issues we differ absolutely. . . . The General Zionists cannot be with us together, even as we could not be with them together, in one Government."[40]

Within less than two weeks, the General Zionists turned around with identical objections against the leftist parties.[41] They declared themselves unwilling to join a government at whose center would be the three Labor parties, dominating the program, policies, priorities, and portfolios. They stated that "under the conditions proposed at present," and particularly since they were offered only one portfolio, they must decline the offer to join the government.[42]

Bargaining for Power: Standpoint of the Leftist Parties

The large selection of parties that Mapai seemed to have soon dwindled down to the two leftist parties. The Progressives, who were ready to join the government, were by themselves too weak to buttress Mapai's position.

Throughout the negotiations, the left-wing parties had been hedging over Mapai's proposals for tighter rules of collective Cabinet responsibility. Mapai insisted that the agreement reached by a former Cabinet,[43] calling upon Ministers and parties to resign from the government if they cannot actively back its policies, should be given the force of law. Mapam and Ahdut ha-'Avodah countered with the proposal that on specific issues where they would have to face a crisis of conscience— like foreign alliances, military treaties, relations with Germany, or military government over Arab-populated territories—they should have a right to vote against the government.[44] Eventually, a compromise formula was arrived at on Cabinet responsibility according to which Mapam and Ahdut ha-'Avodah were to be permitted to abstain in Kneset votes only on three

40. *Divrei ha-Kneset*, Fourth Kneset, 9th session, 28 (December 16, 1959) :98. Ya'aqov Hazan of Mapam.

41. *Jerusalem Post*, December 2, 1959.

42. *Davar*, December 4, 1959.

43. See preceding chapter, "Breach of Collective Responsibility: The Case of Indiscretion."

44. *Davar*, December 14, 1959.

issues: the question of the sale of arms to Germany, military government, and the support of pioneer youth movements in public schools. They would also be allowed to make statements to the Kneset explaining their abstention.[45]

Together with the two leftist parties and the Progressives, Mapai would have had 74 votes, offering the government a comfortable margin of safety. Only a week before the presentation of the new government to the Kneset, Ben-Gurion pulled the "biggest surprise of the week."[46] He called on the NRP for a meeting to further explore the possibility of its joining the government.[47]

Bargaining for Power: Standpoint of the National Religious Party

Though Mapai emerged from the Kneset elections only nine votes short of an absolute majority, it would have liked the partnership of the General Zionists. It badly needed their support for the contemplated change in the electoral system. It also wanted the Mapam and the Ahdut ha-'Avodah in order to balance the pressures for economic and social reforms from the General Zionists. With the expectation that both of these groups would join the government, Mapai felt that it could dispense with the NRP which, as usual, presented difficult and pressing demands to the government in the religious field.

In addition to its routine demands for a Sabbath law, or better supervision of autopsies, the NRP insisted on two things. First, it wanted to extend the system prevailing in the state elementary schools, with its special religious units, to the newly contemplated state secondary and vocational schools.[48] Second, it demanded the replacement of Rabbi Toledano, the nonparty, Mapai-supported Minister of Religious Affairs, by an NRP Minister.

45. *Ibid.*, December 16, 1959.
46. *Jerusalem Post*, December 11, 1959.
47. *Ha-Zofeh*, December 7, 1959.
48. *Ibid.* The NRP claim was that if the government should make secondary education obligatory without offering religious youth an opportunity for religious instruction on the secondary level, it would lead to outright and flagrant coercion of the affected children to abandon the religious way of life and to embrace secularism.

Mapai initially rejected both NRP demands. If their demands were fulfilled, the state secondary schools would be split into two sections, one following a secular and the other a religious curriculum. The state religious schools on all levels would then be under religious (NRP) control, to insure the hiring of a competent, religiously trained staff and the implementation of a religious curriculum. Mapai wished to avoid a permanent split in the state education system along political-religious lines and refused to go along with the NRP. When negotiations with the General Zionists and the leftist parties ran into serious snags, Mapai had no alternative but to compromise on the issue, if it wanted to present a government to the Kneset in the near future. An agreement was reached that was substantially in accord with NRP demands. The secondary school system would consist of two types of schools, the secular and the religious.

The same agreement provided for the final shelving of the question of "Who is a Jew?" that brought about a Cabinet crisis in June 1958. It also called for the establishment of a permanent Ministerial Committee of Five to examine problems in the religious sphere, particularly Bills and Regulations coming from the Ministry of Religious Affairs. It declared that a committee would be established to examine the question of autopsies, which would not be permitted without the consent of the deceased person's family, that a Sabbath observance law would be duly legislated, and that "status quo" in matters of religion would be guaranteed in the government program.[49]

On the question of the Ministry of Religious Affairs the NRP attitude did not prevail, although an NRP leader expressed his hope that there, too, changes will occur to his party's satisfaction.[50] Mapai insisted upon the retention of Rabbi Toledano as Minister of Religious Affairs. The only concession it made was the establishment of a Ministerial Committee to examine problems in the sphere of religion. Among the problems to be examined were the new regulations issued by Rabbi Toledano for the impending election of a new Chief Rabbi in

---

49. *Ma'ariv,* December 11, 1959. Also *Ha-Zofeh,* December 15, 1959.
50. *Divrei ha-Kneset,* Fourth Kneset, 10th session, 28 (December 17, 1959) : 120. Z. Warhaftig of NRP.

246 THE POLITICS OF COMPROMISE

Israel. The regulations would have given the Minister of Religious Affairs, a government servant, ultimate control over the election procedure and a decisive vote in the selection of candidates. The NRP strenuously objected to the relegation of the Chief Rabbinate to a position subordinate to the government and its employees,[51] especially since the Ministry was not in their hands. Mapai, however, remained obdurate, offering NRP, at best, a Deputy Ministership of Religious Affairs.[52]

The Government and its Program

On December 16, 1959, Ben-Gurion presented the new government and its program to the Kneset. The portfolios were distributed among the coalition parties as follows: Mapai—9; NRP—2; Mapam—2; Ahdut ha-'Avodah—1; Progressives—1; nonparty—1. The Cabinet of sixteen Ministers commanded the support of 86 votes in the Kneset.

Basic Principles of the Government Program

In place of the brief statement of former government programs, calling for joint responsibility of all members of the Cabinet and their affiliated parties in the Kneset, the new program projected an amendment to the Transition Law that would authorize the Prime Minister to dismiss a Minister breaking the agreement of collective responsibility. The proposed amendment read as follows:

Collective responsibility is obligatory for members of the Cabinet and the representatives of their parties in the Kneset. A vote in the Kneset by a member of the Cabinet or the representatives of his party in the Kneset against a decision of the Cabinet, or abstention from voting in the Kneset by a member of the Cabinet or the representatives of his party in the Kneset on a decision of the Cabinet without the Cabinet's permission, shall be equivalent to the resignation of that member of the Cabinet. This resignation shall take effect on

51. *Ma'ariv*, December 9, 1959.
52. Conflict between Chief Rabbinate and the Ministry described in Chapter 5.

its announcement by the Prime Minister in the Kneset. This announcement shall not require the approval of the Kneset.[53]

Incorporated in the program was a waiver of Cabinet responsibility "on the question of the electoral system." Since all of Mapai's partners were unalterably opposed to it, Mapai had to offer them "complete freedom" on the matter.

Although the term "status quo" had been frequently applied to religion, for the first time a government program unequivocally stated: "The Government will maintain the status quo in the state in matters of religion" (Chapter 8, 62). Two other articles on "religion in the state," guaranteeing prevention of "any religious or antireligious coercion from whatever side it may come," were taken over from the government program of November 1958.

The articles providing for "Compulsory Health Insurance" were another novel feature of the program (Chapter 9, 63–66). A National Insurance Law would provide "health insurance for the ctizens of the state as a whole" without, however, interfering in the functioning of the existing sick-funds maintained by the Histadrut for its members.

One brief article in the government program declared that "No party propaganda will be permitted among the pupils in state schools of all kinds" (Chapter 6, 58).

The balance of the government program established basic principles in economics, foreign affairs, immigration, education, civil service, basic laws, and minorities that did not differ essentially from the basic principles of the former government. According to a member of the opposition, "anyone could subscribe to them without protest, from Member of Kneset Bernstein (General Zionist) to Member of Kneset Mikunis (Communist). None would have any objections to them. Everything is smooth, everything is optimistic, everything is good, everything is general, everything is without content."[54]

The controversial issues that caused difficulties in the formation of the government and that could threaten its survival

---

53. "Basic Principles of Government Program," approved by the Kneset on December 17, 1959. *Israel Government Yearbook 5720 (1959/60)*, p. 89.

54. *Divrei ha-Kneset*, Fourth Kneset, 11th session, 28 (December 17, 1959) :123. Y. Bader of Herut.

were hardly touched upon in the government program. They were embodied, instead, in separate coalition agreements between Mapai and the parties of the coalition.

Analysis of New Government

Contrary to expectations, Mapai's numerical preponderance offered no real advantage in the formation of the new government and in the realization of its goals. Mapai's main objective, to change the electoral system, could not be accomplished since, together with the General Zionists, it would have been one vote short of the required majority. The lack of one vote was sufficient to defeat Mapai's purpose. Since the other prospective coalition partners were unequivocally opposed to a change in the electoral system, Mapai had to guarantee them in the government program "complete freedom on the question," should it ever come up for a vote in the Kneset.

Despite Mapai's voting strength, it was unable to make its weight felt during the coalition bargaining any more than in the past. It seems that Mapai's increase in strength worked to its disadvantage since it motivated the coalition parties to secure their positions in clearly defined coalition agreements and in more advantageous portfolios.

An agreement between the leftist parties and Mapai undermined Mapai's attempt to tighten Cabinet discipline which it wished to accomplish through the passage of a new law demanding better enforcement of collective responsibility. Relations between Ahdut ha-'Avodah and Mapam, on the one hand, and Mapai, on the other, were further strained at the session when the Cabinet was presented to the Kneset. Their speakers spent more time expostulating their differences concerning collective responsibility than their underlying unity. Despite the exceptions allowed in the agreement, Mapai managed to incorporate in the government program provisions for collective responsibility, promising a more stable Cabinet Government for the future.

The Progressives extracted an agreement from Mapai entitling them to follow the dictate of their conscience and permitting them to disagree with the Cabinet on matters of religion. In return, the Progressives renounced their demand for the complete nationalization of the existing sick funds, particularly those of the Histadrut.

The agreement with the NRP threatened to be the most costly to Mapai, since it was diametrically opposed to prevailing popular sentiment. It guaranteed religious entrenchment on the secondary school level and the introduction of a Sabbath observance law.

A *Jerusalem Post* editorial expressed dread at such a prospect.

> The present Sabbath restrictions already put Israel back into the Middle Ages for some thirty-six hours each week. Ships do not dock, aircraft do not take off, passenger trains do not run, and bus transport, with few exceptions, does not function, although "sherut" taxis do. Telegrams and cables are not delivered, so that messages concerning matters of life and death may be hopelessly delayed.[55]

Yet, the religious parties want a Sabbath Law that would largely abolish the operation of many functions of state and industry and, in addition, they demand the splitting of the secondary schools into two separate units.

> In the past, numerical necessity has too often forced him (Ben Gurion) to narrow his broad vision by compromise. With the direct command of 52 seats out of the 61 needed for an absolute majority in the Kneset, the Prime Minister no longer need allow any considerations to weigh other than those of principle. The present freedom to maneuver should make it possible to admit the religious parties to the Government only on condition that religious observance remains a matter for the individual to decide for himself.[56]

Mapai's command of fifty-two votes, contrary to the great expectations of Mapai and its sympathizers, did not free it of its dependence on the religious parties. Mapai leaders recognized that "if the NRP secured sixty-one seats, it would certainly have installed Orthodoxy officially, and not been content

55. *Jerusalem Post*, November 24, 1959.
56. *Ibid.*

to make sure of freedom of religious practice for those who want it." Mapai, however, found the NRP indispensable as a counterweight to the leftist parties in the coalition.[57]

Although Mapai bowed to numerous demands of its partners in the coalition agreements and in the government program, in the realm of portfolios it did not yield at all. Ahdut ha-'Avodah's demand for two portfolios, one of them the Ministry of Agriculture, was rejected outright. Instead, they had to be content with the Ministry of Transport alone.[58] Mapam had to accept the Ministry of Development without the district of Eilat, which was going to be annexed to the Ministry of Commerce and Industry, in the hands of a Mapai Minister. The NRP was given the important Ministry of Interior and the Ministry of Posts. Its attempts to acquire the Ministry of Religious Affairs were foiled. Mapai left it in the hands of the nonparty Minister, Rabbi Toledano. The Progressives once again inherited the Ministry of Justice. Mapai was willing to bend on principles; it was not willing to relinquish power.

57. *Ma'ariv,* December 11, 1959. Article by Moshe Dayan of Mapai.
58. *Jerusalem Post,* December 13, 1959.

Part IV
Religion and State in Israel

The religious establishment, or institutionalized religion, which includes the religious parties, the Ministry of Religious Affairs, the Rabbinical Councils, the Rabbinical Courts, and the Chief Rabbinate, has asserted itself in the affairs of the nation most conspicuously through coalition politics. With its process of bargaining accompanying the formation, composition, and functioning of government, coalition politics has offered the religious parties the opportunity to embody religious standards into the laws of the state. The configuration of political forces, with Mapai (now Israel Labor Party) as the only party able to form a government and succeeding thus far only with the cooperation of the religious parties, has given the religious parties the leverage and power to attain many of their objectives.

The power of the religious parties has asserted itself most forcefully and decisively on the Cabinet level, since the Cabinet has been the fulcrum of power in the state. In return for their support of Mapai in the government, the religious parties were able to obtain many concessions. These included the maintenance of status quo, which meant the safeguarding of the whole autonomous religious establishment inherited from the British Mandate, the defeat of a written constitution, the determination of "Who is a Jew?" in terms of religious law, and many more.

The Arab-Israeli war of June 1967 did not affect the power of the religious parties to any noticeable extent. The war resulted in a stunning victory by Israel over its Arab belligerents on all fronts. In the course of six days the defense forces of Israel occupied the Sinai Peninsula from Egypt, the Golan Heights from Syria, and recaptured the Old City of Jerusalem and the western bank of the river Jordan from the Kingdom of Jordan.

Though the Six Day War and the international crisis that preceded it elicited a response of national unity in Israel, they contributed little to the elimination of the religious problem of the Israeli society. Indications suggest the reverse. Possession of the Western (commonly referred to as the Wailing) Wall in Jerusalem offered new ground for acrimony between the religious and the secular elements. They have differed on the interpretation whether the Wall is a religious or national shrine. If it is the former, access to the greater part of the Wall could be barred for women, and archeologists could be prohibited from conducting excavations at the site by the Ministry of Religious Affairs. If it is the latter, anyone could approach any section of the Wall and archeological digs could be undertaken by permission of the Ministry of Interior.

Another novel problem arose with the administrative unification of the Old (Arab) and the New (Jewish) sectors of Jerusalem. In the divided city the religious elements could demand Sabbath observance in public places. In the united city, could anything be done to close the night spots on Friday evening, or at least bar Jews residing in the New City from crossing into the Old City and, in violation of a religious prohibition, enjoy the night clubs?

The intensification of the Arab-Israel conflict brought to the fore another problem from an unexpected source. In order to counter the blast of Arab propaganda, that penetrates many homes of Arab residents in Israel by means of television, the Kneset voted to extend Israel's TV broadcasting from six to seven days a week. Religious opposition, on the grounds that this is a breach in the "status quo" and an official act of Sabbath desecration, was fierce. The seven-day broadcasting was to begin, by enormous miscalculation, during the week of Kneset elections. This circumstance immediately projected the issue into the political arena, making it a trump card for bargaining. The religious parties extorted a concession from Prime Minister Meir that the first of the Sabbath broadcasts would be postponed until the establishment of a new government. Only owing to a direct Court order, in contravention of the Prime Minister's promise and religious protests, did the Sabbath broadcast get under way as scheduled.

In similar instances lie the seeds for future coalition bargaining, which may require a reinterpretation of the "status quo" and the application of ingenuity by the party negotiators. In other terms, herein lies the danger of possible further violation of the democratic system through governmental interference with the private actions of individuals—actions that would have no direct bearing on the public good.

14

Coalition Government After the Election to the Sixth Kneset

The new configuration of political forces that emerged during the Sixth election on November 2, 1965, did not alter the pattern of Cabinet formation or functioning. Neither did the religious parties mellow and learn to respect the wishes of the majority. In the attempt to create a new government after the election to the Sixth Kneset, the religious parties posed the most serious obstacles to the Prime Minister designate Levi Eshkol.[1] They forced him to apply for an extension of the permissible time limit allowed for the creation of a government. Their demands included a strict Sabbath observance law, a restrictive anatomy and pathology law, a higher budgetary allowance for religious education, and the closing of the new Port Ashdod on Sabbath.

The renewal of the demand for a Sabbath observance law came about in a characteristic manner. The coalition agreement of the former government in November 1961 between Mapai and the NRP included the adoption of a Sabbath law. The matter, however, received low priority on the legislative agenda of the Cabinet. It became a subject of protracted maneuvering between the Minister of Religious Affairs, Zerah Wahrhaftig (NRP), and the Labor Minister, Yigal Allon (Ahdut ha-

---

1. Although elections to the Sixth Kneset were held on November 2, 1965, the Thirteenth Government was presented to the Kneset on January 12, 1966.

'Avodah), each of whom demanded the right to be in control
of the proposed draft measure. After much procrastination the
Labor Minister submitted a bill which was found unacceptable
by the NRP. The Prime Minister then appointed a committee
headed by Mapai Kneset whip, Israel Kargman, to draft a
compromise measure. His intention was to bury the issue in
committee.

An unexpected circumstance came to the aid of the NRP.
Herut introduced a motion of no-confidence in the Kneset
concerning a recent remark by Levi Eshkol that "things were
not in order" during Ben-Gurion's reign. Levi Eshkol solicited
the support of the NRP to vote down the opposition. The NRP,
capitalizing on the situation, made the passing of the Sabbath
law the condition for its support. Mapai was immediately forced
into action.

The NRP wanted closing strictures imposed on cafés, restaurants, pharmacies, medical facilities, beaches, and soccer games,
in addition to those already applied elsewhere. No theaters
were to perform on Friday evening; music was to be prohibited
in hotels and restaurants, and non-Jews were to be forbidden
to work in Jewish areas. The NRP also demanded that the
Minister of Religious Affairs should have a decisive influence
in the implementation of the law. Mapai, however, was only
willing to "freeze" the existing status quo without additional
concessions and with the Labor Minister in charge of the bill.
It was only due to the filibustering tactics of Labor Minister
Alon that a new draft law on Sabbath observance did not
reach the floor of the Kneset before its closing session.[2]

Frustrated by their setback, the religious parties stiffened
their demand for the necessary guarantees that a Sabbath bill
be given high priority. They insisted on these guarantees before
joining the new government.[3] A compromise was eventually
worked out between the Ma'arakh (alignment) and the NRP
on the eve of the new government's presentation to the Kneset.
According to the compromise, new regulations would be introduced in the form of an amendment to the Work Hours and
Rest Law. They would prohibit the operation of any plant

2. *Jerusalem Post,* July 2, 1965.
3. *New York Times,* November 28, 1965.

on Sabbath, even in irreligious settlements, unless classified as essential by the Minister in charge of the bill's implementation.[4]

A half year before the sixth Kneset elections, spokesmen of the various religious parties were already arguing as to who had done most "against the stain of post-mortem operations."[5] This was clearly competitive election propaganda. Nevertheless, the religious parties, charging large-scale abuses of the autopsy provisions, launched a concerted effort to introduce drastic changes in the Anatomy and Pathology Law.[6] The main objective was to reduce autopsies to a minimum. Professor Henry Ungar, the head of the Pathology Department of the Hebrew University Medical School, concerned with the progress of medical science in Israel, stated, "If we cease performing post-mortems, we will be accepting responsibility bordering on murder."[7]

As with the Sabbath law, so also with regard to autopsy, the Ma'arakh agreed to initiate amendments imposing severe restrictions on post-mortems. The implementation of the law was to be in the hands of the Minister of Health. Once again the "Ministerial factor" proved decisive. As long as Moshe Shapiro of the NRP was Minister of Health things were quiet. When Israel Barzilai of Mapam succeeded him, however, the ultra-Orthodox charged that the number of post-mortems had drastically increased.[8] It was expected that the issue would crop up again with the next Cabinet crisis.

Demands for additional budgetary allocations for religious education came from two sources: the NRP wanted the funds in order to extend religious studies in the state religious primary schools by two hours a week; the Po'alei Agudat Israel requested increased aid for the private religious schools. The Ma'arakh declined the NRP demand, since any additional allocation for one part of the national system would have necessitated a proportional allocation for the other, costing 20 million pounds.[9] The Ma'arakh–Po'alei Agudat Israel agree-

4. *Jerusalem Post*, January 11, 1966.
5. *Ibid.*, May 28, 1965.
6. *Laws of the State of Israel* 7 (August 26, 1953) :135.
7. *Jerusalem Post*, July 2, 1965.
8. *New York Times*, September 23, 1966.
9. *Jerusalem Post*, December 5, 1965.

ment, however, accorded additional financial support for the private ultra-orthodox school network.[10]

Perhaps the most controversial issue in the negotiations between the Ma'arakh and the religious parties was the matter of Port Ashdod, a new harbor whose opening coincided with the creation of the new government. The religious parties demanded that the status quo applied to the Jaffa—Tel Aviv harbor be extended to Ashdod and that, consequently, the port should be closed to all shipping beginning with sunset on Friday afternoon through Sabbath. The Ma'arakh, concurring with the view of the Ports Authority, wished to abide by the status quo in accordance with the Haifa model, where work has been carried on late into the night on Friday.[11] According to experts, Israel shipping has been suffering a loss of one million dollars yearly by forbidding ships to enter ports on Sabbath. It was also noted that such a prohibition is contrary to shipping regulations in all countries.[12]

Religious leaders did not deny the loss to the country's economy resulting from the closing of the harbor. Ya'aqov Katz, of the Po'alei Agudat Israel, admitted in a Kneset debate that holding up a ship for one day would cost the state 3000 pounds, but who would dare to say that observing the Sabbath is not worth more than that? he asked dramatically.[13] Zerah Wahrhaftig, the Minister of Religious Affairs, adopted the same idealistic approach, stating that it is not a necessity to operate the port on Friday afternoons, since all that was involved was merely a matter of money and the state could make up the difference.[14]

Once again the religious parties attained most of their ob-

---

10. *Ibid.*, December 6, 1965.
11. *Ibid.*, December 14, 1965.
12. *Yediot Aharonot*, March 11, 1965.
13. *Jerusalem Post*, December 16, 1965.
14. *Ibid.*, December 15, 1965. Another maritime problem that led to a minor government crisis resulted from the prohibition of the Rabbinate to approve two kitchens, a kosher and a nonkosher one, on the Zim Line ship *Shalom*. Similar recognition has been granted to foreign-owned vessels. The government initially favored two kitchens for practical purposes. However, under religious pressures the government changed its mind and the SS *Shalom* could operate only a kosher kitchen, which is usually more expensive. As a result the ship could not compete with other lines, and had to be sold at a loss by the Zim Lines.

jectives, despite the fact that it was the first time in six Kneset elections that the NRP lost votes and had to relinquish one of its seats in the Kneset. Repeatedly, the attainments of the religious parties were recognized not as a triumph of religious rights but as a victory for political extortion. The *Jerusalem Post* wrote: "These matters involve major issues concerning the economy as a whole, and they cannot be settled by a public last minute ultimatum and threats not to re-enter the Government, nor can any government expect to survive for long if it yields to such threats."[15]

In the establishment of this government, more than ever before, secular parties protested against the coercion used by the religious parties. Gideon Hausner, of the Independent Liberal Party, spoke in favor of joining the Cabinet in order to prevent the adoption of new religious legislation.[16] Mapam insisted, as a condition for joining the government, that the status quo on religious questions should not be changed.[17] The minor partner in the Ma'arakh, the Ahdut ha-'Avodah, initially also urged the exclusion of the NRP from the coalition. In his own Mapai Party, Levi Eshkol was confronted by a group of younger members of Kneset, trying to persuade him to consider the creation of a coalition without the NRP.[18] These strong secular pressures were neutralized, however, by cross-currents of political aspirations. Thus, despite the strong vocal opposition, the NRP could further its objectives.

Though initially opposed to the NRP, after almost two months of negotiations with the various parties, the Ahdut ha-'Avodah was ready to accept a compromise with the religious parties. This was because of its apprehension that a narrow coalition may be forced to seek Rafi's support—a grave threat to the maintenance of the Ma'arakh.[19] Simultaneously, Pinhas Sapir, the Minister of Finance, "expressed apprehension at the difficulties on the economic front that a narrow-based government might encounter," because of the influence of left-wing Mapam

15. *Ibid.*, editorial.
16. *Ibid.*, December 3, 1965.
17. *Ibid.*, November 10, 1965.
18. *Ibid.*, November 30, 1965.
19. *Ibid.*, December 28, 1965.

ana Ahdut ha-'Avodah.[20] In order to protect the government (that is, Mapai) from left-wing pressures, including the influence of the Ma'arakh partner, Ahdut ha-'Avodah, the incorporation of the NRP became a strategic necessity. Since Mapai, for the first time, had no more than a parity in the coalition, nine out of 18 Ministers, the indispensability of the NRP became very real.

Certainly, the NRP also had to make concessions to its partners. At the demand of Ahdut ha-'Avodah, no separate agreement was to be reached between the NRP and the Ma'arakh's Mapai section which would be kept secret from the other coalition partners.[21] More painful to the NRP was the demand of the Ma'arakh that the Chief Rabbinate should not have the final say in matters of dispute concerning the Kashrut Law and that an appellant should have the right to appeal to the High Court.[22] According to a Mapam spokesman, a coalition agreement provided that "the Rabbinate will not be able to revoke a *hehsher* [imprimatur necessary for the service of kosher food] given to hotels or other establishments for reasons unrelated to actual kashrut observance. . . . Heretofore a hotel could lose its *hehsher* if it opened its cabaret on Friday night. Now the only criterion of kashrut will be observance of dietary laws."[23] Thus, the NRP had to yield on some issues in order to make strides in others.

In the balance, when "after nearly two months of wrangling, the tortuous stylized dance of establishing a new coalition was finally reaching a successful end,"[24] two things were certain: the cleavage between the religious and the nonreligious was as great as ever, and there was, as yet, no end to the erosion of individual freedom of the nonobservant section of the population. This was manifest not only on the Cabinet, but also on the non-Cabinet level.[25]

Sixteen months after its inception the Thirteenth Govern-

20. *Ibid.,* December 24, 1965.
21. *Ibid.,* January 2, 1966.
22. *Ibid.,* December 5, 1965.
23. *Ibid.,* January 21, 1966.
24. *Ibid.,* December 31, 1965.
25. See Part IV, Chapter 15 for "Religious Problems on the Non-Cabinet Level."

ment terminated on May 31, 1967, during a grave international crisis threatening the existence of Israel. Owing to Arab threats, to the withdrawal of United Nations Emergency Forces from Gaza, Sinai, and Sharm-al-Sheik, to the imposition of a blockade on the Gulf of Aqaba by Egypt, to the entry of Iraqi and Saudi troops into Jordan, and to the signing of a mutual defense pact between King Hussein and President Nasser, Levi Eshkol moved to establish a broadly based Government of National Unity. The Prime Minister invited Rafi and Gahal to join the government, offering Rafi the portfolio of the Foreign Minister, and the Gahal two Ministerships without portfolio. Rafi rejected the proposal. Simultaneously, the Independent Liberal Party and the National Religious Party threatened to withdraw from the coalition should Rafi's Moshe Dayan, the hero of the Sinai Campaign of 1956, not be offered the Ministry of Defense. Within Mapai a bitter debate ensued over the portfolio of Defense. Levi Eshkol, supported by the Secretary General of the party, Mrs. Golda Meir, opposed giving the vital portfolio to Rafi. However, yielding to Mapai circles that were hopeful of a rapprochement with Rafi and to strong popular pressure, the Prime Minister called upon Moshe Dayan to accept the portfolio of Defense. Dayan accepted, and on June 2 the reconstituted Cabinet was presented to the Kneset as the Fourteenth Government of Israel. A half year later the Mapai, Rafi and Ahdut ha-'Avodah parties announced their merger into the newly formed Israel Labor Party.

The Fourteenth Government had several unique characteristics: It was the largest Cabinet to date, consisting of twenty-one members; it included all the parties except the Communists; it was the first time that the portfolio of Defense was entrusted to a non-Mapai Minister; and it was the first Cabinet in which Mapai did not have at least a parity of Ministers.

Toward the Seventh Kneset

The government of National Unity was established on June 1, 1967 in response to Arab threats to the survival of the State of Israel that required the mobilization and concentration of all available resources. After the peak of the crisis, the broad-based coalition government was maintained in order to cope more effectively with the sustained emergency of the post Six-Day War phase of the Arab-Israel conflict.

Hardly were the guns silenced on the Golan Heights when the Mapai Secretariat unanimously decided to pursue merger negotiations with its Alignment partner, Ahdut ha-'Avodah, and with its socialist offspring party, Rafi, which split off from Mapai on the eve of the elections to the Sixth Kneset. Mapam was also approached regarding the merger. The wave of euphoria and good will that enveloped Israel as a result of its astounding victory was conducive to the delicate merger negotiations. However, it took over five months to hammer out a merger agreement with Ahdut ha-'Avodah and Rafi.

At the Rafi convention in December 1967 the merger proposal slipped through with a bare majority (58 percent) in favor. It took Mapam another ten months to commit itself to an alignment with the newly formed Israel Labor Party.

The Labor-Mapam Alignment commanded a majority of 63 votes in the Kneset. For the first time in Israel's history a majority government became a real prospect, eliminating future dependence on the minor parties. Hardest hit by this turn of events would have been the NRP, which benefited most by Mapai's dependence on its support.

The interests of the religious parties and of the Mapai became diametrically opposed regarding the success of the merger. The NRP had cause for concern that its fortunes would be adversely affected by the presence and influence of anti-religious groups in the inner councils of the dominant Labor party. Indeed, Meir Ya'ari, the leader of Mapam, declared that "our Kneset majority will stop the blackmail of the clericalists and the reactionaries." Though Mr. Ya'ari promised that his party would not press for separation of religion and state because the country could ill afford a struggle on this subject at present, this was meager comfort to the religionists. Nor was the Mapai Secretary General's, Golda Meir's, assurance that efforts would be made to maintain NRP participation in the government able to dispel NRP forebodings. Their concern was warranted, especially since, in the same statement, Mrs. Meir voiced agreement with Mr. Ya'ari that the new Labor alignment would deprive the religious parties of their advantageous position of holding the balance in Israel's politics.

Minister of Interior and leader of the NRP, Haim Moshe Shapiro, voiced the sentiments of the religious groups when he declared that, "the alignment of Mapam with the Labor party will certainly not be to the country's good." He expressed faith in the establishment of a united religious front that, under the circumstances, had become crucial to combat opposition to the religionists. The NRP leader, together with other nonsocialist party leaders, was hopeful and guardedly confident that labor unity would not last. This hope was not mere wishful thinking.

From the very outset, the factions of the Labor party did not present a solid phalanx. Though the merger on the party machine level was complete, the constituent factions agreed that each group would be allowed to establish an ideological circle within the framework of the broader party, to continue the separate identity of their youth movements, and to maintain their newspapers and kibbutz organizations (for Mapai, Ihud ha-Kibbutzim; for Ahdut ha-'Avodah, Kibbutz ha-Me'uhad). However, even on the political level, where the party strove for the attainment of complete unity, seething conflicts soon became noticeable. These could be classified as twofold: disagreements regarding national policy and personal rivalries among the leaders of the factions. On occasion, the two areas overlapped and national policy problems became intensified because of personal antagonisms.

Disagreements over national policy were slow in emerging. They centered around Israel's attitude to the administered territories and around the United Nations Security Council Resolution of November 22, 1967. The initial readiness of the Israel leaders to return to the Arab countries a substantial portion of the territory occupied in the June '67 war for a reciprocal peace treaty underwent substantial modification in the face of increasing Al Fatah terrorism, the implacable hostility of the neighboring Arab governments, the one-sided resolutions of the United Nations, and the involvement of the Great Powers.

There appeared to be unanimous agreement in the Cabinet

that Israel would keep Jerusalem, Gaza, and the Golan Heights. Regarding the Western Bank, opinions differed. Allon, the leader of Ahdut ha-'Avodah and Minister of Labor, proposed the creation of a string of paramilitary settlements along the Jordan River that would encircle the Western Bank, except for a corridor connecting it with Jordan. Upon reaching an agreement that the disputed territories be demilitarized, Israel would return them to King Hussein.

Dayan, the leader of Rafi, as Minister of Defense in charge of the administered areas, pursued a policy aiming at co-existence and integration of the Arabs into the Israel labor market and economy. The objective of Dayan's policy may have been eventual complete integration of the administered areas into Israeli life on all levels.

Sapir, a star leader of Mapai and Minister of Finance, supported by Foreign Minister Abba Eban, objected strongly to Dayan's policy of economic integration. Sapir saw a grave security risk in the Arabs who were allowed to work in Israel. He further contemplated and feared the eventual Arabization of Israel by sheer weight of numbers, should complete annexation of the territories be undertaken.

The NRP and the Gahal supported Dayan's policy in the Cabinet. They soon discovered that their strategy served a dual purpose. It allowed them to pursue their objectives of working toward the annexation of the administered areas, and it helped to bring to the fore and sharpen the cleavage in the Labor alignment.

The Labor ranks were beset by bitter personal rivalries. After the June '67 war, the rumor became widespread that Mr. Eshkol would not aspire for another term as Prime Minister after the 1969 parliamentary elections. Immediately, three aspirants sprang up, Allon, Dayan, and Sapir. Of the three, Dayan seemed to have the greatest popular backing. He was the mastermind of the '56 Sinai Campaign and his name was flatteringly associated with the victorious '67 Six Day War. His followers began taunting Eshkol, claiming that he was not fit for the Prime Ministership, and demanding that he resign in favor of Dayan. These taunts only strengthened Eshkol's distaste for Dayan, whom he thoroughly distrusted for several reasons. Dayan had betrayed him by helping to form the anti-Eshkol Rafi party and by forcing him out of the Defense Ministry at a critical juncture on the eve of the 1967 war, snatching from him the personal laurels of victory. Furthermore, upon returning to the Mapai, Dayan expressed his intention of forcing the party to reform from within by making the Rafi platform its own.

In June 1968 Eshkol took a step to strengthen Allon's position vis-à-vis Dayan by appointing him Deputy Prime Minister and Minister of Absorption. The action was first approved by the Labor Party Leadership Bureau attended by all labor ministers except Dayan. The six former Rafi members of the Bureau were also absent. The NRP, Gahal, and Independent Liberal Party members of the Cabinet protested that they were not consulted on the Premier's action and that the move was highly irregular. Less than two months later, a second reshuffle occurred in the Cabinet when Pinhas Sapir was appointed Labor Party Secretary General and Minister without Portfolio, with his portfolio of Finance transferred to Mapai Minister of Commerce and Industry, Ze'ev Sharef.

In September 1968, Eshkol established a new Cabinet Committee to wield overall authority in the administered areas. Its unmistakable intent was to curtail the authority and power of Dayan as Defense Minister.

In January 1969, when the Labor-Mapam Alignment was completed, Mapam, with eight members in the Kneset, received six places in the top ranking "Management" bureau of the party, whereas Dayan's Rafi Party, with nine members in the Kneset, had only two. Despite Rafi protests, the Labor leadership did not yield, evidently considering Mapam a valuable ally against Dayan and his faction.

Only one week later, Allon, by a clever maneuver, scaled even higher on the ladder of power. By resigning from four key Ministerial Committees, claiming to have been slighted, he forced the Cabinet, over the protests of the NRP, Gahal, and the Independent Liberal Party, to offer him the post of Arab affairs and probable access to all information pertaining to security and defense. Simultaneously, anti-Dayan groups were being formed by Allon and Sapir supporters and pronouncements against the "frightening phenomenon of the personality cult" grew louder.

On February 26, 1969 Prime Minister Levi Eshkol died of a heart attack. The struggle for the premiership that would have splintered the party was narrowly averted by summoning Golda Meir from retirement to save the party by accepting the position of Prime Minister. With the death of a Prime Minister, tenure of a government automatically ends. On March 17, therefore, Golda Meir presented her new government of National Unity to the Kneset, receiving its confidence by 106 votes, the largest support the Kneset ever gave to a newly constituted government.

The new government was identical to its predecessor in its composition. The proximity of the national elections and the continued national emergency prompted Mrs. Meir to pledge that her government would be maintained as a "government of continuity." No change in policy was contemplated. Since Mrs. Meir was not expected to remain as Prime Minister after the expiration of the Kneset term, individual rivalries continued unabated. Only when Mrs. Meir's intentions to stay on as Premier became known did the factions of the Labor Party close ranks and adopt a compromise election platform that incorporated the resolve of securing strategic borders and of introducing electoral reform, at least on the municipal level, before the next elections.

The election campaign was comparatively mild. Since all the big parties were in the coalition and anticipated the continuation of the National Unity Government after the elections, they refrained from offending potential partners. A growing consensus on security matters also began to prevail among them, particularly after the Labor Party Convention endorsed in substance Dayan's line of economic integration, open borders, and strong response to terrorism, coupled with Allon's plan for settlement and Eban's lofty aspirations for a negotiated peace.

In contrast to the 1965 elections, Gahal did not aspire to become the alternative government. It tacitly recognized the Labor-Mapam Alignment's preponderant lead, and all it aimed at was to cut into Alignment vote. The NRP had similar short-term ambitions, hoping to woo the religious voter from Mapai, which had recently aligned itself with the anti-religious Mapam. Possibly, since the emergence of a one-party government following the elections seemed likely, the religious demands of the NRP program were couched in generalities. Emphasis was placed on observance of religious law and support for religious education.

Elections to the Seventh Kneset took place on October 28, 1969. They resulted in a setback to the Labor-Mapam Alignment which gained 56 seats in the Kneset, five short of a majority and seven short of its representation in the former Kneset. By contrast, the Gahal emerged with 26 seats, regaining the four mandates it had lost to the Free Centre in the last Kneset. The NRP gained one seat, raising its total to 12 (with the other religious parties to 18).

Though the Labor Alignment maintained its position as the strongest list in the Kneset, the result of the elections amounted to a not inconsiderable defeat for its constituent factions. Expectations were that sociological and psychological factors would play into the hands of the Alignment. The demographic composition of the nation had stabilized to some degree. The heterogeneity of the Jewish population, which contributed to the great variety and number of parties, has receded in the pressure-cooker of the Israel society. For the first time in Israel's history a generation of Sabras, born under the flag of independent Israel, marched to the polls and were expected to cast their lot with the progressive socialist forces. A majority party promised to redress the inequities of minority pressure on the government, to introduce stability into the country's electoral system, and to offer clear-cut ideological alternatives to the voter.

The elections demonstrated that the Israeli voter was not willing to change the prevailing political system and wished to maintain the division of political power. Though often voicing unhappiness with the by-products of the Israel type coalition government, he seemed to prefer it to what could conceivably have become a perpetual one (and always the same) government. And so, when the results of the seventh parliamentary elections were tabulated, it became clear that the coalition game had not ended.

Once again, as always in the past, the NRP found itself in a preferential bargaining position. To enable it to establish a viable government, the Labor-Mapam Alignment had a choice of only two partners, the Gahal and the NRP. The Mapam faction of the Labor Alignment categorically rejected the inclusion of Gahal in the government, fearing their influence in social and economic affairs. Some Ahdut ha-'Avodah leaders—among them notably Yizhak Ben Aharon, who was slated to become Histadrut Secretary General—and even some Mapai Ministers, like Abba Eban, objected to Gahal participation in the Cabinet. Among the Labor leaders, however, there seemed to be virtually unanimous agreement that the NRP would be the less dangerous and therefore the more preferable partner in a coalition.

In view of the deteriorating border situation and the prospect of increasing Great Power pressure for concession to return the administered areas to the neighboring belligerent Arab states, Golda Meir and the Alignment's Political Committee expressing the prevalent Mapai sentiment, preferred the reestablishment of the National Unity Government, based on the principles of the outgoing Cabinet. The inclusion of both the Gahal and NRP in the next Cabinet would have the additional advantage of freeing the government from complete dependence on any one supporting party.

Whatever the outcome of the coalition negotiations, the NRP was in a key position from the outset. Its leader, Moshe Hayim Shapiro, made it clear that the NRP would insist on the reconstitution of the National Unity Government. He further emphasized that his party "will stand firm on its demand to revoke TV broadcasts on Sabbath eve" (see Preface) and will seek the recently vacated Kneset speakership.

As so often in the past, the ex-Mapai leadership responsible for establishing a working coalition found the NRP demands less exacting than the demands of other parties or factions. The NRP bargained mainly for principles, while the other parties bargained for power. The Gahal expected to be represented in the new government in positions of responsibility and in accordance to its parliamentary strength. Whereas in the former government the Gahal had only two Ministers without Portfolio, in the new government it aimed for five Ministers, at least one of them occupying a major portfolio. Similarly, the ex-Rafi faction of the Labor Alignment insisted on two portfolios for two Ministers, as opposed to the one it held in the preceding government. Fearing the decline of its own power, Mapam fought against "a Gahal-Dayan take-over" and threatened to withdraw from the government. As in former coalition negotiations, so now again the ex-Mapai leadership was ready to compromise on principles like Sabbath TV, even if it awakened widespread criticism in the nonreligious majority, but would not compromise an inch on yielding power.

15

Problems and Prospects for a Solution of the Religious Impasse

A significant aspect of the religious problem in Israel is the ability of the religious parties, with the backing of only fifteen per cent of the electorate, to impose the rule of the Torah (religious law) on the Jewish community. The mechanism through which the religious parties have exercised their influence has been the machinery of government. The opportunity to initiate such influence was offered by the systems of government and quasi-government that Israel inherited from the British Mandatory power, the Jewish Community under the Mandate (Kneset Israel), and the Zionist Organization.

The contributions of the coalition government and of the historic antecedents to the religious problem have been examined in the preceding pages. However, neither the key role of the religious parties in the machinery of government, nor the inheritance from the past could fully explain the grudging submissiveness of eighty-five percent of the Jewish population to a system of laws that it does not seem to consider in harmony with the outlook of modern man.

A thoroughgoing study of the religious problem in Israel would have to assess the feelings and attitudes of the population that contribute to the creation of a climate of religious acceptance or rejection. An examination and analysis of such intangibles are beyond the scope of this inquiry, but the presence of emotional and psychological factors must, nevertheless, be duly noted and their impact be taken into consideration.

The problem is compounded by the ambivalent attitude of a substantial segment of the Jewish population to the Jewish religion on the one hand, and the religious institutions that claim to represent it on the other. Individuals who decry the influence of religious institutions in the country may nevertheless wish to strengthen the influence of religion.

Many avowedly secular circles readily accepted the teaching and dissemination of "Jewish consciousness," which rests on religious foundations, in the public school system. This stemmed from an awareness and grudging recognition that the Jewish religion may have been an instrument of survival for the Jewish people throughout its 1900 years of statelessness, and may continue to serve the same purpose in the future. The preservation of the Jewish religion by a Jewish state could, therefore, be considered not merely a gesture of gratitude. It may also be dictated by the instinct of national survival.

The average Israeli's willingness to hold on to the Jewish religion and his eagerness to do away with the religious establishment results in an ambiguous and hesitant stance. He is caught in a vicious cycle by his concern that a forthright and vigorous attack on the religious establishment may inadvertently knock out the underpinnings of religion, whereas support of religion through the only channels now available would fortify the religious establishment.

The secular-minded Israeli Jew has an intense dislike for the religious establishment, whose interference in private life he finds, at best, irritating and, at worst, destructive of the democratic ideals as envisioned by the founders of the state. This intense dislike is heightened by the inability of the religious establishment to adapt itself to changing circumstances. The Chief Rabbinate has demanded rigorous adherence to a system of laws that was last codified 400 years ago in the days of darkest exile for the Jewish people. The law, though periodically reinterpreted, has not been brought up to date. The Chief Rabbinate has been unwilling, or unable, to confront the reality of an independent Jewish state with a new set of circumstances and requirements. The application of a code, created in exile and adapted to exilic conditions, in the independent State of Israel appears to many as a glaring anachronism.

An important contributory factor to the antagonism against the religious establishment has been the method utilized by it in imposing religious law without heed as to the occasional tragic consequences suffered by the individuals affected. The Israeli is very sensitive to the infringement on his religious freedom by legally constituted authorities. Religious freedom in Israel, as interpreted by many Israelis, would consist of the ability to eat, travel, work, get married or divorced, contribute to an eye or kidney bank, and even take a swim in a mixed swimming pool without interference by rabbinic authorities. What adds insult to the injured sensibilities of the secular Israeli is that the rabbinic authorities are empowered to act as agents of the judiciary and are backed by the punitive arm of the state.

Yet, the dislike felt by the secular Israeli for the religious establishment does not necessarily carry over to the institution of religion itself. In recent years there has been a gradual thawing of antireligious sentiment. The emergence of a sympathetic approach to newly developing religious forms has become clearly discernible.

Initially the pioneering workers' movement, that played a decisive role in the establishment of the state, was militantly antireligious. The founders of the socialist settlements (kibbutzim) and of the Histadrut identified religion with a passive attitude of patient waiting in exile for God's redemptive help. This identification was strengthened by the anti-Zionism of numerous religious spokesmen and the Aguda group. The pioneers substituted for the religion of the synagogue the religion of labor.

From a historic perspective the rebellion against traditional religion may have accomplished a useful purpose. It led to self-help, the creation of a Jewish working class in Israel, the reclamation of the land and the establishment of the state. Presently there are signs of searching for a new and contemporary meaning in the Jewish religion among Jewish working class intellectuals. The once prevalent notion that religion and democracy, and religion and progress are not compatible is giving way to a search for new forms of religion that could be in harmony with democracy and man's technological advancement.

This chapter will deal with the practical impact of the religious establishment on the everyday life of the Israeli citizen, and with possible approaches of solving the religious impasse.

Religious Problems on the Non-Cabinet Level

Not all of the accomplishments of the religious elements found expression on Cabinet level. Some of their attainments, extremely irritating to the nonreligious, seemed to have nothing to do with the bargaining process or with agreements reached within the Cabinet. They were directly connected with the routine of personal, municipal, or national life. Only an isolated few of the numerous occurrences that raised the ire of the nonreligious will be mentioned here.

A typical instance was a local rabbinical council's refusal to grant permission to a young Falasha (Ethiopian Jew) to marry a Jewish woman unless he consented to undergo ritual immersion with the intent to convert. The young Falasha, Benjamin Gettye, happened to be the son of a well-known Hebraic scholar-teacher who had come to Israel in 1955 with the help of Youth 'Aliyah. He had been born and brought up as a Jew by Jewish parents.[26] The reason for the refusal was that the Falashas were suspected by the Rabbinate of having intermarried in Ethiopia in the course of the ages. This was but one of many instances considered a flagrant interference in personal life, with negative effects on the individual's state of mind and on his attitude to Judaism.

A cause célèbre was the case of Mrs. Rina Eitani, who lived as a Jewess all her life, had been persecuted by the Nazis as a Jew, had been interned by the British on Cyprus, had been married to a Jew in the Jewish tradition, and had been living on a kibbutz in Israel. After all this, she was declared not Jewish by the Ministry of the Interior, under an NRP Minister,

---

26. *Jerusalem Post*, February 23, 1966. In March 1968 Gettye's suit against the Rabbinate was rejected (March 11, 1968, p. 11).

because her mother was not Jewish.[27] The zeal of the religious militants to maintain the "racial, national, or religious purity" of the Jewish people seemed to have overstepped the moral bounds by going contrary to the spirit of the tradition in whose defense they have claimed to act.

Perhaps even more pointed is the instance of a ten-year-old boy who was refused burial in a Jewish cemetery by the rabbinical authority in Pardes Hanna because his mother was not Jewish. Since the father was Jewish and the child was raised in the Jewish faith, the family would not inter him in any other cemetery. He was, therefore, buried outside the Jewish cemetery precincts.

This incident was followed by a sharp debate in the Kneset, during which a number of representatives gave expression to their indignation. A member of the Mizrahi Party, verbalizing the thinking in religious quarters, exclaimed in the heat of the debate, "We don't want them (the non-Jewish spouses of recent immigrants) here; we want to preserve the purity of our race."[28]

Less tragic, but more ironic, was the refusal of the Rabbinical authorities in February 1968 to register the forthcoming marriage of Ben Gurion's granddaughter, Galia, since her mother could not produce a conversion certificate issued by an orthodox rabbi. As reported by the *Jewish Chronicle* of London (March 1, 1968), the Rabbinical Court stated: "We have no doubt that Mrs. Mary Ben Gurion became a convert to Judaism before her marriage took place in England, but we wish to be sure that an orthodox rabbi approved of her conversion."

Religious endeavors, many of them successful on a municipal level, were cited before. Among them were their protests against the opening of an industrial exhibit in Haifa on Sabbath, the

---

27. *New York Times,* January 19, 1965, p. 30. See also Part III, Chapter 8, "Who Is a Jew?" The Ministry's decision was eventually reversed.

28. Mendel Kohansky, "A Problem of Religion," *Jewish Frontier,* February 1958, p. 21. It was in direct retaliation for the Pardes Hanna episode that the Minister of Interior, Ben-Yehudah, (Ahdut ha-'Avodah) issued new regulations concerning "Who Is a Jew?" that in turn brought about the resignation of the NRP from the Cabinet. The religious coercion involved in the Pardes Hanna episode elicited accusations from the Vatican organ, *Osservatore Romano,* that the Israel government is forcibly converting Christians!

running of the Haifa subway (the Carmelit) on Sabbath, and the building of a mixed playground and mixed swimming pool in Jerusalem. A new swimming pool recently constructed at the Hebrew University in Jerusalem also became an issue in municipal politics, when in February 1969, a number of religious teachers, among them two full professors, threatened to resign should it be allowed to operate on Sabbath. Much more shocking than these protests were the direct threats of the Rabbinate, like the one against the B'nai B'rith House in Tel Aviv, that it would be deprived of its *kashrut* certificate if it permits a liberal religious service on its premises.

Two more recent examples deserve mention. In January 1968, Jerusalem was hit by a blizzard that brought damage to electric installations and left wires trailing dangerously. Many homes were left without heat and light. The Electric Company sent out emergency crews to repair the damage. With the approach of Sabbath the Minister of Labor issued a permit for the emergency work to continue. The Minister of Religious Affairs immediately countemanded that order, calling by radio broadcast for stoppage of all work. This episode once again brought to the fore a clash between two Ministries, sharpened the conflict between religious and irreligious, and deprived people of what seemed to be essential needs in the name of religious law.

On July 4, 1968, the Conference of Progressive Judaism (Reform), meeting in Jerusalem, scheduled a mixed service of men and women at the Western Wall. By official order the service was canceled at the last moment. The leaders of the Conference, after meeting with Prime Minister Eshkol on the matter, accepted the government's assurances that "all Jews have a right to worship at the historic and religious site according to their own customs," but concurred that it was necessary to cancel the service because of the threat of disruption by "irresponsible elements."

On the national level, religious pressures threatened to destroy the budding paper industry in the country and to bring to an end proper archeological exploration. In the beginning of 1958, Chief Rabbi Nissim imposed a ban on the printing of religious books on paper produced by the Hadera Mills, the only one in the country, unless all work on Sabbath would be stopped or only non-Jewish employees would work on that day. The management claimed that stopping the machines every week would be prohibitive and that non-Jewish workers were not sufficiently skilled for the task. In view of the Chief Rabbi's stubborn stand, publishers applied to the Minister of Trade and Industry for a license to import paper from abroad. This was refused in order to prevent the bankruptcy of the Hadera Mills. After much procrastination, a compromise was reached, according to which Arab workers were to operate the machines on Sabbath, supervised by Jewish workers who would not actually take part in the process of work. Thus, "no workers will have to be discharged, no Jew will desecrate the Sabbath, no lack of skill will endanger the machines, and the publishers will get their paper."[29]

In February 1956, while laying the foundation for a private home, workmen discovered a Hasmonean burial cave dating back to the Second Temple, in the heart of Jerusalem. Immediately the Chief Rabbinate objected to the desecration of Jewish graves and issued instructions that none of the human remains be moved nor the bones disturbed. Work on the excavation had to be halted, despite the danger of rapid deterioration to the remarkably well-preserved find. The Ministry of Religious Affairs stated that excavation on additional niches would be restricted. This position was supported by hundreds of fanatical religious youth, Naturei Qarta, who were picketing the cave.

It was learned that the government bought up the plot with the cave for the purpose of halting any further excavation. This decision affecting an archeological find may have had far-reaching ramifications. "As a precedent," stated an archeologist, "it could mean the end of practical archeological exploration in Israel."[30]

Special mention should be made of the controversy periodically stirred up by the question, "Who is a Jew?" One such instance, discussed in Chapter 8, led to a Cabinet crisis and the resignation of NRP Ministers from the government. Though

---

29. *Israel Weekly Digest* 1, no. 17 (January 23, 1958) :3.
30. *Jerusalem Post*, February 22, 1956. See also editorial, February 23, 1956.

in that particular case the issue involved (registration of religion and nationality on identity cards) had no practical significance, the religious elements vigorously protested against the attempt of non-Rabbinic authorities to determine "who is a Jew."

A case better known for its notoriety than for its importance is Brother Daniel's request to be accorded Israel citizenship under the Law of Return. That law automatically guarantees citizenship to any Jew settling in Israel. Brother Daniel, though a Catholic monk, had a Jewish mother. According to religious law, he should therefore be considered a Jew. The Court rejected the Brother's request, arguing that a Christian would not be regarded as a Jew by the Jewish people, regardless of descent.

In November 1968, Binyamin Shalit, a captain in the Israel Navy, stirred up a hornet's nest with his appeal to the Supreme Court that it order the Minister of Interior to register his children as Jewish nationals, though their mother is not Jewish. The question posed once again was, "Can a person be Jewish by nationality and not by religion?" Captain Shalit argued that his children should have a greater right to be considered Jewish nationals, though of a non-Jewish mother, than the notorious Fatah terrorist, Nimri, who is deemed a Jew because his mother was Jewish. The Court referred the case for advisement to the Kneset with the recommendation that registration of nationality be deleted from the Population Register. It is expected that the Kneset will defer a decision on the matter indefinitely.

These were some instances where the Cabinet was not directly involved in aiding the attainment of religious goals. Yet, despite the objections of the secular majority and the angry criticism of thousands of Israelis against the "arbitrary and cruel ruling" and the "streak of bigotry" in religious authorities, the religious minority was able to exploit its indispensability to Mapai. The religious parties took full advantage of their power to paralyze the government with the threat of their withdrawal from the coalition.

Politization of Religion and Crisis of Faith

As early as January 1949, before the election to the First Kneset, secular spokesmen demanded that religion be left in the realm of individual conscience and that it not be subjected to legislation, where it would inevitably introduce an element of coercion. In order to accomplish this, they proposed that "religious parties should be dissolved and religious Jews should enter into the existing parties."[31]

During the budget debate of the Ministry of Religious Affairs in June 1966, the NRP, the largest religious party, was attacked by its secular opponents. "We must warn our friends from the NRP against the continued politization of religion, in order to eliminate the impression that the religion of Israel exists in order to serve the NRP."[32] stated member of Kneset Aram of Gahal. A member of the Ma'arakh, addressing himself to the NRP, added, "There is no greater sin than the exploitation of religion for governmental purposes and for the satisfaction of political and social needs."[33]

The official religious organs of the state, like the Chief Rabbinate, the Religious Councils, and, especially, the Ministry of Religious Affairs, "give the impression much more often than would be expected that they serve the needs of the NRP and not the needs of religion in the state,"[34] said Gahal member Joseph Shofman. In the local Religious Councils, for example, that are entitled to the same numerical membership as the City Councils, the NRP takes possession of 50 per cent of the seats, while simultaneously holding on to their seats in the secular representative bodies. In this way, Mapai pays the NRP for its participation in the coalition and offers the NRP additional opportunities to reward its faithful with positions of value.[35] Thus, "every Religious Council is turned into a fortified stronghold" for the NRP.[36] Another member of the coalition did not find the elections to the Religious Council satisfactory and acceptable. The Councils offer services, like marriage, dietary laws, and burial to all citizens of the community, secular as well as religious.

---

31. *Ha-Zofeh,* January 9, 1949, quoting Levi Yizhaq ha-Yerushalmi's article in *Hador.*
32. *Divrei ha-Kneset,* Sixth Kneset, 73rd session, 44 (June 21, 1966): 1836.
33. *Ibid.,* p. 1838. Moshe Aram of Ma'arakh.
34. *Ibid.*
35. *Ibid.*
36. *Ibid.*

They should, therefore, be democratically elected institutions, instead of being imposed upon the population by the Rabbinate and the Ministry of Religious Affairs.[37]

The NRP has also been severely criticized for subverting the Rabbinate. "A rabbi cannot be appointed and a rabbi could not advance if he is not loyal to the NRP."[38] The election of rabbis does not take place on the basis of learning, humility, and fear of God, but is usually dependent on faithfullness to and enthusiasm for the religious party in the Government."[39]

The NRP was most strongly condemned, however, for its control of the Ministry of Religious Affairs, considering it a personal possession of the party.[40] Doubt was cast on the need for a special Ministry of Religious Affairs whose functions could be fulfilled by the Ministry of the Interior. Its critic felt that it was only established to fulfill the demands of the religious parties in the coalition.[41]

Even those who saw a need for the Ministry of Religious Affairs found it wanting. One of the Ministry's main objectives was to contribute to the unification of the Jewish people. Instead, it has served the opposite purpose of driving a wedge between its constituent parts.[42] A speaker of the Po'alei Agudat Israel complained that the Ministry concentrates its efforts on fulfilling religious ritual needs, instead of spreading the knowledge of the Torah among the people.[43] But the most devastating criticism came from Miss Rahel Zabari of the Ma'arakh who pointed out that the population is suffering from a "crisis of faith in the Ministry as a result of its activities that are intolerable in a democratic country."[44]

A "crisis of faith" has gripped the Jewish population of Israel and does not seem to be nearing a solution. Religion has been identified with belonging to a religious political party, instead

---

37. *Ibid.*, p. 1835. Rahel Zabari of Ma'arakh.

38. *Ibid.*, Sixth Kneset, 63rd session, 44 (May 31, 1966) :1564. Joseph Shofman of Gahal.

39. *Ibid.*, 73rd session, 44 (June 21, 1966) : 1838. M. Aram of Ma'arakh

40. *Ibid.*, 63rd session, 44 (May 31, 1966) :1565, 1571. J. Shofman of Gahal and Shulamit Aloni of Ma'arakh.

41. *Ibid.*, p. 1564. J. Shofman.

42. *Ibid.*, p. 1565. Mordecai Zar of Ma'arakh.

43. *Ibid.*, p. 1575. Ya'aqov Katz.

44. *Ibid.*, 73rd session, 44 (June 21, 1966) :1834.

of with adherence to the tenets and spiritual values of the Jewish faith. "A twisted attitude prevails in the Ministry of Religious Affairs and among the members of the NRP according to which only such a person could be considered a religious and traditional Jew who is a member of a party that designates itself as a religious party, that is to say, a party that uses the problem of religion as a political weapon."[45]

Religious values have been overshadowed by the imposition of religious practices on people who consider them a flagrant interference with their individual freedom. Laws of marriage and divorce, Sabbath observance, and holiday travel have been made to apply equally to the religious and to the irreligious person, despite their being a meaningless formality, an irritating procedure, an object of derision, and sometimes a source of personal tragedy to the irreligious.

The irreligious young girl may consider the prerequisite of a ritual bath (mikvah) for the licensing of her marriage nothing more than a nuisance. The young irreligious widow who is not allowed to remarry until her brother-in-law releases her in a formal ceremony called *halitza,* while her brother-in-law may marry without her permission, would consider the situation imposed by religious law humiliating.[46] The woman whose husband has disappeared (*aguna*), or the man of priestly descent (a *Kohen*) who falls in love with a divorcee, both of whom are forbidden by religious law to marry in their particular circumstance, will identify their personal tragedy with the archaisms of a religious faith that their experiences teach them to despise instead of to respect.

No less tragic are the applications of religious laws to mixed marriages and to the fate of their offspring, whether raised as Jewish or not. The ill-masked approval by religious institutions of the breaking up of families by whisking a child into hiding in order to protect him from his irreligious parents and assure him religious instruction, as was witnessed in the Yosele Schumacher case, has not helped improve the image of religion.

---

45. *Ibid.,* 63rd session, 44 (May 31, 1966) :1564. J. Shofman of Gahal.
46. Female members of the Kneset found it particularly objectionable that the religious law still treats them as second-class citizens and deprives them of their equality in what should be a democratic society. See Emma Talmi of Mapam, *Ibid.,* p. 1570.

The prohibitions against the enjoyment of the day of rest have been a source of irritation. Religious interference with private Sabbath travel and interference by Religious Councils and the Ministry of Religious Affairs with lectures, educational and athletic events on the Sabbath, has been greatly resented by a majority of the population.[47] The religious establishment's insistence on Orthodoxy as the only legitimate form of Judaism, and the repression of Conservative and Reform variants, have decreased respect for religious institutions.

Spokesmen of various parties have demanded freedom of religious (or irreligious) expression in Israel, befitting a democratic country "even if it is not in the accepted version of this or that political party."[48] "The religion of Israel does not thrive only within the framework of Orthodoxy. . . . Not one movement has a monopoly on religious faith."[49] "The Ministry of Religious Affairs and the Chief Rabbinate assume that they have the right to force upon us, by the authority of the law of government, one single body of religious customs and commandments, religious ritual, and style of life. And not only upon the secularists, but also upon divergent movements in Judaism, on the Conservatives and the Reform."[50]

The religious establishment has produced a "crisis of faith" and social unrest. The crisis may be attributed to the following: Interference with individual freedom, repression of variant interpretations of Judaism, imposition of ancient laws whose meaningfulness could be challenged and which introduce inequality of sex (*haliza* and *aguna*) or aristocratic descent (*Kohen* versus ordinary Israelite). Strong religious entrenchment in the political system of the state, particularly in the Cabinet, and the secular majority's restraint made this situation possible.

Suggested Remedies for the Problem of Religion in Israel

Miss Shulamit Aloni, a spokesman for the young element in Mapai that has been opposed to the participation of the NRP

47. *Ibid.*, p. 1566. M. Zar of Ma'arakh.
48. *Ibid.*, p. 1565. J. Shofman of Gahal.
49. *Ibid.*, p. 1573. G. Hausner of Independent Liberal Party.
50. *Ibid.*, 73rd session, 44 (June 21, 1966) :1837. M. Aram of Ma'arakh.

in the government, pointed to the confusion over the concepts of the "People of Israel" and the "State of Israel." The "People of Israel" may be guided by religious laws and may be concerned with Jewish religious instruction, but the "State of Israel" is a secular entity and its arms must be secular Ministries. "In a secular state it is forbidden for the Government to get involved in questions of spirit, faith, and belief. Therefore it is forbidden for us to determine, even by the majority of the Kneset, that the Government should take an interest in religious matters."[51] Miss Aloni was quick to underscore that separation of religion and state would be proper not only from a legal and democratic point of view, but also from the point of view of religion, since respect for religion and the synagogue would increase by raising them above political controversy.[52]

It was, however, left to Uri Avineri, the most controversial though not the most influential member of the Kneset, to spell out in detail what separation of religion and state would entail:

Separation of religion and state—what does it mean?

1. There should be no other binding justice in the state except the justice of the national court based on the laws accepted by the majority of the people through their elected representatives. It should not be possible by means of the secular law to impose upon the public such laws that find their source in Holy Scriptures, that are not subject to change by means of the democratic process, and that establish a Rabbinical dictatorship, relying on divine inspiration.

2. No religious institution should be supported on behalf of the state at the expense of the taxpayer.

3. There should be no law, neither national or municipal, limiting an individual's right in freedom of movement, freedom of diet, freedom of occupation, and freedom of entertainment for religious reasons.

4. There should not be in any of the schools supported by the taxpayers a curriculum that includes religious education in an open or hidden manner.

5. There should be complete separation between the Government, which cannot coerce a majority or a minority (not

---

51. *Ibid.*, 63rd session, 44 (May 31, 1966) :1571. Shulamit Aloni.
52. *Ibid.*, p. 1573.

even a small minority) on religion, ideology, basic beliefs, and ritual, and between religion, which is the private matter of every individual and group interested in it.[53]

At the other extreme, most of the religious elements are totally opposed to the idea of separation of religion and state. "We are all convinced," stated an NRP leader, "that separation of religion and state would lead to a split in the people and to brotherly hatred."[54] An Agudah leader put it as follows: "The Torah and religion are the essence of our existence. Every thought that borders on separation of religion and state is identical with the separation of the soul from the body. Our people is not a people except by virtue of its Torah."[55]

Most American Jewish observers place great trust in the separation of religion and state on the basis of the American experience and urge its adoption in Israel. A number of important considerations have, however, effectively restrained even the most outspoken Israeli secularists from taking any concrete measures in that direction.

First, international as well as domestic considerations have militated against the step. Israel, as the "cradle of three religions," has to be very circumspect on religious matters. It has to extend official protection to the holy places of all faiths and to their representatives. In order to avoid repercussions attributable to the Arab-Israel conflict, the state felt compelled to offer its substantial Arab minority the same privileges it enjoyed during the British Mandate, that is, communal autonomy based on religious, as opposed to national, loyalties. To underscore its interest in protecting all religions and in safeguarding the rights of the Arab minority, a special Ministry of Religious Affairs has been kept in operation as an agency of the government. Though this deferential attitude of the government toward religion may have been motivated mainly by external considerations, its most potent effects have been within the

---

53. *Ibid.*, p. 1576.
54. Bezalel Cohen, "Religion and State according to the Sources," *Iyunim b'Ba'ayot Dat u-M'dinah* (Jerusalem: Merkaz Olami Shel ha-Mizrahi v'ha-Po'el ha-Mizrahi, 1964) , p. 13.
55. *Divrei ha-Kneset*, Sixth Kneset, 73rd session, 44 (June 21, 1966: 1834. M. Porush of Agudat Israel.

Jewish community itself. This is evident in the power and influence of Jewish religious institutions.

Second, there are historical, sociological, and psychological factors. Despite the resentment against the "impossible affront to human conscience" inherent in the imposition of Jewish religious law, the majority of the Jews in Israel carry an awareness of the role of the Jewish religion in preserving the Jewish people through 1900 years of homelessness.[56]

Third, an important consideration is the recognition that Israel is continually exposed to external aggression. This requires the avoidance of internal clashes on issues that certain segments of the population feel strongly about, like religion, that may divide the people. (Such internal conflict, or the prospect of it, is often referred to as the *Kulturkampf*.)

The climate of opinion, resulting from this situation, discourages the majority of the population from advocating a complete separation of religion and state. The majority would, however, like to see a separation by degrees, starting, perhaps, with the withdrawal of the religious parties from politics.

Should there be Religious Political Parties?

Would the abolition of religious parties solve the problem of the relationship of state and religion in Israel? There are three points of view on the question. The majority of the vocal religious leadership is militantly in favor of retaining and strengthening the religious party machine. Many secularists have been the proponents of a complete dissolution of religious parties. A minority of the religious people advocate an apolitical orientation for religious Jewry.

Would it be possible to imagine, asked a Mizrahi leader, that all the legislation favoring the traditional Jewish approach would have been attainable without the instrumentality of the religious parties? He answered his own question in the negative. He then stated that those who are opposed to a religious political party see religion as a private matter that ought not be introduced at all into the framework of the state. This would amount

56. B. Eliav, "A Letter from Israel," *Jewish Frontier,* (February 1959), p. 4. A. S. Super, "Who Is a Jew?" *Ibid.* (March 1959), p. 7.

to complete separation of religion and state or, in his opinion, to the breakdown of religion in Israel.[57]

The religious political parties have determined, as their goal, the defense of the interests of religion and have considered themselves its official representatives. The Minister of Religious Affairs, Zerah Wahrhaftig, declared,

> The function of the religious party, as a Jewish religious party, is to . . . determine the direction of things in the light of the "halaha" [Jewish religious law]. The religious party cannot limit itself to strictly religious preoccupations in the narrow sense, although these issues are of particular concern to the NRP. The religious party must take an interest and take a stand on any issue, be it in the realm of economics, or foreign or domestic policy. For everything is connected with religion, and on all issues a religious position can be taken. It is impossible to say: on such and such matters we will rely on other parties, and we will occupy ourselves only with religious questions—it would, therefore, be possible to disperse among the [other] parties. The truth of the matter is that there is not a single thing, not a single law that does not touch—or that could not, God forbid, infringe upon—religious principles, or that could not be solved in line and in harmony with the "halaha."[58]

And at a later point he stated that the struggle around constitutional legislation by itself justifies the establishment and the organization of a religious party. "If a party seeks any right and justification for its existence, the religious party has it."[59]

To the NRP diehards, the dissolution of their party would mean the end of religion, whereas to the contrary, the strengthening of the party would lead to the solution of the religious problem. If successful, the party would impose a uniform religious legislation upon the Jewish population which, though initially resentful, would learn to understand that therein lies the survival of Israel.

---

57. B. Cohen, "Religion and State according to the Sources," *Iyunim b'Ba'ayot Dat u-M'dinah* (Jerusalem: Merkaz Olami Shel ha-Mizrahi v'ha-Po'el ha-Mizrahi, 1964) , p. 16.

58. Zerah Wahrhaftig, "Religious Party Determines the Way of Life," *ibid.,* p. 20.

59. *Ibid.,* p. 25.

Many secularists have taken a radically different stand on the issue of religious parties, advocating their abolition and the dispersal of their membership among the secular parties. The religious parties were repeatedly warned that they have no monopoly on religion and that they do not represent Judaism. Ben-Gurion, Golda Meir, and other leaders of Mapai have consistently claimed that the needs of the religious people would be safeguarded without the presence of religious parties in the coalition.[60]

Despite the religious parties' fear that their withdrawal from political life would result in the separation of religion and state, there is no necessary connection between the two phenomena. The withdrawal, or even the dissolution, of religious parties does not necessarily have to result in the abolition of the Ministry of Religious Affairs, the Chief Rabbinate, the local Religious Councils, or the Religious Courts. All these institutions could be safeguarded on a nonparty basis, lifting them above political bargaining. Although the secular majority may, by democratic procedures, curtail the work of any of these institutions, religion stands to benefit less and lose more by the continued functioning of the religious parties and by their high pressure, extortionist, and predatory activities.

The observation that the activities of the religious parties defeat the purpose of their existence and cause more harm than good to religion elicited voices of concern in the religious camp. In 1964, a leader of Orthodox Jewry in the United States called upon the religious parties to withdraw from politics.[61] He made a similar statement following the elections to the Sixth Kneset while negotiations were in progress for the formation of the Thirteenth Government. He urged the religious parties not to join the government because their identification with politics has weakened their purpose and appeal.[62]

60. See above, Part III, Chapter 6, "Crisis over Religious Education: Act Two."

61. Rabbi Soloveitschik, as quoted by Y. Bernstein, "Separation of Religion from State Equals Separation of Religion from People," Bezalel Cohen, "Religion and State according to the Sources," *Iyunim b'Ba'ayot Dat u-M'dinah* (Jerusalem: Merkaz Olami Shel ha-Mizrahi v'ha-Po'el ha-Mizrahi, 1964) , p. 26.

62. *Jerusalem Post*, November 26, 1965.

In the beginning of 1966, Professor Efraim Urbach of the Hebrew University, a prominent member of the NRP, announced his withdrawal from the political party and, with a group of professionals and public figures, announced the establishment of a nonpolitical "Torah Jewry Movement." The aims of the group were the depolitization of the institutions of the Rabbinate and of religious-oriented schools and the ensuring of freedom of religion. He strongly criticized the political parties' handling of the question of Sabbath work at Port Ashdod, terming it a "catastrophe." He stated that, "political bargaining over religious issues had driven many from the Jewish tradition and had given rise to manifestations of opposition and hatred for religious values. Not legislation, but teaching and information, should be utilized in seeking to inculcate Jewish values."[63]

Another suggestion is to have the religious political parties work together with an a-political religious movement, trying to heighten the potential receptivity of the Jewish population to a religious message. "In the last analysis, the entire policy of the religious parties is doomed to failure so long as it is not supplemented by a serious effort on the nonpolitical level to bring the nonreligious to a serious confrontation with the religious issue on the level of faith and personal commitment."[64]

A nonpolitical religious movement is now a reality. It remains to be seen, however, whether the religious parties will learn to accept it and at least tolerate it, if not support it. One thing is beyond any doubt: the religious parties will not break up their political machinery and will not abdicate their political influence. They seem to be determined to continue to exploit their strategic position in the political configuration of the country. This could be the consequence of true, though misguided, conviction or of the dynamics of any movement that has already picked up momentum. Perhaps the Israeli observer is basically justified in claiming that "every religious party in the whole world, and not only with us, is also a political party."[65] This fact may have to be accepted, and the remedy

---

63. *Ibid.*, January 24, 1966.
64. Eliezer Goldman, *Religious Issues in Israel's Political Life*, p. 105.
65. *Davar*, October 7, 1963. K. Shabatai, "Religion Conquers the Religionist."

to the problem of religion in Israel may have to be sought for in a different direction.

Reform of Religious Law

It is probable that antagonism toward the religious parties and the religious elements would lessen if Jewish religious law reflected the conditions of a modern democratic society. In some areas, involving important aspects of individual freedom, Jewish religious law is anachronistic.

Suggestions have been made to reform religious law to bring it up to date. When such proposals come from the secular camp, they are taken in stride as something to be expected.[66]

On occasion, however, voices of influential leaders from the religious camp clamor for much-needed religious reforms. Tova Sanhedrai, a leader of the NRP, recently issued an urgent call to the Rabbinate to amend religious law in line with modern concepts of equality and democracy. Regarding marriage, she asked for a solution to the problems of the abandoned wife who is not allowed to remarry (aguna), the childless widow who needs her brother-in-law's permission to marry again (haliza), and the person of priestly descent (Kohen) who wishes to marry a divorcee (gerusha). She indicated that, without a solution to these personal problems, she can well sympathize with those demanding civil marriage. As for inheritance, where religious law has been interpreted in such a way that women are excluded, she demanded a stand from the Rabbinate guaranteeing full equality, regardless of sex. In other realms, too, she urged that pressure be applied upon the Rabbinate to force it to face up to the practical problems of modern man and to seek solutions to them that would harmonize the spirit of the tradition with the needs of the day.[67]

Demands for religious reform, whatever their source, do not advocate anything contrary to the Jewish tradition. Tova San-

66. *Divrei ha-Kneset,* Sixth Kneset, 73rd session, 44 (June 21, 1966) : 1836. Sh. Z. Abramov of Gahal.

67. T. Sanhedrai, "The Rabbinate is Dutybound to Formulate New Regulations," Bezalel Cohen, "Religion and State according to the Sources," *Iyunim b'Ba'ayot Dat u-M'dinah* (Jerusalem: Merkaz Olami Shel ha-Mizrahi v'ha-Po'el ha-Mizrahi, 1964) , p. 93.

hedrai accompanied her plea for reform with several examples of a religious law being circumvented, reinterpreted, or abandoned. A secular government speaker, Moshe Aram of the Ma'arakh, produced a multitude of instances where changes in Jewish religious law took place in the course of the ages and pleaded for a similar dynamic approach today. "In the Talmud,[68] as well as in the later Commentaries upon the Talmud, are scattered innumerable warnings and commands to adapt the law to reality, in the spirit of 'And thou shalt live by it' and not die or suffer by it," he stated.[69] "But what is to be done," asked a commentator, "when Orthodoxy's leaders close their eyes to reality and refuse to budge or to permit a natural and necessary religious development to fit our times?"[70]

To the Orthodox, religious law is divinely inspired and, therefore, not subject to change, unless a precedent can be found within the tradition itself. It would be helpful if the Orthodox leaders would recognize that the force of reality will eventually grind away at the *halaha*, leading the nation out of confusion. Religious leadership could promote this process. Abandoning legislative coercion, recognizing twentieth-century reality, and introducing much-needed religious reforms would benefit both religion and state.

Is there a Solution to the Problem of Religion and State in Israel?

The fear that Israel may become a theocracy through the imposition of religious law by legislative or institutional means, has been somewhat lessened in recent years. Taking a step in the right direction, the secular state courts asserted their au-

---

68. First and largest Jewish code of law and lore.

69. *Divrei ha-Kneset,* Sixth Kneset, 73rd session, 44 (June 21, 1966): 1838. Aram quoted from a number of sources to prove his point. "In the Tractate, *Sabbath,* p. 40, it says: 'Should you see that the issue cannot be abided by, absolve yourself from it.' In the *Toseftah Shevi'it,* chapter 3, it says: 'They promulgated laws only within limits of feasibility.' In *K'tubot,* p. 60: 'Laws were not promulgated to inflict pain or loss. . . ! In *Yerushalmi Yevamot,* 80:12, it says: 'Custom supersedes law,' to teach you that the law was placed into your hands and not you into the hands of the law," etc.

70. Joseph Badi, *Religion in Israel Today* (New York: Bookman Associates, 1959), p. 61.

thority over religious institutions in 1964.[71] The solution to the religious problem in Israel will, however, not be found in an occasional courageous stand by a secular judge, though such instances serve as a forceful reminder that Israel abides by the "rule of law" (and not religious law) .

The remedies to Israel's religious problem that have been projected in this chapter may improve the situation. In the present circumstances, however, they are either not workable, or they need to be supplemented. Reform of religious law, both plausible and viewed favorably by most parties concerned, is at best a tedious and slow process that may produce satisfactory results if accompanied by an easing of political aggressiveness by the religious parties. But the religious parties find their *raison d'être* in aggressive manipulations for additional religious legislation.

The suggested solution that religious parties should withdraw from political activity remains purely in the realm of the theoretical. An attempt of such a nature was tried in another country that has been shackled with religious problems. In France, during the Vichy and the Restoration period, the Catholics divorced themselves from political battles, making it "easier for the Church to put more attention on action in society."[72] But social action undoubtedly proved less fruitful than political action, since by the time of liberation in 1944, the Church had once more become interested in politics. Although it did not establish a party with the prefix "Christian," as in some other continental countries, it affected its influence through the MRP. (When the RPR was created in 1947, it, too, became the political champion of the Church.) By 1951 the Catholic forces felt powerful enough to establish a "Committee for Educational Freedom," causing a major political crisis by pushing through the "Barange Bill," which called

71. *The New York Times,* August 12, 1964. "Israel's High Court of Justice overruled today rabbinical objections and held itself competent to examine decisions by the Supreme Rabbinical Council. The rabbinate had maintained that decisions of the Supreme Council, the highest authority on the interpretation of religious law, were not subject to review by any lay authority because they were based on the law of God."

72. Stanley Hoffman, ed., *In Search of France,* Paradoxes of the French Political Community (Cambridge, Mass.: Harvard University Press, 1963) , p. 37.

for state subsidies to Church schools.[73] It would be purely utopian to expect the withdrawal of the religious parties from political activity.

A declaration of separation of religion and state, even if possible, would not solve the problem in the prevailing circumstances. It would not terminate religious interference with individual freedom. It would not put an end to the coercive measures applied by the religious minority upon the majority. It would not halt the abuse of religious institutions for political purposes, nor the abuse of ministries as party strongholds for patronage and narrow party interests.

A declaration of separation would be an empty gesture as long as the configuration of political forces encourages the religious parties to play a crucial role in the dynamics of coalition government. Radical changes need to be introduced in Cabinet formation and functioning in order to halt the deterioration of democratic processes in the country and the harassment of the majority by a strategically well-situated minority.

---

73. Philip Williams, *Politics in Post-War France.* (London: Longmans, Green & Co., 1955), p. 330. The Barange Bill was only a temporary culmination of an ongoing bitter feud between the clerical and lay forces in France for the control of the school system. The survival of Church schools, made possible only by public subsidies, is of crucial importance to the French Catholic Church, because the schools are practically the sole reservoir of candidates for priesthood. The radical and socialist parties are fighting subsidies to the Church schools because of their traditionally conservative character. Francois Goguel, *France Under the Fourth Republic.* (Ithaca, N.Y.: Cornell University Press, 1952), p. 125.

16

Coalition Government and the Future of Democracy

The end of World War II signaled the beginning of a new surge of nationalism and the birth of scores of new nation states in Africa and Asia. Among these was the State of Israel. The Jewish people had as an additional impetus the need for a homeland in the wake of the murder of six million Jews under Nazi rule. This event catapulted the Jewish people into action for the establishment of a sovereign State of Israel, and simultaneously marshaled the sympathy in the United Nations to Israel's side. Thus, a chief motivation for the creation of Israel can be found *outside* the territorial boundaries of the state: in the tragic events of Nazi occupied Europe during World War II.

Similarly, *outside* forces seem to have a decisive impact on shaping the State of Israel since its inception. A study of coalition government in Israel indicates that inner tensions and personality conflicts could rip the body politic apart were it not for the threat to Israel's survival by the neighboring Arab states. It may sound ironic, and nevertheless be true, that Israel managed to evolve and maintain a dynamic social and political system owing to the constant danger of an Arab attack. Israel's unenviable geographical position may be its most important single asset—an effective stabilizer of internal politics during the critical period of building the state.

Outside pressures and motivations for creating the state and maintaining an orderly government are intrinsically not beneficial to the welfare of the state. They pose a dangerous situation. A reduction of the pressures from abroad could result in a new feeling of national security, and a prolonged period of this deeper peace may be ruinous to the country: interparty conflicts may paralyze the machinery of democratic government.

Outside motivations may therefore have to be replaced by inner drives and constructive attitudes to the government. Mutual suspicion among the parties would have to yield to vigilant trust. Such a change, of course, cannot be accomplished by compulsion. But it could be stimulated by governmental action.

Depoliticizing the Civil Service

Ministries would cease to function as party fortresses by making the appointment, removal, promotion and demotion of all civil servants, with the exception of the Minister and the Director of the Ministry, subject to the authority of a nonpartisan Civil Service Commission. Law could provide for the summary dismissal of civil servants on all levels who utilize their position in a partisan manner for the promotion of the interests of their party or its adherents. These and similar regulations could be accompanied by an intensive educational campaign on all echelons of the civil service concerning the crucial need of subordinating party preferences to a comprehensive loyalty to the nation. The nonpartisan Civil Service Commission, or the Office of the Comptroller General, could be available to receive, investigate and act on complaints of abuse of a civil service position, and the general population could be kept aware of this recourse for redressing grievances.

Clamping down on the civil service by eliminating patronage and neutralizing it politically would go a long way toward minimizing the destructive effects of coalition bargaining. As was stated earlier, the coveted prize in coalition negotiations has been the acquisition of an influential Ministry with all the partisan benefits that accrue from it. Once these benefits are substantially trimmed, an important area of haggling and distrust would be eliminated.

Other areas where possible changes would contribute to the strengthening of the nation and to the safeguarding of democracy are the electoral process, the polarization of the political forces, the creation of a vital constructive opposition, and the evolution of a stable consensus of opinion among the parties and in the nation.

Electoral Reform

Let us look into the possibility of reforming the electoral system and the value it would have to the solution of the problem. A change in the prevailing political system and orientation was one of the great ambitions of Mapai leadership prior to the formation of the Ma'arakh in 1965. It is presently an integral article of the platform of the Rafi faction of the Israel Labor Party. For years Ben Gurion, supported by the majority of Mapai, has advocated amending the electoral system of the state. His aim has been to develop a two-party system that would offer the electorate a clear-cut choice in the establishment of government. He, therefore, has proposed that the system of PR (Proportional Representation), with the whole country as one constituency, be replaced by a number of single member constituencies with majority representation. This would eliminate the small parties that manage to accumulate a sufficient number of votes on a country-wide basis to seat one or several candidates, but whose votes within small constituencies would become dissipated and ineffectual. The expected outcome would be the polarization of the party structure, with a resultant strong Government party and a strong opposition party that, nevertheless, would be a loyal opposition, tempered by the prospect of being the alternative government.

Ben-Gurion's proposal may be sound in theory. If successful, it might eliminate the destructive aspects of coalition politics. It might eradicate the danger to the democratic process inherent in the religious minority's power over the secular majority. Its practical application, however, faces difficulties.

First, an absolute majority of sixty-one votes is required to amend the electoral law in force. Ben-Gurion was never able to muster the required strength to push an amendment through the Kneset, though once he was only one vote shy of the necessary majority. In November 1968, a Labor Party committee, headed by Dov Josef, recommended that the existing PR system be blended with a constituency system. According to the committee's recommendations, the country could be divided into 30 constituencies, each electing three members to the Kneset. The remaining 30 representatives would be chosen by the PR system from the whole country. In view of the setback suffered by the Labor Alignment in the elections to the Seventh Kneset, however, there is little likelihood that a majority for electoral reform would be available.

Second, should a two-party system be established in Israel, it would probably lead to the creation of a permanent Mapai government in perpetuity. The effects of rule by one party that has no competent political challenger for power, even though it be in a two-party or multiparty setup, are corrupting, as demonstrated by examples of Italy, Turkey, or Pakistan.[1]

Third, the change to single majority constituencies is no guarantee that a two-party system would evolve. The "model of the two-party system" is an example to the point. Throughout the 1920s, Great Britain had three parties competing for power.

Fourth, the two-party system has no inherent merit. The

---

1. "As the governing party in Italy since the end of 1945, it (the Christian Democratic Party) has had an uninterrupted tenure of office which has led to complacency, corruption, and the feeling that it has a God-given right to permanent rule," Norman Kogan, *The Government of Italy* (New York: Crowell, 1965) , p. 52.

For Pakistan, G. W. Choudhury points out that the Muslim League had been the sole force between 1937 and 1947, leading to the establishment of an independent Pakistan. It then continued as the predominant leading party, suffering from internal corruption, until its disintegration. G. W. Choudhury, *Democracy in Pakistan* (Dacca: Green Book House, 1963) , p. 279.

In Turkey, the rule of the Republican People's Party (1919–1945) would not be relevant, since it offered a one-party regime. The Democratic Party, its successor, however, ordered the confiscation of its opponents' assets, closed down the Nation Party, and applied repressive measures against the press. Geoffrey Lewis, *Turkey* (London: Ernest Benn Ltd., 1955) , p. 132.

system of representation should be fitted to the inherent consciousness of the electorate and to the prevailing notions of representative justice.[2] The extreme ideological awareness of the Israeli may revolt against the two-party straitjacket and may do its best to prevent its imposition.

It must, however, be recognized that the change of the PR system to a majority constituency system, though possibly not offering the required cure, could at least raise the likelihood for the creation of a sounder basis of democratic government.[3]

Party Amalgamation and Polarization

The responsible political leadership of the major parties in Israel has placed its hope in the progressive amalgamation of the parties leading to the eventual polarization of the political forces. Such, indeed, has been the trend in Israel, as evidenced by the formation of the Ma'arakh (Mapai and Ahdut ha-'Avodah) and Gahal (Herut and the Liberals) in 1965, and the Israel Labor Party (Ma'arakh and Rafi) in 1968.

This welcome trend of polarization has been accompanied, however, by a disconcerting phenomenon of depolarization. The formation of the Ma'arakh resulted in the creation of a new party, the Rafi; the merger that brought to life the Israel Labor Party was the incentive for the new State List; the creation of Gahal brought about a new split in Liberal ranks and the rejuvenation of the old Progressive Party under the name of Independent Liberal Party (ILP) ; it also resulted in a Herut splinter group, the Free Centre. Thus, centrifugal and centripetal forces have been operating side by side, neutralizing each other.

In 1961 the number of party lists in the Fifth Kneset elections was drastically reduced (14 as compared to 24 in the Fourth Kneset in 1959) , but this was only because of the 5000-pound fine to be imposed upon any party that would fail to gain one percent of the total vote. In 1965 the figure

2. Herbert J. Spiro, *Government by Constitution* (New York: Random House, 1959) , p. 357.
3. Robert A. Dahl, *Political Oppositions in Western Democracies* (New Haven, Conn.: Yale University Press, 1966) , p. 350.

began increasing again to 17 and in 1969 to 19, indicating depolarization rather than polarization of parties.

The hopes that the process of amalgamation would eliminate the exploitation of the political system by the religious minority were dashed in the aftermath of the elections to the Sixth Kneset. The formation of the Liberal-Herut Bloc (Gahal) eliminated the Liberals (formerly General Zionists) as prospective partners because of Mapai-Herut enmity. This reduced Mapai's alternatives in the creation of a new government. Rafi has remained an improbable partner, owing to the personality conflicts between the leaders of the two parties. Mapai was left with the unpalatable alternative of creating a government consisting of its Ma'arakh (45 votes), Mapam (8 votes), ILP (5 votes), and the Minorities (4 votes), giving it a total of 62 votes. This would have left Mapai dependent on every one of its partners, since the withdrawal of even the smallest of them could bring down the government. Therefore it became clear that the elimination of the Liberals as a prospective coalition candidate made Mapai dependent on the religious parties. The hope that the first majority government in Israel's history would be elected in the October 1969 parliamentary elections, and would thereby terminate the extortionist politics of minority parties, were dashed on the will of the Israel electorate. Once again the ex-Mapai leadership remained dependent on the minority parties, particularly the NRP, in setting up a government.

It should, nevertheless, be recognized that the process of amalgamation, accompanied by other favorable circumstances, is a beneficial and encouraging phenomenon; it can lead to the strengthening of the democratic foundations of the country.

A Vital Opposition

The safeguarding of democracy in Israel may depend upon the preservation of the coalition form of government and the politics of compromise until an effective opposition is able to develop. But the existing safeguards for democracy are very meager, allowing the tyranny of the religious minority over the secular majority. They are not at all a satisfactory alternative to a vital opposition.

The development of a vital opposition is intimately linked with the polarization of the party system and electoral reform. The electoral reform would presumably eliminate the small parties, thereby contributing to the polarization of the larger ones and to the creation of a powerful government party and a strong opposition. Such are the hopes but not the prospects. There are no indications that Israel is heading in the direction of a two-party system. There is no sign of a strong but loyal opposition. The glimmer of promise offered by the merger of the Herut and Liberal parties into the Gahal Bloc before the Sixth Kneset election soon faded. Whereas in the 1965 Kneset elections Gahal boldly aspired to become the alternative government, in the elections to the Seventh Kneset, it did not even make a pretense of such ambition.

The emergence of a responsible and vital opposition is of paramount importance to the survival of an effective and progressive political system. Although Mapai would be inconvenienced by a strong, functioning opposition, it is in need of it to hold its supporters in a disciplined alert and to prevent the repetition of internal upheavals, like the Lavon Affair. The other parties need a vital opposition to avoid the perpetuation of a "Mapai government" and a sense of bitter frustration that all legitimate efforts to capture the government would fail. The country needs it to prevent the exploitation of the present political system by an ambitious minority for its own partisan purposes and against the wishes of the majority.

Without a strong and responsible opposition, any political system courts the danger of the decline and degeneration of its democratic processes.

The Experience of Other Countries

It may be helpful to examine briefly what the experience of other countries has to offer to the understanding, if not the solution, of the religious-political problem in Israel.

Regrettably, from the outset we hit a blank wall. Although

the study of foreign political institutions is useful in ascertaining and evaluating the position of the Israel political system, it is difficult to dispute Professor Sartori's contention that "Israel is definitely atypical." In discussing the features of the multipolar systems which characterize such states as Italy, the Fourth French Republic, and the Weimar Republic, he refers to the "unique syndrome" of Israel as revealed in its party structure, "which defies any generalization."[4]

Professor Sartori's statement about Israel requires some modification. Although Israel may be "atypical" in its overall political system, viewed from an historical and sociological standpoint none of the individual features of the political system are unique. The only possible exception is the Mapai Ministerial majority in all Cabinets prior to 1965.

Religious involvement in politics and religious group pressures on state authority are certainly not unique to Israel. A glimpse at these manifestations in other countries may offer some useful insight. Professor Sartori describes the situation in Italy as follows:

There is no conflict between religions, such as we find, for instance, in Holland: Italians are all Catholics. There is, however, a religious cleavage between church and state, and perhaps in no Western country as much as in Italy the problem of the place of the church in the society remains a burning issue. The DC—Christian Democratic Party—is resented as being the "priest's party," and in Italy no less than in France governmental coalitions are blocked—and fall apart—on the traditional issue of state subsidies to private schools (which actually are church schools).

. . . Italians have been ruled since 1948 by a predominant Catholic party that receives a great deal of overt electoral support from the clergy, that would never dare defy a veto of the Vatican, and that permits a very consistent amount of daily church interference at all levels. It is, then, the overbearing and tiresome daily presence of the DC which produces, by way of reaction, a very definite cleavage between

4. J. La Palombara and Myron Weiner, *Political Parties and Political Development* (Princeton: Princeton University Press, 1966). Chapter by Giovanni Sartori, "European Political Parties: The Case of Polarized Pluralism," p. 160.

Catholic and laical policy orientation, a cleavage which deeply affects the recruitment of political leadership and accounts for many of the paralyzing complications of the party system.[5]

From the Italian experience it can be derived that,

A centrifugal development of the political system is likely whenever a religious-confessional criterion of political affiliation is superimposed upon the left-right distribution of the party alignment, and, more precisely, whenever a religious party adopts a clerical policy orientation and affirms itself as a predominant party by means of a special link with the dominant church. Under these circumstances an anticlerical polarization is likely to follow.

This centrifugal development will not follow, however, if the religious party does not exploit the confessional appeal and becomes integrated in the spectrum of party alignments by acquiring an inter-confessional dimension in terms of both leadership recruitment and electoral support (e.g., Belgium). Also, an anticlerical polarization is likely not to follow if the religious party is not a predominant party, if it is specifically concerned with the protection of minority rights, or if there is more than one religious party (e.g., Holland).[6]

The generalizations derived from the Italian experience indicate that religious involvement in politics seems to elicit antireligious reaction; that the stronger the dominance and pressure exercised by the religious parties, the more powerful become the corresponding anti-pressures; that religion would benefit most by limiting its concern to social issues. How this objective could be accomplished has not been projected. Evidently, democratic European countries like Italy, Holland, Belgium, Sweden, and Greece and Asiatic countries like India and Pakistan are each grappling with the problem with varied levels of intensity.[7]

---

5. *Ibid.*, p. 143. The DC in the 1963 general elections gained only 38.2 percent of the vote.

6. *Ibid.*, p. 169.

7. Church and state are not separated in Italy (J. La Palombara, *Interest Groups in Italian Politics* [Princeton: Princeton University Press, 1964], p. 105) even though Article 7 of the Constitution of Italy provides: "The

Perhaps the Chief Rabbinate of Israel would be willing to consider the Belgian experience where the Popes, after initial resistance, finally consented to the reinterpretation of Catholic doctrine. The religious parties might learn from the Dutch experience where, despite the control of a parliamentary majority, the religious elements used means of persuasion rather than force in their approach to power.

Although the experiences of these countries may suggest an approach to eliminate the danger to the democratic process in Israel, they do not solve the problem.

---

state and the Catholic Church are, each in its own order, independent and sovereign." (Norman Kogan, *The Government of Italy* [New York: Crowell, 1965], p. 189.)

In Holland, "Ever since 1918, the religious parties have jointly obtained a majority of seats in Parliament. . . . Their impact made itself felt only gradually. For a long time their leaders hoped to achieve their aims by action within the elite, through persuasion, petition, and protest. They sought to convert existing authority rather than challenge it." (Dahl, *Political Opposition in Western Democracies,* p. 201, chapter by Hans Daalder, "The Netherlands: Opposition in a Segmented Society.")

In Belgium, "The Constitution did not separate church and state, as many Belgians like to say. But it set new patterns of freedom for both. If for Catholics the church was to be free of control by the state, for Liberals the state had to be free of control by the church. The Constitution set forth a number of the liberal freedoms that were anathema in other Catholic lands, where error was not permitted to compete with revealed truth. Rome grudgingly recognized the liberal hypothesis of the special 'Belgian case' as the best it could obtain. Not until Leo XIII, however, did Rome fully accept the Belgian constitutional charter and its modern liberties." (Dahl, Robert A., *Political Opposition in Western Democracies,* chapter by Val R. Lorwin, "Belgium: Religion, Class, and Language in National Politics") , p. 150.

In Sweden, the Lutheran Church is supported by the state. Unless one goes to the trouble of declaring otherwise, the Swedish citizen is presumed to be a member of the "state church." The tax for church administration and support of pastors is minimal. There appears to be little resentment of it. In addition to their religious function, traditionally the Lutheran clergy maintain personal records such as marriages, births, and deaths, and perform other quasi-civil functions.

There seems to be little anti-clericalism or overt antireligion, but only a vast yawning indifference to the church. *New York Times,* December 14, 1966, article by John Cogley, "Religion in Sweden."

In Greece, "In 1928 about 96 percent of the population were members of the Orthodox Church. Since 1833 the Church in Greece has been autocephalous under a Holy Synod with the King at its head. . . . (Religion has ceased to possess something of the spiritual force it once had) ," Beckham Sweet-Escott, *Greece,* Royal Institute of International Affairs, London, 1954, p. 4.

Political Reorientation

The Cabinet has been the scene of party conflicts, owing to its position as the focus of power in the state. It can, however, maintain its central position only as long as its majority reflects a consensus of opinion in the Kneset. One hope for the future lies in a stable consensus of opinion.

Concerning the basic goals of government, a consensus of opinion and attitude is now readily available. This did not hold true in the first decade of statehood when the parties were in violent disagreement over the goals and the means of attaining them. On the extreme right, the greatest ambition of Herut was to expand the boundaries of Israel to its historic frontiers. At the right-center, the General Zionists aimed for a free enterprise society. At the extreme left, the Communists practically denied the need of independent statehood. The more moderate left-wing Mapam and Ahdut ha-'Avodah considered their mission the establishment of a labor society, based on a Marxist-Leninist platform. With the exception of Mapai, the parties were unbending in their ideological orientation, delaying the formation of a political consensus.

In recent years, under the impact of realities, the situation has changed. The parties have achieved a *modus vivendi*, to a fairly large extent, on issues they once considered paramount, such as expansionism, free enterprise, or the privileges of labor. Herut would probably still demand a firmer defense policy or quicker retaliation for an Arab raid than the parties on its left. The Liberals would still watch with suspicion certain moves of the Histadrut. The Mapam would still demand higher wages for the workers. Nevertheless, a greater readiness to listen to the others' view, a readier acceptance of each other than in former years, and a decrease in militancy on ideological issues has been noted in Israel.

A consensus of opinion and attitude has been evolving that seems to embrace all parties, except the Arab Communists and the Religious Bloc. The former offer but a thin facade for Arab irredentist and Communist aspirations, aiming to overthrow an independent Israel. The latter digress from the consensus by declaring that religion takes precedence over the state itself.

A protracted state of emergency that may solidify the existing consensus and may force the labor factions to minimize their internal differences could decisively affect the status of religion in Israel. It could be of direct and immediate significance in changing the composition of the Cabinet and in relieving the state of the continual menace of abuse by minority parties. It would be a step beneficial to the democratic process, to the orderly procedure of coalition government, and to the resolution of the religious problem in Israel.

Democracy at Work

The state of emergency resulting from Arab belligerence contributed significantly to a peaceful resolution of domestic conflicts in Israel by means of democratic processes of bargaining and compromise. The inheritance of the British Mandate and the experience in self-rule in Zionist bodies and the Jewish Community Organization helped to shape the thinking of the Jewish population in a democratic mold.

Yet, neither the dangers threatening from the outside, nor the inheritance from the past could fully explain the success of the democratic system in Israel. The Arab states claimed to be threatened by Israel, as much as Israel claimed to be threatened by them, forcing the neighboring Arab states to maintain their vigilance. These states also shared with Israel a heritage of Western European (English or French) Mandatory rule. The situation is not much different in Pakistan and other countries, that maintain a state of belligerence with one or more neighboring states and that emerged to independence from a former Mandate wherein the laws and customs of a democratic Western country were applicable. Yet, many of the African and Asiatic countries are still struggling with an array of domestic problems and powerful military juntas that crush democratic institutions and practices before they could assert themselves.

What makes democracy in Israel work? Perhaps the most important single cause is the will of the people to see Israel survive. The trauma of persecution suffered by the Jewish people through history has strengthened its determination to prevent the recurrence of Jewish homelessness. The people's will to secure the state's survival has produced a mutual, though somewhat grudging acceptance of clashing ideologies in the political spectrum. The parties may dislike each other intensely and may berate and vilify each other publicly without reservation, yet would refrain from resorting to violent measures against each other. Thus, by a combination of circumstances and historical experience the people have evolved the necessary self-discipline and the tolerance of opposing views, both of which are preconditions for the functioning of a democracy.

Mapai could have assumed absolute control over the country's economic and political life, particularly prior to 1965 when it dominated the Histadrut. Similarly, the efficient military machine could have tried to stage *coups d'état* to terminate numerous Cabinet stalemates. But either of these steps would have alienated a sufficiently large segment of the population to weaken and even jeopardize the people's will to survive. Fear of loss of morale, which a small nation facing overwhelming odds needs, would keep Mapai and the military in check more than any other single cause. Thus, the basic premise of Israel's democracy is that every view be allowed freedom of expression and organization, every individual be permitted freedom of choice and action, in full trust of their exercise of self-restraint and sense of responsibility, in order to adequately insure the nation's will to survive. From this basic premise of Israel's democracy have mushroomed the multitude of parties, the electoral system of proportional representation in a single national constituency, the religious status quo, or the unfettered freedom of opposition.

Despite the overriding consensus of most parties to protect the survival of Israel, elements who are ready to drive its democratic system to the brink of paralysis are not lacking. The sustained pressures exercised by the religious parties upon the government and the people seem to pose a potential threat to the democratic system. The religious parties manage to attain their objectives in defiance of the will of the majority by skillful utilization and manipulation of the very freedoms guaranteed by the system they would replace by theocracy. Their efforts are met by protests of parties who represent the majority and who claim that the imposition of religious law on the private lives of the citizens is an infringement of individual rights.

Despite the influence of the religious minority parties on the government and its process of decision-making, and despite the need of governmental action to buttress the democratic principles on which the state is founded, the system of democracy has found a sound ally in the government and people of Israel.

Appendixes

FRAGMENTATION OF PARTY VOTES IN THE KNESET

Kneset	First	Second	Third	Fourth	Fifth	Sixth	Seventh	Total
Year elected	1949	1951	1955	1959	1961	1965	1969	
Lists registered with the Central Elections Committee	21	20	23	26	15	18	19	
Lists allowed to run	21	17	18	24	14	17	16	
Lists gaining less than one per cent of the vote (no representation)	9	2	6	12	3	4	4	40
Lists gaining 4 seats or less	6	7	4	4	3	7	9	40
Lists gaining between 5 and 9 seats	2	4	3	5	4	2	0	20
Lists gaining between 10 and 15 seats	1	2	4	1	1	2	1	12
Lists gaining between 16 and 19 seats	2	0	0	1	2	0	0	5
Lists gaining 20 seats and up	1	2	1	1	1	2	2	10
Number of votes required for each seat	3592	5692	6938	7800	8332	10,056	11,274	
Number of Deputy Speakers elected in the Kneset	2	4	8	5	7	8	2	

POLITICAL PARTIES: EXTENT OF PARTICIPATION
IN GOVERNMENT COALITIONS

(January 25, 1949–October 28, 1969)

Name of Party	*Number of Coalitions Participated in*
1. Israel Labor Party	
a) Mapai	15
b) Ahdut ha-'Avodah	9
c) Rafi	
(prior to split with Mapai: *All*	
governments; since then:)	2
2. Mapam	6
3. Religious Parties	
a) NRP	15
b) Po'alei Agudat Israel	9
c) Agudat Israel	3
4. Gahal	
a) Liberal (or General Zionist) Party	4
b) Herut	2
5. Independent Liberal (or Progressive) Party	11
6. Arab Parties: have consistently supported Mapai in the coalition	

DISTRIBUTION OF VOTES BY MAJOR BLOCS IN KNESET ELECTIONS

	1949	1951	1955	1959	1961	1965	1969	Fluctuations
SOCIALIST BLOC	69	65	65	66	64	67	64	64 — 69
Mapai	46	45	40	47	42	45		
Ahdut ha-'Avodah	19	15	10	7	8			
Mapam			9	9	9	8	56	
Rafi						10		
Communists	4	5	6	3	5	4	4	
State List							4	
NON-SOCIALIST BLOC	30	34	33	31	34	31	32	30 — 34
Herut	14	8	15	17	17			
Liberal Party	7	20	13	8	17	26	26	
Independent Liberal	5	4	5	6		5	4	
Sefardim	4	2						
Free Centre							2	
RELIGIOUS BLOC	16	15	17	18	18	17	18	15 — 18
Ha-Po'el ha-Mizrahi	16	8	11	12	12	11	12	
Mizrahi		2						
Po'ale Agudat Israel		2	6	6	6	2	2	
Agudat Israel		3				4	4	

FLUCTUATION OF COALITION ALIGNMENTS

TENURE	GOVERNMENT	NON-SOCIALIST GROUPING			RELIGIOUS GROUPING	SOCIALIST GROUPING				
March 10, 1949 to Oct. 16, 1950	First	HERUT	GEN. ZION.	S P	REL. BLOC	M A P A I		MAPAM	C	O
Nov. 1, 1950 to Feb. 14, 1951	Second	HERUT	GEN. ZION.	S P	REL. BLOC	M A P A I		MAPAM	C	O
Oct. 8, 1951 to Dec. 19, 1952	Third	HERUT	GENERAL ZIONIST	S P	N.R.P. / T.R.F.	M A P A I		MAPAM	C	O
Dec. 23, 1952 to Dec. 7, 1953	Fourth	HERUT	GENERAL ZIONIST	P	N.R.P.	M A P A I		MAPAM	C	O
Jan. 26, 1954 to June 29, 1955	Fifth	HERUT	GENERAL ZIONIST	P	N.R.P. / T.R.F.	M A P A I		MAPAM	C	O
June 29, 1955 to Aug. 15, 1955	Sixth	HERUT	GENERAL ZIONIST	P	N.R.P. / T.R.F.	M A P A I		MAPAM	C	O
Nov. 3, 1955 to Dec. 31, 1957	Seventh	HERUT	GEN. ZION.	P	N.R.P. / T.R.F.	M A P A I	AHDUT HA AVODAH	MAPAM	C	O
Jan. 7, 1958 to July 5, 1959	Eighth	HERUT	GEN. ZION.	P	N.R.P. / T.R.F.	M A P A I	AHDUT HA AVODAH	MAPAM	C	O
Dec. 17, 1959 to Jan. 31, 1961	Ninth	HERUT	GEN. ZION.	P	N.R.P. / T.R.F.	M A P A I	AHDUT HA AVODAH	MAPAM	C	O
Nov. 2, 1961 to June 16, 1963	Tenth	HERUT	LIBERAL PARTY		N.R.P. / A.Y. / P.A.Y.	M A P A I	AHDUT HA AVODAH	MAPAM	C	O
June 26, 1963 to Dec. 15, 1964	Eleventh	HERUT	LIBERAL PARTY		N.R.P. / A.Y. / P.A.Y.	M A P A I	AHDUT HA AVODAH	MAPAM	C	O
Dec. 22, 1964 to Nov. 22, 1965	Twelfth	HERUT	LIBERAL PARTY		N.R.P. / A.Y. / P.A.Y.	M A P A I	AHDUT HA AVODAH	MAPAM	C	O
Dec. 1, 1966 to May 31, 1967	Thirteenth	GAHAL		I.L.P.	N.R.P. / A.Y. / P.A.Y.	A L I G N M E N T	MAPAM	RAFI	C	O
June 1, 1967 to	Fourteenth	GAHAL		I.L.P.	N.R.P. / A.Y. / P.A.Y.	A L I G N M E N T	MAPAM	RAFI	C	O

Abbreviations

S — Sefardim
T.R.F.— Torah Religious Party
P — Progressives
I.L.P.— Independent Liberal Party
A.Y.— Agudat Israel
P.A.Y.— Po'ale Agudat Israel
N.R.P.— National Religious Party
C.— Communists
O.— Other: Includes the Arab Parties, as well as splinter factions, whether part of a Government or not.

▓ Members of Government

PORTFOLIOS OF THE ISRAELI CABINET
AND THEIR DISTRIBUTION BY PARTY

PORTFOLIO	G 1ST	O 2ND	V 3RD	4TH	E 5TH	R 6TH	N 7TH
Prime Minister	Mapai	Mapai	Mapai	Mapai	Mapai	Mapai	Mapai
Defense	Mapai	Mapai	Mapai	Mapai	Mapai	Mapai	Mapai
Finance	Mapai	Mapai	Mapai	Mapai	Mapai	Mapai	Mapai
Foreign Affairs	Mapai	Mapai	Mapai	Mapai	Mapai	Mapai	Mapai
Education & Culture	Mapai	Mapai	Mapai	Mapai	Mapai	Mapai	Mapai
Agriculture	Mapai	Mapai	Mapai	Mapai	Mapai	Mapai	Mapai
Police	Mapai	Mapai	Mapai	Mapai	Mapai	Mapai	Mapai
Trade & Industry	Mapai	Indep.	Mapai	G.Z.	G.Z.	Mapai	Mapai
Labor	Mapai	Mapai	Mapai	Mapai	Mapai	Mapai	Mapai
State			Mapai Mapai	Mapai Mapai	Mapai		Mapai
Development				Mapai	Mapai	Mapai	Mapam
Posts			NRP	NRP	NRP	NRP	NRP
Religious Affairs	NRP	NRP	NRP	NRP	NRP	NRP	NRP
Social Welfare	Aguda	Aguda	Aguda	NRP	NRP	NRP	NRP
Interior	NRP	NRP	NRP	G.Z.	G.Z.	NRP	Ahdut
Health	NRP	NRP	NRP	G.Z.	G.Z.	Mapai	Mapam
Justice	Prog.	Prog.	Mapai	Prog.	Prog.	Prog.	Prog.
Communications	Mapai	Mapai	NRP	G.Z.	G.Z.	Mapai	Ahdut
Immigration	NRP	NRP					
Supply & Rationing	Mapai						
War Victims	NRP	NRP					
Housing							
Diaspora							
Deputy P. M.							
Tourism							

Abbreviations: ILP—Independent Liberal Party; Prog—Progressives;

PORTFOLIOS OF THE ISRAELI CABINET
AND THEIR DISTRIBUTION BY PARTY

M E N T S

8TH	9TH	10TH	11TH	12TH	13TH	14TH	Total
Mapai	Mapai	Mapai	Mapai	Mapai	Mapai	Mapai	All Mapai
Mapai	Mapai	Mapai	Mapai	Mapai	Mapai	Rafi	13 Mapai; 1 Rafi
Mapai	Mapai	Mapai	Mapai	Mapai	Mapai	Mapai	All Mapai
Mapai	Mapai	Mapai	Mapai	Mapai	Mapai	Mapai	All Mapai
Mapai	Mapai	Mapai	Mapai	Mapai	Mapai	Mapai	All Mapai
Mapai	Mapai	Mapai	Mapai	Mapai	Mapai	Mapai	All Mapai
Mapai	Mapai	Mapai	Mapai	Mapai	Mapai	Mapai	All Mapai
Mapai	Mapai	Mapai	Mapai	Mapai	Mapai	Mapai	11 Mapai; 2 G.Z.; 1 Indep.
Mapai	Mapai	Ahdut	Ahdut	Ahdut	Ahdut	Ahdut	9 Mapai; 5 Ahdut
Mapai	Mapai	Mapai				Gahal Gahal	9 Mapai, 2 Gahal
Mapam	Mapam	Mapai	Mapai	Mapai	ILP	ILP	6 Mapai; 3 Mapam; 2 ILP
NRP Mapam	Mapai PAI	Mapai	Mapai	Mapai	Mapai	Mapai	6 Mapai; 6 NRP (1 Mapam; 1 PAI)
NRP Indep.	Indep. Mapai	NRP	NRP	NRP	NRP	NRP	13 NRP; 2 Indep. (1 Mapai)
NRP Mapai	NRP	NRP	NRP	NRP	NRP	NRP	11 NRP; 3 Aguda (1 Mapai)
Ahdut	NRP	NRP	NRP	NRP	NRP	NRP	10 NRP; 2 Ahdut; 2 G.Z.
Mapam	Mapam	NRP	NRP	NRP	Mapam	Mapam	6 NRP; 5 Mapam; 2 G.Z.; 1 Mapai
Prog.	Prog.	Mapai	Mapai	Mapai	Mapai	Mapai	8 Prog.; 6 Mapai
Ahdut	Ahdut	Ahdut	Ahdut	Ahdut	Ahdut	Ahdut	8 Ahdut; 3 Mapai; 2 G.Z.; 1 NRP
						2 NRP	
						1 Mapai	
						2 NRP	
		Mapai	Mapai	Mapai	Mapam	Mapam	3 Mapai; 2 Mapam
					Ahdut	Ahdut	
			Mapai	Mapai			
				ILP	ILP		

G.Z.—General Zionist (Liberal) Party; PAI—Po'ale Agudat Israel; Aguda—Agudat Israel; NRP—National Religious Party; Ahdut—Ahdut ha-'Avodah

GOVERNMENTS IN OFFICE

Governments	period in office till resignation	as caretaker Gov't	parties in coalition	no. of seats in Kneset	no. of Ministers
FIRST KNESET					
First Gov't 10/3/49– 16/10/50 12 Ministers 73 votes in Kneset	19 months & 5 days	16 days	Mapai Rel. Bloc Progress. Sephardim Minorities	46 16 5 4 2	7 3 1 1 –
2nd Gov't 1/11/50– 14/2/51 13 Ministers 73 votes in Kneset	3 months & 14 days	7 months & 24 days	Mapai Rel. Bloc Progress. Sephardim Minorities (non-party)	46 16 5 4 2	7 3 1 1 – 1
SECOND KNESET					
3rd Gov't 8/10/51– 19/12/52 13 Ministers 67 votes in Kneset	14 months & 11 days	5 days	Mapai NRP Minorities Agudat Is. Poalei Ag. Sephardim	45 10 5 3 2 2	9 3 – 1 – –
4th Gov't 23/12/52– 7/12/53 16 Ministers 87 votes in Kneset	11 months & 14 days	1 month & 20 days	Mapai Gen. Zion NRP Minorities Progress.	45 23 10 5 4	9 4 2 – 1
5th Gov't 26/1/54– 29/6/55 16 Ministers 87 votes in Kneset	13 months & 3 days	none	Mapai Gen. Zion. NRP Minorities Progress.	45 23 10 5 4	9 4 2 – 1
6th Gov't 29/6/55– 15/8/55 12 Ministers 64 votes in Kneset	1 month & 18 days	2 months & 18 days	Mapai NRP Minorities Progress.	45 10 5 4	9 2 – 1
THIRD KNESET					
7th Gov't 3/11/55– 31/12/57 16 Ministers 80 votes in Kneset	25 months & 27 days	7 days	Mapai NRP Ahdut Av. Mapam Progress. Minorities	40 11 10 9 5 5	9 2 2 2 1 –
8th Gov't 7/1/58– 5/7/59 16 Ministers 80 votes in Kneset	18 months	5 months & 12 days	Mapai NRP Ahdut Av. Mapam Progress. Minorities	40 11 10 9 5 5	9 2 2 2 1 –

fissure in Cabinet

date	party	cause
February 1950	Rel. Bloc	1. demand for religious education in immigrant camps; 2. breach of collective cabinet responsibility.
October 1950	Rel. Bloc	protest co-optation of nonparty Minister, leading to resignation of Prime Minister
February 1951	Rel. Bloc	on vote of no confidence concerning education; though government not defeated, Prime Minister resigned over breach of collective cabinet responsibility
June 1952		reorganization of government, with nonparty Minister of Justice appointed
September–December 1952	Agudat Is. & Mizrahi	Ministers resign on conscription of women, leaving government with a narrow basis of 60 votes—hence resignation of Prime Minister
May 1953	Gen. Zion.	resignation over display of red flag in schools; crisis resolved in June 1953
December 1953	Prime Minister	resignation for reasons of health
February 1954	Mapai	resignation of Lavon and return of Ben Gurion to Ministry of Defense
June 1955	Gen. Zion.	abstention on vote of no confidence on Kastner case, leading to resignation of Prime Minister over breach of collective cabinet responsibility

caretaker government for election to Third Kneset

February 1956	Progress.	resignation at nonfulfillment of promises made to academicians by gov't; demands settled by end of month and resignation withdrawn
June 1956	Mapai	resignation of Sharett on internal party differences
December 1957	Ahdut Av.	refused Cabinet's request to resign for breach of collective responsibility, forcing Premier to resign
July 1958	NRP	resigned over disagreement with Minister of Interior (Ahdut ha-'Avodah) on definition of "Who is a Jew"
July 1959	Mapam & Ahdut Av.	voted against government in no confidence motion over sales of arms to West Germany; refused to resign, forcing Prime Minister to resign

GOVERNMENTS IN OFFICE

Governments	period in office till resignation	as caretaker Gov't	parties in coalition	no. of seats in Kneset	no. of Ministers
FOURTH KNESSET 9th Gov't 17/12/59– 31/1/61 16 Ministers 86 votes in Kneset	13 months & 14 days	9 months	Mapai NRP Mapam Ahdut Av. Progress. Minorities (non-party)	47 12 9 7 6 5	9 2 2 1 1 – 1
FIFTH KNESSET 10th Gov't 2/11/61– 16/6/63 16 Ministers 68 votes in Kneset	19 months & 15 days	10 days	Mapai NRP Ahdut Av. Minorities Poalei Ag.	42 12 8 4 2	11 3 2 – –
11th Gov't 26/6/63– 15/12/64 15 Ministers 68 votes in Kneset	17 months & 19 days	7 days	Mapai NRP Ahdut Av. Minorities Poalei Ag.	42 12 8 4 2	10 3 2 – –
12th Gov't 22/12/64 22/11/65 15 Ministers 68 votes in Kneset	11 months	1 month & 21 days	Mapai NRP Ahdut Av. Minorities Poalei Ag.	42 12 8 4 2	10 3 2 – –
SIXTH KNESSET 13th Gov't 12/1/66– 31/5/67 18 Ministers 75 votes in Kneset	16 months & 19 days	none	Ma'arakh NRP Mapam ILP Minorities Poalei Ag.	45 11 8 5 4 2	12 3 2 1 – –
14th Gov't 1/6/67– 6/2/69 21 Ministers 111 votes in Kneset	21 months & 5 days	1 month & 5 days	Ma'arakh Gahal NRP Rafi Mapam ILP Minorities Poalei Ag.	45 26 11 10 8 5 4 2	12 2 3 1 2 1 – –
15th Gov't 11/3/69– 28/10/69 21 Ministers 106 votes in Kneset	7 months & 17 days	1 month & 17 days	Ma'arakh Gahal NRP Rafi Mapam ILP Minorities Poalei Ag.	45 22 11 9 8 5 4 2	12 2 3 1 2 1 – –

fissure in Cabinet

date	party	cause
January 1961	Prime Minister	resigned after cabinet decision on Lavon Affair with which he disagreed
June 1963	Prime Minister	Ben Gurion resigned for personal reasons
December 1964	Prime Minister	Levi Eshkol resigned over interparty differences on Lavon; resignation withdrawn
		elections; expiration of Kneset term
		Arab threat leading to Six Day War forces reorganization of government into a "Government of National Unity"
	Prime Minister	death of Prime Minister Levi Eshkol in office
		elections; expiration of Kneset term

KNESET MEMBERS BY PARTY LIST

List	Seventh Kneset 28/10/ 1969	Sixth Kneset 2/11/ 1965	Fifth Kneset 15/8/ 1961	Fourth Kneset 3/12/ 1959	Third Kneset 26/7/ 1955	Second Kneset 30/7/ 1951	First Kneset 25/1/ 1949
Total	120	120	120	120	120	120	120
Israel Labor Party —Alignment	56	–	–	–	–	–	–
Mapai	–	45	42	47	40	45	46
Ahdut ha-'Avodah	–	(3)	8	7	10	(4)	(4)
Rafi	–	10	–	–	–	–	–
Mapam	–	8	9	9	9	15	19
State List	4	–	–	–	–	–	–
National Religious Party	12	11	12	12	11	10	16 (5)
Agudat Israel	4	4	6	6	6	5	
Po'ale Agudat Israel	2	2	(6)	(6)	(6)	(6)	
Gahal	26	26	–	–	–	–	–
Herut	–	–	17	17	15	8	14
Liberal Party (1)	–	–	17	8	13	20	7
Independent Liberal Party (2)	4	5	(7)	6	5	4	5
Free Centre	2	(8)	–	–	–	–	–
Ha-'Olam Hazeh	2	1	–	–	–	–	–
Communists	1	1	5	3	6	5	4
New Communists	3	3	–	–	–	–	–
Minorities lists	4	4	4	5	5	5	2
Other lists	–	–	–	–	–	3	7

(1) Until Fourth Kneset—General Zionists
(2) Until Fourth Kneset—Progressive Party
(3) Ma'arakh combined Mapai and Ahdut ha-'Avodah
(4) Ahdut ha-'Avodah was included in Mapam
(5) Religious Bloc list included all religious parties
(6) Torah Religious Front combined Agudat Israel with Po'ale Agudat Israel
(7) Liberals and Independent Liberals combined in one list
(8) Split off Herut faction of Gahal—its four members counted in Gahal total

RESULTS OF ELECTIONS TO THE KNESET
(Percentages)

Lists	Seventh Kneset 28/10/ 1969	Sixth Kneset 2/11/ 1965	Fifth Kneset 15/8/ 1961	Fourth Kneset 3/12/ 1959	Third Kneset 26/7/ 1955	Second Kneset 30/7/ 1951	First Kneset 25/1/ 1949
Total	100.0	100.0	100.0	100.0	100.0	100.0	100.0
Israel Labor Party —Alignment	46.2	–	–	–	–	–	–
Mapai	–		34.7	38.2	32.2	37.3	35.7
Ahdut ha-'Avodah	–	36.7 (3)	6.6	6.0	8.2	(4)	(4)
Rafi	–	7.9	–	–	–	–	–
Mapam	–	6.6	7.5	7.2	7.3	12.5	14.7
State List	3.1	–	–	–	–	–	–
National Religious Party	9.7	8.9	9.8	9.9	9.1	8.3	12.2 (5)
Agudat Israel	3.2	3.3	5.6	4.7	4.7	3.6	
Po'ale Agudat Israel	1.9	1.8	(6)	(6)	(6)	(6)	
Gahal	21.7	21.3	–	–	–	–	–
Herut	–	–	13.8	13.5	12.6	6.6	11.5
Liberal Party (1)	–	–	13.6	6.2	10.2	16.2	5.2
Independent Liberal Party (2)	3.2	3.8	(7)	4.6	4.4	3.2	4.1
Free Centre	1.2	(8)	–	–	–	–	–
Ha-'Olam Hazeh	1.2	1.2	–	–	–	–	–
Communists	1.1	1.1	4.2	2.8	4.5	4.0	3.5
New Communists	2.8	2.3	–	–	–	–	–
Minorities lists	3.6	3.8	3.9	4.7	4.9	4.7	3.0
Other lists	1.9	1.3	0.3	2.2	1.9	3.6	10.1

(1) – (8) See notes on p.

RESULTS OF ELECTIONS TO THE KNESET
(Numbers in Hundreds)

Lists	Seventh Kneset 28/10/ 1969	Sixth Kneset 2/11/ 1965	Fifth Kneset 15/8/ 1961	Fourth Kneset 3/12/ 1959	Third Kneset 26/7/ 1955	Second Kneset 30/7/ 1951	First Kneset 25/1/ 1949
All eligible voters	1,758,7	1,499,7	1,274,3	1,218,5	1,057,8	924,9	506,6
Voted	1,428,0	1,244,7	1,037,0	994,3	876,1	695,0	440,1
Valid votes	1,367,7	1,206,7	1,007,0	969,3	893,2	587,5	436,7
Israel Labor Party —Alignment	632,0	–	–	–	–	–	–
Mapai	–	443,4 (3)	349,3	370,6	274,7	256,5	155,3
Ahdut ha-'Avodah	–	(3)	66,1	58,0	69,5	(4)	(4)
Rafi	–	95,3	–	–	–	–	–
Mapam	–	80,0	75,7	69,5	62,4	86,1	64,0
State List	42,7	–	–	–	–	–	–
National Religious Party	133,2	108,0	99,0	95,6	78,0	56,7	53,0 (5)
Agudat Israel	44,0	39,8	56,7 (6)	45,6 (6)	39,9 (6)	25,0 (6)	
Po'ale Agudat Israel	25,0	22,0					
Gahal	296,3	257,0	–	–	–	–	–
Herut	–	–	138,6	130,6	107,2	45,7	50,0
Liberal Party (1)	–	–	137,3	59,7	87,1	111,4	22,7
Independent Liberal Party (2)	44,0	45,3	(7)	44,9	37,7	22,2	17,8
Free Centre	16,4	(8)	–	–	–	–	–
Ha-'Olam Hazeh	16,9	14,1	–	–	–	–	–
Communists	15,7	13,6	42,1	27.4	38.5	27.3	15.1
New Communists	38,8	27,4	–	–	–	–	–
Minorities lists	48,0	45,4	39,3	46,2	42,3	32,3	13,4
Other lists	14,8	15,4	3,2	21,4	16,1	24,4	43,6

(1) – (8) See notes on p.

CABINET MEMBERS WHO WERE NOT MEMBERS OF THE KNESET

Second Government:	Ya'aqov Geri,	Minister of Commerce (non-party)
Third Government:	Ben-Zion Dinur,	Education and Culture (Mapai)
	Haim Cohen,	Justice (Mapai)
Fourth Government:	Ben-Zion Dinur,	Education and Culture (Mapai)
Fifth Government:	as above	
Sixth Government:	as above	
Seventh Government:	Moshe Karmel,	Communications Ahdut ha-'Avodah)
	Pinhas Sapir,	Commerce and Industry (Mapai)
Eighth Government:	as above	
Ninth Government:	Rabbi Moshe Toledano,	Religious Affairs
Tenth Government:	Eliahu Sason,	Posts (Mapai)
	Dov Joseph,	Justice (Mapai)
Eleventh Government:	as above	
Twelfth Government:	Haim Gvati,	Agriculture (Mapai)
	Eliahu Sason,	Posts (Mapai)
	Dov Joseph,	Justice (Mapai)
Thirteenth Government:	Israel Barzilai,	Health (Mapam)
	Mordehai Bentov,	Housing (Mapam)
	Moshe Karmel,	Transport and Communications (Ahdut)
	Haim Gvati,	Agriculture (Mapai)
	Moshe Kol,	Development & Tourism (ILP)
	Yaaqov Shimshon Shapiro	Justice (Mapai)
Fourteenth Government:	as above	
Fifteenth Government:	as above	

For dates of the Governments see relevant tables in Appendix.

Bibliography

Official Publications

B'nei Israel: Piskei Halaha u-Meqorot l'Birur Dinam u-Sh'eilat Mozaam (B'nei Israel: Legal Decisions and Sources for the Clarification of Their Status and the Question of Their Origin) . Jerusalem: Publication of the Chief Rabbinate, 1962.

Divrei ha-Kneset (Israel Parliamentary Proceedings) . vols. 1–44. Jerusalem: Government Printer, 1949–1966.

Facts About Israel 1966. Israel: Ministry for Foreign Affairs, 1966.

Ha-Rabanut ha-Rashit l'Israel (The Chief Rabbinate of Israel) , ed. Ya'aqov Even-Hen. Ministry of Religious Affairs, 1964.

The Israel Digest: A Bi-Weekly Summary of News from Israel. Vols. 2–9. Jerusalem: Israel Information Office, January 1951–April 1958.

Israel's 18th Year. Israel: Government Press Office, April 25, 1966.

Israel Government Yearbook, 1949–1966. Jerusalem: Government Printer for Central Office of Information, Prime Minister's Office.

Israel Weekly Digest. vols. 1–9. New York: Jewish Agency, American Section, October 1957–August 1966.

The Jewish Agency's Digest of Press and Events. vols. 1–10. Jerusalem: Information Department of the Jewish Agency and the World Zionist Organization, September 1948–September 1957.

Laws of the State of Israel. Jerusalem: Government Printer, 1949–1963.

Official Gazette of the Government of Palestine, "Religious Communities Organization Ordinance," no. 157, 15 February 1926.

Palestine Gazette, "Elections of Rabbinical Officers and Rabbis of Local Communities." vol. 9, supplement 1, 9 April 1936.

Party Platforms. State of Israel Government Press Division, 1951.

Reshumot (Bills of the Kneset). Jerusalem: Government Printer, 1966.

Sefer ha-Huqim (Laws of the State of Israel). Jerusalem: Government Printer, 1963–1966.

Selected Judgments of the Supreme Court of Israel, ed. E. David Goitein. 2 vols. Jerusalem: Ministry of Justice, 1963.

Statistical Abstract of Israel, no. 17. Jerusalem: Central Bureau of Statistics, 1966.

A Survey of Palestine, "The Statutory Jewish Community," vol. 2. Palestine Government Printer, 1946.

Zionisten—Kongress 11, 1913, Stenographisches Protokoll der Verhandlungen. Berlin: Juedischer Verlag, 1914.

Zionisten—Kongress 12, 1921, Stenographisches Protokoll der Verhandlungen. Berlin: Juedischer Verlag, 1922.

Books and Pamphlets

American Jewish Yearbook 5684. Philadelphia: Jewish Publication Society, 1923.

Attias, Moshe. *Kneset Israel b'Erez Israel: Yesodah v'Irgunah* (The Community of Israel in Palestine: Its Foundation and Its Organization). Jerusalem: Va'ad Leumi, 1944.

Badi, Joseph. *Religion in Israel Today.* New York: Bookman Associates, 1959.

Baker, H. E. *The Legal System in Israel.* Tel Aviv: Steimatsky, 1961.

Bernstein, M. H. *The Politics of Israel.* Princeton, N.J.: Princeton University Press, 1957.

Burstein, Moshe. *Self-Government of the Jews in Palestine Since 1900.* Tel Aviv: Ha-Po'el ha-Za'ir, 1934.

Choudhury, G. W. *Democracy in Pakistan.* Dacca: Green Book House, 1963.

Cohen, Israel. *A Short History of Zionism.* London: F. Muller, 1951.

Dahl, Robert A., ed. *Political Opposition in Western Democracies.* New Haven, Conn.: Yale University Press, 1966.

Davis, Helen Miller, ed. *Constitutions, Electoral Laws, Treaties, and States in the Near and Middle East.* Durham, N.C.: Duke University Press, 1953.

Davis, Moshe, ed. *Israel: Its Role in Civilization.* New York: Harper, 1956.

Daykan, Paltiel. *Dinei Nesuin u-Gerushin* (Laws of Marriage and Divorce). Tel Aviv: Yavneh, 1956.

Dinim v'Heshbonot 'Al Kinusei Hug "Amana" b'Shanim 5722–5724 (Accounts of the Meetings of the "Amana" Group in the Years 5722–24.) Jerusalem: Reuven Mas, 1965.

Drayton, R. H. *The Laws of Palestine.* London: Government of Palestine, 1939.

Dunner, Joseph. *The Republic of Israel, Its History and Its Promise.* New York: McGraw-Hill, 1949.

Duverger, Maurice. *Political Parties.* Science Edition, 1963.

Eisenstadt, S. N. *The Absorption of Immigrants.* London: Routledge, 1954.

Elston, D. R. *Israel, The Making of a Nation.* London: Oxford University Press, 1964.

Feinberg, Nathan. *Erez Israel bi-T'qufat ha-Mandat u-Medinat Israel.* Jerusalem: Hebrew University, 1963.

Freudenheim, Yehoshua. *Government in Israel.* New York: Oceana, 1967.

Goadby, Frederic M. *International and Inter-Religious Private Law in Palestine.* Jerusalem: Ha-Madpis Press, 1926.

Goguel, François. *France Under the Fourth Republic.* Ithaca, N.Y.: Cornell University Press, 1952.

Goldman, Eliezer. *Religious Issues in Israel's Political Life.* Jerusalem: Mador Dati, The Youth and he-Haluz Department of the World Zionist Organization, 1964.

Hasin, Eliyahu. *Ha-Parasha.* Tel Aviv: 'Am ha-Sefer, 1961.

Herring, Pendleton. *The Politics of Democracy.* New York: Rinehart, 1940.

Hoffman, Stanley, ed. *In Search of France: Paradoxes of the*

French Political Community. Cambridge: Harvard University Press, 1963.

Hurewitz, J. C. *Struggle for Palestine*. New York: Norton, 1950.

Inhoff, Christoph von. *Israel: Die Zweite Generation*. Stuttgart: Deutsche Verlags-Anstalt, 1964.

Iyunim b'Baayot Dat u-Medinah. Jerusalem: Merkaz Olami Shel ha-Mizrahi v'ha-Po'el ha-Mizrahi, 1964.

Jabotinsky, Vladimir. *Die Idee Des Betar*. Lyck: Arthur Kaulbars Verlag, 1935.

———— *State Zionism*. New York: Zionist Revisionist Organization of America.

Jennings, Sir Ivor. *The British Constitution*. Cambridge: Cambridge University Press, 1961.

————. *Cabinet Government*. Cambridge: Cambridge University Press, 1951.

Kahana, Kalman. *The Case for Jewish Civil Law in the Jewish State*. London: Soncino, 1960.

Koestler, Arthur. *Promise and Fulfillment*. London: Macmillan, 1949.

Kogan, Norman. *The Government of Italy*. New York: Crowell, 1965.

Kraines, Oscar. *Government and Politics in Israel*. Boston: Houghton Mifflin, 1961.

La Palombara, J. *Interest Groups in Italian Politics*. Princeton, N.J.: Princeton University Press, 1964.

———— and Weiner, Myron. *Political Parties and Political Development*. Princeton, N.J.: Princeton University Press, 1966.

Lewis, Geoffrey. *Turkey*. London: E. Benn, 1955.

Matras, Judah. *Social Change in Israel*. Chicago: Aldine, 1965.

Middle East Record, 1961. vol. 2. Tel Aviv: Tel Aviv University, Reuven Shiloah Research Center, 1965.

Patai, Raphael. *Israel Between East and West: A Study in Human Relations*. Philadelphia: Jewish Publication Society, 1953.

Pickels, Dorothy. *The Fifth French Republic*. New York: Praeger, 1962.

Political Parties in Israel. Pamphlet published by the Jewish Agency, 1948.

Preuss, Walter. *Die Judische Arbeiterbewegung in Palestina.* Vienna: Fiba-Verlag, 1936.

Prittie, Terence. *Israel, Miracle in the Desert.* New York: Praeger, 1967.

Rackman, Emanuel. *Israel's Emerging Constitution 1948–1951.* New York: Columbia University Press, 1955.

Rubner, Alex. *The Economy of Israel; A Critical Account of the First Ten Years.* New York: Praeger, 1960.

Safran, Nadav. *The United States and Israel.* Cambridge, Mass.: Harvard University Press, 1963.

Sanders, Ronald. *Israel: The View from Masada.* New York: Harper, 1966.

Schechtman, Joseph B. *Fighter and Prophet: The Vladimir Jabotinsky Story.* 2 vols. New York: Thomas Yoseloff, 1961.

Sefer ha-Mizrahi (The Book of the Mizrahi) . Jerusalem: Mosad ha-Rav Kuk, 1946.

Seligman, Lester G. *Leadership in a New Nation; Political Development in Israel.* New York: Atherton, 1964.

Sharashavsky, Benzion. *Dinei Mispaha* (Family Laws) . Jerusalem: Hebrew University, 1958.

Sicron, Moshe. *Immigration to Israel.* Jerusalem: Central Bureau of Statistics, 1957.

Spiro, Herbert J. *Government by Constitution.* New York: Random House, 1959.

Sweet-Escott, Beckham. *Greece.* London: Royal Institute of International Affairs, 1954.

Tedeschi, Guido. *Studies in Israel Law.* Jerusalem: Hebrew University, 1960.

Tsidon, Asher. *Beit ha-Nivharim.* Jerusalem: Ahiasaf, 1964.

———. *Ha-Kneset l'Halaha u-l'Ma'aseh.* Jerusalem: Ahiasaf, 1954.

Una, Moshe. *Bi-Shevilei ha-Mahshavah v'ha-Ma'aseh.* Tel Aviv: Kibbutz Dati, 1955.

Weiner, Herbert. *The Wild Goats of Ein Gedi.* New York: Doubleday, 1961.

Weingrod, Alex. *Israel: Group Relations in a New Society.* New York: Praeger, 1965.

Williams, Philip. *Politics in Post-War France.* London: Longmans, 1955.

Yaari, Meir. *What Faces Our Generation.* Tel Aviv: D'fus he-Hadash, 1958.

Articles

Abramov, S. Z. "The Danger of Religious Split in Jewry." *Midstream,* 12 (October, 1966), pp. 3–13.

———. "The Lavon Affair." *Commentary* 31 (February 1961) : 100–105.

Alexander, Mark. "Israel's Left Reels to the Shock of Prague." *Commentary* 15 (April 1953) : 379–89.

Antonvsky, Aron. "Ideologia u-Ma'amad b'Israel." (Ideology and Class in Israel), *Amot* 2 (August-September 1963) : 21–28.

Akzin, Benyamin. "Al Menahem Begin v'Al T'nuat Herut" (Concerning Menahem Begin and the Herut Movement). *Hadoar* 46 (August 5, 1966) : 559–60.

Avineri, Shlomo. "Sofa Shel T'qufah." (End of an Era). *Amot* 4 (October-November 1965) : 7–17.

Barkatt, Reuven. "Mapai: Zionist Socialist Party." *Jewish Frontier* 29 (July 1962) : 3–7.

Bar-Natan, Moshe. "Cabinet Poker." *Jewish Frontier* 28 (November 1961) : 5–8.

———. "The Challenge to Ben-Gurion." *Jewish Frontier* 29 (June 1962) : 4–6.

———. "Forming a Coalition." *Jewish Frontier* 27 (January 1960) : 4–7.

———. "Israel Says 'Yes' to Ben-Gurion." *Jewish Frontier* 26 (December 1959) : 8–11.

———. "The Rabbinate Elections." *Jewish Frontier* 31 (May 1964) : 4–7.

———. "The Rabbinate in Israel." *Jewish Frontier* 31 (November 1964) : 12–14.

———. "Storm Over the Rabbinate." *Jewish Frontier* 27 (September 1960) : 6–8.

———. "Yossele and the B'nei Israel." *Jewish Frontier* 29 (August 1962) : 4–6.

Bar-On, Uri. "Religion in the Kibbuz." *Jewish Frontier* 27 (September 1960) : 16–21.

Ben-Dor, Leah. "An Analysis of the Elections." *Jewish Frontier* 26 (December 1959) : 3–5.

———. "Elections: No Alternative." *Jewish Frontier* 28 (June 1961) : 7–10.

Ben-Gurion, David: "Histadrut and the State." *Jewish Frontier* 23 (May 1956) : 6–9.

———. "How is Israel Different?" *Jewish Frontier* 29 (August 1962) : 7–14.

Benor, Y. L. "Religion, Community and State." *Zionist Newsletter* 4 (October 30, 1951) : 12–14.

Bentwich, Norman. "Seder in an Israeli Kibbuz." *Jewish Frontier* 28 (March 1961) : 43–44.

Berger, Herzl. "Mapai Faces Elections." *Jewish Frontier* 26 (September 1959) : 3–8.

Blanshard, Paul. "Israel: Church and State." *The Nation* 170 (27 May 1950) .

Cohen, Jack J. "Compromise is a Religious Principle." *Jewish Frontier* 31 (February 1964) : 21–24.

———. "The Religious Search in Israel." *Jewish Frontier* 29 (October 1962) : 23–25.

Daniel, Ruth. "Parties in the Histadrut." *Jewish Frontier,* 26 (June 1959) : 6–11.

David, Ilana. "The Law and the Adopted Child." *Jewish Frontier* 26 (June 1959) : 23–25.

Eban, Abba. "Democracy or Anarchy?" *Midstream* 9 (September 1965) : 33–38.

Eliav, Benjamin. "Factionalism in Government." *Jewish Frontier* 25 (February 1958) : 4–7.

Eshkol, Levi. "After the Alignment." *Jewish Frontier* 32 (July-August 1965) : 3–4.

Etzioni, Amitai. "Behind the Lavon Affair." *Jewish Frontier* 28 (February 1961) : 11–13.

Frenkel, Erwin. "The Lavon Affair: Its Political Implications." *Midstream* 7 (Spring 1961) : 60–69.

Friedberg, Maurice. "The Split in Israel's Communist Party." *Midstream* 12 (February 1966) : 19–28.

Galanter, Marc. "A Dissent on Brother Daniel." *Commentary* 36 (July 1963) : 10–17.

Gillon, Philip. "Sources of the Law." *Jewish Frontier* 29 (April 1962) : 26–29.

Grodzinsky, Shlomo. "Hearot lo-Politiyot l'Hahraah Politit" (Non-Political Explanations to a Political Phenomenon). *Amot* 3 (April-May 1965) : 7–10.

———. "Hearot she-Eynan Yafot l'Onat ha-B'hirot" (Unwelcome Explanations in the Election Season). *Amot* 4 (August-September 1965) : 7–10.

Guttman, Emanuel. "Israel: Dimension of Participation." *International Social Science Journal* 12 (1960) : 53–62.

Halpern, Ben. "Dark Days Ahead of Mapam." *Jewish Frontier* 20 (January 1953) : 13–15.

———. "Faith and Unbelief." *Jewish Frontier* 24 (April 1957) : 7–11.

———. "Rafi." *Jewish Frontier* 32 (September 1965) : 7–11.

———. "Who is a Jew?" *Jewish Frontier* 26 (January 1959) : 7–10.

Heid, Gal. "What is a Jew in Israel?" *Jewish Frontier* 26 (February 1959) : 7–11.

Heiman, Leo. "Religion in Israel's Army." *Jewish Frontier* 22 (April 1957) : 25–27.

Himmelfarb, Milton. "How Many Israels?" *Commentary* 37 (January 1964) : 64–67.

Jabotinsky, Vladimir. "About Cassandra." *Jewish Standard* (28 May 1943) p. 5.

Johnston, Scott D. "Election Politics and Social Change in Israel." *Middle East Journal* 16 (Summer 1962) : 309–27.

———. "Party Politics and Coalition Cabinets in the Kneset of Israel." *Middle Eastern Affairs* 13 (May 1962) : 130–38.

Josephtal, Giora. "Reflections on Trends in Israel's New Society." *Jewish Frontier* 27 (September 1960) : 11–13.

Kelman, Wolfe. "Judaism in Israel." *Conservative Judaism* 19 (Winter 1965) : 1–19.

Kimche, Jon. "A Mandate for Change." *Midstream* 12 (January 1966) : 56–61.

———. "The People vs. Ben Gurion's Government." *Commentary* 14 (September 1952) : 237–244.

Kohansky, Mendel. "A Problem of Religion." *Jewish Frontier* 25 (February 1958) : 21–22.

Korn, Izhaq. "Habad, or Religious Parties." *Jewish Frontier* 28 (December 1961) : 23–25.

———. "State and Religion: Toward a Solution of the Problem of Coexistence." *Jewish Frontier* 26 (December 1959) : 25–27.

Laqueur, W. Z. "The Kastner Case." *Commentary* 20 (December 1955) , pp. 500–511.

———. "The Oren Case: A Fellow-Traveler Comes Home." *Commentary* 22 (August 1956) : 110–118.

Lavon, Pinhas. "Histadrut Economy: New Ways for Old." *Jewish Frontier* 25 (September 1958) : 4–8.

Lehrman, Hal. "Ben-Gurion Wins and Loses an Election." *Commentary* 12 (November 1951) : 415–424.

Levenberg, Aliza. "Israel's Elections, 1965." *Jewish Frontier* 33 (January 1966) : 3–7.

Lindsey, Robert L. "Israel's Coming Crisis over 'Jewishness.' " *Commentary* 18 (July 1954) : 16–25.

Livneh, Eliezer. "The Elections in Israel." *Midstream* 12 (January 1966) : 48–55.

———. "Israel's Electoral System." *Jewish Frontier* 21 (February 1954) : 17–19.

Luft, Gerda. "Israel's Conservative Voters." *Commentary* 31 (November 1961) : 426–428.

Meron, Theodore. "The Authority of Religion in Israel." *Jewish Frontier* 22 (January 1955) : 22–26.

Morris, Ya'aqov. "Clericalism vs. Religion." *Jewish Frontier* 29 (October 1962) : 26–27.

"The Oswald Rufeisen (Brother Daniel) Case." *Midstream* 9 (March 1963) : 78–96.

Peres, Shimon, "What Ben Gurion's Group Stands For?" *Midstream* 9 (September 1965) : 38–39.

Peretz, Don. "Reflections on Israel's Fourth Parliamentary Elections." *Middle East Journal* 14 (Winter 1960) : 15–28.

Petuchevsky, Jacob J. "Who is a Jew?" *Jewish Frontier* 26 (June 1959) : 6–10.

Rottenstreich, Nathan. "I-Nahat Datit" (Religious Disquiet) . *Amot* 3 (October-November 1964) : 7–28.

Salpeter, Eliahu. "Israel Kneset Elections." *Middle Eastern Affairs* 12 (November 1961) : 262–268.

Samuel, Edwin. "The Ottoman Legacy to Israel." *Jewish Frontier* 27 (August 1960) : 11–16; 28 (January 1961), pp. 19–23.

Sharett, Moshe. "Socialism in Israel," *Jewish Frontier* 22 (September 1955) : 9–15.

Sherman, A. V. "Can Ben Gurion Reshape Israeli Politics?" *Commentary* 28 (December 1959) : 461–470.

Shulewitz, Malka Hillel. "The B'nei Israel versus the Rabbinate." *Jewish Frontier* 30 (October 1963) : 7–11.

Simon, Ernst. "Are We Israelis Still Jews?" *Commentary* 15 (April 1953) : 357–364.

Stock, Ernest. "Grassroots Politics—Israel Style." *Midstream* 12 (June-July 1966) : 3–14.

Super, Arthur Saul. "Religion: Ritual or Spiritual?" *Jewish Frontier* 25 (April 1958) : 17–19.

Syrkin, Marie. "Orthodoxy on the Rampage." *Jewish Frontier* 20 (September 1953) : 5–8.

Teller, Judd L. "The Israeli Voter Ponders the 'Moral Crisis.' " *Commentary* 11 (February 1951) : 145–52.

———. "Religious Modernism Stirs in Israel." *Commentary* 15 (June 1953) : 576–83.

———. "The Spartan Youth of Israel: A Generation Searches for Its Soul." *Commentary* 10 (July 1950) : 7–14.

Weiner, Herbert. "Church and State in Israel." *Midstream* 8 (Winter 1962) : 3–14.

———. "The Liberal Religious Impulse in Israel." *Commentary* 20 (July 1955) : 38–49; 20 (August 1955) : 146–54.

Weingrod, Alex. "The Two Israels." *Commentary* 33 (April 1962) : 313–19.

Werner, Alfred. "Israel's Zealots in Gaberdine." *Commentary* 11 (January 1951) : 61–67.

Yaron, M. "The Arabs in Israel." *Jewish Frontier* 24 (February 1957) : 10.

Newspapers and Periodicals
State of Israel

Ha-Arez. Independent daily.
'Al ha-Mishmar. Mapam daily.

Amot. Quarterly, published by the American Jewish Committee in Israel.

Ha-Boqer. General Zionist daily.

Davar. Daily organ of the Histadrut with largest circulation of all newspapers in the country. Voices Mapai viewpoint.

Herut. Herut Party daily.

Igeret la-Golah. Monthly, published in English by the ha-Po'el ha-Mizrahi.

Jerusalem Post. Independent, English language daily with strong Mapai leanings.

Maariv. Independent afternoon daily.

La-Merhav. Ahdut ha-'Avodah daily.

Ha-Zofeh. National Religious Party daily.

Yediot Aharonot. Independent afternoon daily.

United States

American Zionist. Monthly, published by the Zionist Organization of America.

Commentary. Monthly, published by the American Jewish Committee.

Ha-Doar. Hebrew weekly, published by the Histadrut Ivrit of America.

Forward. Yiddish language daily with strong labor leanings.

Jewish Frontier. Monthly, issued by the Farband Labor Organization.

The Jewish Horizon. Monthly, published by the Religious Zionists of America.

JTA Bulletin. Published daily by the Jewish Telegraphic Agency.

Middle Eastern Affairs.

Middle East Journal.

Midstream. Monthly, published by the Theodore Herzl Foundation.

Newsletter. Monthly, published by the United Zionist-Revisionist Organization of America.

New York Times.

Der Tog. Yiddish daily with religious bent.

Zionist Newsletter. Published by the Information Department of the Jewish Agency.

Index